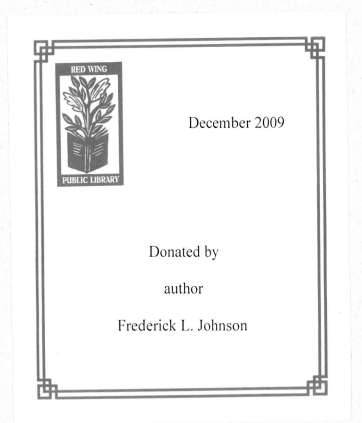

SUBURBAN DAWN

First Printing
November 2009

Published by the Richfield Historical Society
6901 Lyndale Avenue South
PO Box 23304
Richfield, MN 55423
612-798-6140

Editing: Diane Johnson and Thomas U. Tuttle

Layout and Design: David Thofern

Printing: Sexton Printing, St. Paul, MN

Printed in the United States of America

ISBN: 978-0-578-03917-6

Also by Frederick L. Johnson

The Sea Wing Disaster
Goodhue County, Minnesota: A Narrative History
Sky Crashers
Uncertain Lives
Red Wing: A Portable History
Richfield: Minnesota's Oldest Suburb

SUBURBAN DAWN

THE EMERGENCE OF RICHFIELD, EDINA AND BLOOMINGTON

FREDERICK L. JOHNSON

WITH THOMAS U. TUTTLE

Richfield Historical Society

CONTENTS

—◆—

Acknowledgements

—◆—

Suburban Dawn examines the histories of three Minnesota communities through a review of themes critical to their development. It is a story that could not have been told without the assistance of the historical societies of Edina, Bloomington and Richfield. Unless linked to important historical themes or incidents, communities are responsible for researching and reporting their own histories. That is exactly what these suburban Twin Cities caretakers of the past have accomplished.

Sarah Tapper assumed the directorship of the Richfield Historical Society, the sponsoring agency for this book, just as the project started. The Richfield organization previously published my sesquicentennial history of their city in 2008. Ms. Tapper generously shared her time and expertise as the project moved forward, and made the collections of the society readily available.

A willingness to routinely do more than requested proved to be a common trait among all three historical society directors. Bloomington's Vonda Kelly opened the doors of the refurbished 19th century town hall—today's history center—outside normal business hours. She even brought in, for my use, her own personal collection of materials regarding professional sports in Bloomington.

Marci Mattson, executive director of the Edina Historical Society, proved a most versatile guide to the organization's formidable resources and collections. If Mattson didn't know the answer to a question, she knew who did. She's an "idea" person and provided useful insights on a number of topics. Ms. Mattson immediately grasped the thrust of the project and repeatedly volunteered her time.

A key to the success of these historical societies is their network of dedicated members. Operating with very modest budgets, these organizations must rely upon volunteers in order to survive. I've met dozens of these stewards of local history in the last few years, and marvel at their dedication. It is not possible to list all who have helped me, but the membership rolls of each group would be a starting point. That said, I will mention Edina's knowledgeable and affable Bob Kojetin as a source on almost anything related to that community; it is no wonder they named a park after him.

Susan Larson-Fleming, archivist of the Hennepin County History Museum, was also of great assistance in, once again, working to make my research tasks easier. Also of help during the research phase of this project was the skilled cadre of assistants at the Minneapolis and St. Paul Public Libraries. The versatile and knowledgeable staff members of the Minnesota Historical Society were, as always, ready to help with insights and suggestions.

Volunteers at the Northwest Airline History Centre located in the NWA Federal Credit Building in Bloomington shared their fascinating collection of airline-related materials, as well as their own experiences. Noel Allard, Minnesota's estimable resource on aviation and auto racing history, was particularly helpful. Allard, executive director of the Minnesota Aviation Hall of Fame, is a knowledgeable and generous ally of those studying his historical specialty. He provided many of the photographs of aircraft and auto racing in this book. The photo credits page carries a detailed list.

My thanks to the talented, deliberate and patient Dave Thofern, who designed the book and put up with my many special requests. A versatile Rita Thofern served in many roles, grammarian, editor, and photographer among them, and proved to be most helpful. D'Arlyn Marks proofread the book and also made helpful suggestions about content. Her professionalism and talent are much appreciated. As always, my wife Diane immerses herself in my writing projects through first readings to final edits. She wrestles early drafts into shape, and, as copy editor, gets the text ready for printing. Her talent for design is reflected throughout the book. She has contributed innumerable hours of thoughtful, painstaking work. Along with my love, she has my respect and gratitude.

Thomas U. Tuttle's name is found on the title page of this book. From its beginnings roughly two years ago, Tom and I have worked on this book in the hope of providing readers new context and more understanding of Bloomington, Edina and Richfield history. Tom, a past president of the Richfield Historical Society, oversaw the project, conducted interviews and edited its content. It should also be noted that his talented wife, Elizabeth, brought her perspective to the editing process. Like a good ship's captain, Tom used a light touch to keep this undertaking on course and off the rocks. It was a pleasure working with him.

Frederick L. Johnson
Cottage Grove, Minnesota
September 23, 2009

To the members and friends of the Richfield, Edina and Bloomington Historical Societies for their continuing support in keeping alive the history of their communities, and to the directors of those societies whose assistance was essential to the publication of this book:

Sarah Hummel, director, Richfield Historical Society
Vonda Kelly, executive director, Bloomington Historical Society
Marci Mattson, executive director, Edina Historical Society

IMAGE CREDITS

All photographs and images, unless otherwise noted, are from the Richfield Historical Society. Credits for other images used are found below.

Noel Allard, Minnesota Aviation Hall of Fame Collection–82 top and bottom, 83 top and bottom, 84, 85 top and bottom, 87, 88, 90 bottom, 92, 94 top and bottom, 95, 96, 97, 98, 100, 102, 103 top and bottom, 104, 105, right, 107, 213

Bloomington Historical Society–6 lower right, 15, 27 right, 45 bottom, 46 top and bottom, 78, 126, 128 top and bottom, 138, 142 bottom, 144, 145, 156, 174, 178, 179, 180, 182, 183, 184, 185, 193, 195, 196 bottom, 201, 208

Edina Historical Society–47 left and right, 48, 52, 54, 56 top and bottom, 60, 112, 119, 120, 121, 123, 130, 132, 133, 134, 199, 205

Edina Magazine–202 top and bottom

Hennepin County Public Affairs–xvii

Ken Hohag–99

Joe Hoover–41, 139

Minneapolis *Journal*–80, 89, 117, 122, 136

Minneapolis Park Board–64 bottom

Minneapolis *Star*–154, 157

Minneapolis *Tribune*–176

Minnesota Historical Society–4 upper right, 5 upper right, 7 top, 9, 11 top and bottom, 12 top, 13 top, 19 bottom, 21, 22, 25, 29, 31, 34, 35 top and bottom, 36, 61, 64 top, 66, 115, 141

Betty Webster collection–209 top, middle and bottom, 211 top and right

PREFACE

———◆———

This is a book about three neighboring south Minneapolis suburbs and the history they share. In the starring roles are Richfield, Edina and Bloomington, Minnesota, communities linked by nearly two centuries of common experience. Their stories are told through a series of narratives that address historical themes of shared importance. The chronicle begins in the early 19th century as the United States commences settlement of Native American lands in what would become the 32nd state. It concludes in the 1970s with the three subject cities at or near full development.

When Hennepin County was organized in April 1858, Bloomington and Richfield were among the towns its Board of Commissioners laid out. Thirty years later, citizens living around Edina Mills in west Richfield decided to constitute their own village. Residents of the three sparsely-populated agricultural districts moved forward, their fates linked by geography and common concerns. It would take a century for these farm towns to assume their present-day manifestations, that of self-contained suburban cities.

The book's subtitle, *The Emergence of Richfield, Edina and Bloomington*, lists the three communities in the order in which they matured. By the mid-1970s, the approximate endpoint of the volume, Richfield was fully developed, possessing no further available land upon which to build. Edina would be the next in that position, and Bloomington, last. This evolutionary order has no affect on the narrative, however. The book's themes drive it forward.

Readers will typically find self-evident the relationship of individual chapters to a central concept. For example, "Cloud Man's Daughters and Their Anglo-American Husbands" is found in Section One, *Dominion of the Dakota*, and "Squatters in South Hennepin County" is placed in Section Two, *Patrons of Agriculture*. A less obvious placement occurs with "The Murder of Fred Babcock," located in Section Four, *Boomlet to Boom*. This account of a most somber episode in Richfield history is a counterbalance to the presumption that rapidly growing postwar suburbs were immune to big city problems. "Commies! The 1950s 'Red Scare' in South Hennepin" is included with the exciting early years of growth, as portrayed in *Boomlet to Boom*. "Commies" preserves a distant memory of a time when assault against Bloomington, Richfield and Edina by aircraft carrying city-destroying weapons was considered a terrifying possibility.

Suburban Dawn is not a chronological review of subjects pertinent in the histories of these communities. Their local historical societies have already done an excellent job of detailing such episodes. Instead, this account provides consideration and context regarding events significant to the emergence of Richfield, Edina and Bloomington as modern Minnesota suburbs. The author is hopeful the narrative and its annotated endnotes will bring its readers a deeper understanding of the present and past of these three suburban communities.

The sandy, glacial outwash plain that stretched south from Minneapolis proved ideal for post-Second World War developers. Houses soon covered the farm fields of the century-old villages of Richfield, Edina and Bloomington as the three modern suburbs emerged. This late 1950s view looking south shows construction of Interstate-35W as it cuts through south Minneapolis, in the foreground, and skirts Grass Lake then Wood Lake, in Richfield, and heads toward Bloomington in the distance.

EDINA, RICHFIELD, BLOOMINGTON AND SOUTH MINNEAPOLIS

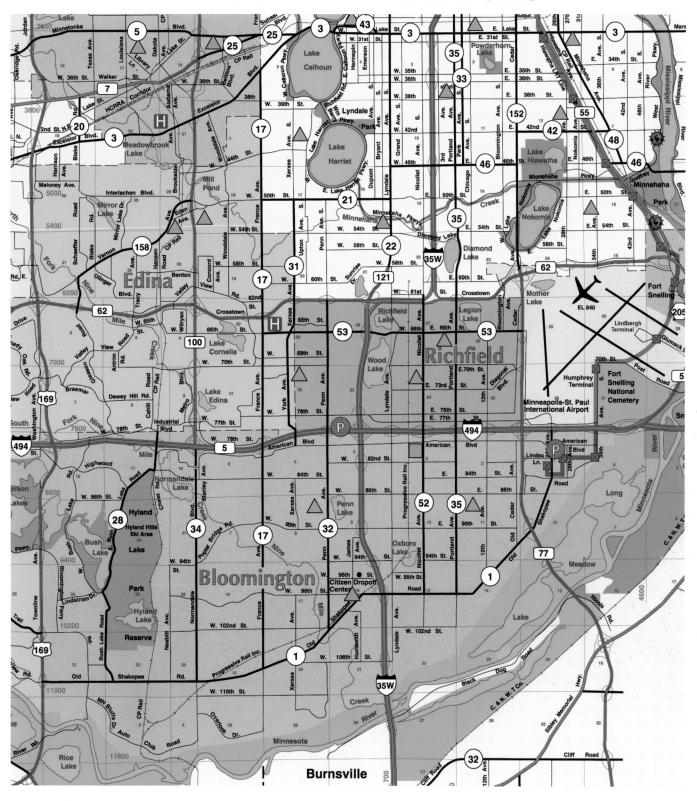

–ONE–
DOMINION OF THE DAKOTA

In August 1819, a contingent of United States soldiers arrived at the confluence of the Mississippi and St. Peter's rivers tasked with constructing a military base. This outpost, Fort Snelling, extended partial American jurisdiction into a territory under the divided control of the Ojibwe and Dakota nations. It was the southern and western sections of this vast area—the dominion of the Dakota—that would later become the focus of the newcomers. Those around the fort, located in future southern Hennepin County, lived near and with the Mdewakanton, the largest tribe of the eastern Dakota.

Whites were no strangers to the Dakota. Indian and white had conducted a flourishing trade for well over a century. During that time, and in the three decades following establishment of Fort Snelling, the Dakota retained control of their far-flung empire. Nonetheless, government agents and traders, many of whom married Indian women, imported American cultural values, assisted by missionaries striving for a religious conversion of the Dakota.

In 1851, an expansive United States successfully coerced the Dakota into selling their vast Minnesota Territory land holdings. Instead of resolving the problems between the whites and Dakotas, tensions only increased. A harsh, remorseless war ensued.

CLOUD MAN'S DAUGHTERS AND THEIR ANGLO-AMERICAN HUSBANDS

Those discussing the increase of present-day racial and ethnic diversity in south suburban Hennepin County often treat the subjects as new phenomena. The people dwelling in that same area during Minnesota's pre-territorial years included Dakota, mixed-bloods, French, British and Anglo-Americans living in close proximity or together, and often inter-marrying. An example of such marriages can be found in the Lake Calhoun band of Mdewakanton. Cloud Man, the village chief, had three daughters, all of whom married prominent Anglo-Americans.

The daughters of Mdewakanton Dakota Chief Cloud Man, The Day Sets, Hushes the Night and Stands Like a Spirit, shared two traits: each was "unusually beautiful and spirited." They would later share a new kind of familial bond. All married prominent Anglo-Americans from the small frontier enclave that would grow into the state of Minnesota.[1]

The Day Sets and Lawrence Taliaferro

In the late 1820s, Cloud Man agreed to take part in an important experimental program devised by Lawrence Taliaferro (pronounced **Tol**-i-ver), the Indian agent at Fort Snelling. President James Monroe personally selected the 25-year-old Virginian to regulate trade in the region and protect the interests of Indians living

Major Lawrence Taliaferro, Indian Agent

Fort Snelling's Round Tower

there. Taliaferro wanted to encourage the Dakota, through Cloud Man's example, to take up agriculture and hence speed their assimilation into American culture. This was the first, but far from the last, attempt in the future Minnesota to impose, as historian Bruce J. White asserts, "...the agricultural way of life on an orderless region that they (Anglo-Americans) believed to be wasted on its inhabitants."[2] Cloud Man took his family and those of several other followers—they previously had been part of Black Dog's small village on the Minnesota River in present-day Burnsville—to the shores of present-day Lake Calhoun. The chief's people were expected to learn cultivation techniques from government-paid farmer Philander Prescott.[3]

In Lawrence Taliaferro's case, marriage to The Day Sets, Cloud Man's daughter, buttressed his kinship ties to the Mdewakanton. His position as son-in-law increased the Indian agent's status and leverage with the Dakota, but likewise put him under obligations to his Indian family. The relationship also proved valuable to the chief, even after Taliaferro left his Indian wife.

Around the year 1835, Drifter, a Mdewakanton challenger to Cloud Man's position of chief, moved to the Lake Calhoun village. Since Cloud Man was not a hereditary leader, his situation was somewhat precarious. But Taliaferro, using his influence as Fort Snelling Indian agent, recognized his former father-in-law's status, thus settling the dispute.[4]

Lawrence Taliaferro's decision to travel to Pennsylvania and marry Eliza Dillon placed The Day Sets in an awkward position. The marriage between Taliaferro and Dillon took place on July 22, 1828. Back at Lake Calhoun, meanwhile, the Indian agent's young first wife gave birth to their daughter, Mary, on August 17.

Taliaferro brought Eliza Dillon, described as dark-haired, attractive and an accomplished pianist, to Fort Snelling in November 1828.[5] Taliaferro's new marriage ended his relationship with The Day Sets. However, he took financial responsibility for Mary and began attempts to create in her a desire to become more

Indian Village on the Mississippi near Fort Snelling
Watercolor by Seth Eastman

Anglo-American than Mdewakanton. This was a daunting task, since by age 11 Mary still lived with her mother and grandmother, Red Cherry Woman, and led a mostly Dakota life. She did, however, attend the Rev. Jedediah Stevens's Lake Harriet mission school.[6]

In 1839 Taliaferro decided to retire as Indian agent at Fort Snelling and move to Pennsylvania near his wife's family. He wrote to Samuel Pond, a Christian missionary to Cloud Man's Mdewakanton, noting that it would "afford me some consolation, and pleasure" if Mary could "…remain with you, and Mrs. (Cordelia) Pond…." He promised to pay for his daughter's board, clothing and tuition. Taliaferro added significantly, "Mary's mother [and] grandmother and others are about to leave the Lake to get wild rice, and they now seem willing to let her stay with you."[7]

Cloud Man's people began moving from the Lake Harriet mission in fall 1839 because they felt too exposed to their Ojibwe (Anishinaabeg) enemies. The Ponds shifted farther south to the Minnesota River bluffs of the future Bloomington and established their new Oak Grove mission in 1843. The Day Sets and Mary were among those Mdewakanton staying near the Ponds.[8]

Mallet head, Indian implement

Mary Taliaferro still lived near Oak Grove in January 1846 when the Ponds received bad news from her father. Samuel Pond had asked Taliaferro about trust funds—monies promised in the 1837 treaty with the Dakota—that he held for Mary and her mixed-blood cousins. The retired Indian agent replied he had been wiped out by failure of the firm "in whose hands the money was placed." He worried about the future of his daughter, now a young woman of 17.[9]

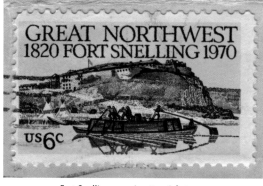

Fort Snelling sesquicentennial stamp

In 1848 Mary Taliaferro married Warren Woodbury, a soldier at Fort Snelling, and soon was a mother. It is not known if Taliaferro saw Mary again. He did keep up a regular correspondence with her and returned to Minnesota at least once (in 1856) but apparently did not visit her. He died in Pennsylvania on January 20, 1871.[10]

The Minnesota Dakota War of 1862 thrust itself into the life of Mary Taliaferro Woodbury and her three children. They were visiting Dakota relatives in western Minnesota—Warren had signed on to fight in the Civil War—when taken captive by rebelling Indians. Mary later reported to her father that the Mdewakanton leader Little Crow had saved them out of friendship and respect for Taliaferro.

Mary's husband Warren died in 1863 of yellow fever contracted while soldiering. Seven years later Mary was listed as living in St. Paul with three children, and in 1880 a city directory showed her at the same address as her oldest son, Warren, Jr., and his non-Indian wife. Mary, along with a daughter and Warren and his family, decided to leave white society permanently in 1887–88 and moved to the Santee Indian Reservation in Nebraska. There they lived among their exiled relatives.[11]

Hushes the Night and Daniel Lamont

Cloud Man's daughter Hushes the Night married Scottish trader Daniel Lamont a few years after the Taliaferro-The Day Sets country marriage. Lamont spent most of his time on the upper Missouri and had become a partner in the Columbia Fur Company of Joseph Renville, William Laidlaw and Kenneth McKenzie. That group sold their holdings to the mighty American Fur Company in 1827. It could have been Lamont's new connection with American Fur that brought him to Mendota and Henry Sibley, who represented the company there.[12]

Lamont married Hushes the Night while at Fort Snelling in the late 1820s,

Samuel Pond

a union that produced a child whom they named Jane. Dan Lamont joined the Upper Missouri Outfit in the early 1830s, heading back to the northern plains and fur trading. In 1834 he was running the trading post at Fort Assiniboine, built in 1833–34 during an expedition up the Yellowstone River. He is believed to have died in that region within the next few years.[13]

Hushes the Night's daughter, Jane Lamont, attended the Rev. Stevens's mission school at Lake Harriet. In spring 1840, when that mission was abandoned, Jane's mother asked Samuel Pond to raise her daughter as part of his family. The Ponds accepted Jane, then about 11. The girl's mother and other Dakota from Cloud Man's band often were found close by, even after the move to Oak Grove mission.[14]

In August 1847 Hushes the Night died and her Dakota relatives left the area. Jane stayed on, living at the Pond brothers' missions at Oak Grove and Shakopee. The Ponds trained her to become a teacher, a task she performed "very well," according to Cordelia Pond.

A somewhat secret romance bloomed between Jane and Samuel Pond's nephew, Starr Titus, who had lived in the Pond household for a number of years. It appears the couple managed to keep their feelings under wraps prior to their 1850 decision to marry. An entry in Gideon Pond's diary soon after

Seth Eastman, soldier and artist

the wedding notes that he, for the first time, had seen Starr speak to Jane in front of the family. He had never heard her speak to Starr.[15]

In 1853 Jane and Starr decided to settle near Samuel and Cordelia Pond's land in Shakopee. They could have moved with the Dakota on their new Minnesota River reserve, but, according to Samuel, "Jane is very unwilling to go with the Indians."[16] She would not reverse that course and continued to live out her life as an Anglo-American woman. It is believed she maintained contact with her Dakota kin.[17]

Commanding Officer's Quarters, Fort Snelling

South Battery and Storehouse, Fort Snelling

Stands Like a Spirit and Seth Eastman

Fifteen-year-old Stands Like a Spirit, Cloud Man's youngest daughter, became the last of the chief's daughters to marry. Seth Eastman, her future spouse, was a recent graduate of the U.S. Military Academy at West Point when he arrived at Fort Snelling in 1829. The 22-year-old officer soon met the attractive Dakota teenager and a romance blossomed.[18]

Musket slits in the South Battery wall

Stands Like a Spirit and Eastman married in what Samuel Pond described as "Indian form," and in short order the young wife was expecting a child. Their daughter Winona (Nancy Eastman) was still an infant when her father received a new assignment and had to leave his young family. Charles Eastman, the soldier's mixed-blood grandson, later recorded family memories of Seth Eastman and the soldier's relationship with his daughter. He wrote that Seth was "...very tender toward his child," adding, during his last visit with Nancy, he "...pressed [the child] to his heart while tears ran down his noble young face." It appears he never saw his Mdewakanton wife again and it would be 1848 before he once more encountered Nancy.[19]

Before departing, Seth Eastman made arrangements for his daughter's future support, telling Stands Like a Spirit, "...whenever she needed anything for the child to go to Wasicum Hanska (Henry Sibley, then still a fur trader) and ask for it and she would have it." Stands Like a Spirit and her mother, Uncheedah, took on the task of raising Nancy Eastman. When the girl reached age 12, her mother approached Samuel Pond with a request to let her daughter stay with his family. Stands Like a Spirit reminded him that Nancy's father was white and a Christian.[20]

At about this same time, the Ponds had consented to take charge of Nancy's cousin Jane Lamont, Hushes the Night's daughter. They agreed Nancy could live with them, but Stands Like a Spirit's mother, Uncheedah, had other ideas. Samuel Pond reported her complaint, "...now that she is able to help me you will take her away...you shall not have her...." It is also likely that her grandmother wanted her raised Mdewakanton.[21]

Nancy Eastman grew into a strikingly beautiful young woman. Her son Ohiyesa, later known as Charles Eastman, did not know her since she died shortly after his birth, but he proudly described her legendary beauty. Writing in English later in his life, Charles said his mother "...was known as the handsomest woman of all the Spirit Lake (Mdewakanton) and Leaf-Dweller (Wahpeton) Sioux."[22] Eastman explained to his English-speaking readers that his mother's adult name meant Demi-Goddess; her Dakota name was Wakantankawin, or Great Spirit Woman.

In fall 1841 Seth Eastman returned to Fort Snelling to assume command. He brought along Mary Henderson Eastman, his 23-year-old Anglo-American wife. Historian Rena Neumann Coen believes a letter written by George Turner, the fort surgeon, provides evidence that Mary encountered Nancy/Great Spirit Woman, her husband's mixed-blood daughter, while at Snelling.[23]

A wintertime attack of scarlet fever struck Mary and her daughter Virginia in 1846. Wrote Dr. Turner, "Mrs. Eastman sent for Mary [likely he meant Nancy] to come quick and take charge of the sick child and seemed willing to resign herself totally to an enemy's care...." [24] It seems probable that Nancy Eastman,

mixed-blood's performance would teach the ailing Mary "a salutary lesson."[25]

Nancy Eastman/Great Spirit Woman soon eloped with the deceptively clever Many Lightnings. According to an oft-told family story, the 17-year-old, high-spirited like her mother, decided to run off with a young man who could not afford the "bride's price" required for her hand. Many Lightnings, an admirer of Nancy, learned of the plan and, with his head covered by a blanket, arrived at the meeting place. He then sneaked off with her before her expected suitor arrived. Despite this deception, their marriage was a success and the couple raised four sons and a daughter. Nancy died of complications from childbirth and scarlet fever in 1858 shortly after Charles was born.[26]

Artist Frank Blackwell Mayer's, *Thunder Dance*, a watercolor painted in 1851

her husband's Dakota daughter, was the "enemy" to whom Turner referred. The doctor had been stationed at Snelling since 1840 and would have known she was the fort commander's daughter even if he didn't recall her Anglo name. Turner reported that Nancy had "not neglected her charge," and hoped the young

As the stories of Cloud Man's daughters illustrate, country marriages—matrimony in the Dakota manner—created significant issues. First, among many, were the marriages themselves. In the cases of the men who married Cloud Man's daughters, such alliances appeared to be casual at best. But the fate of children born of these marriages became a matter of greater consequence.

Clearly, Lawrence Taliaferro wished to see his daughter assimilated into the Anglo-American culture and exerted considerable influence on his daughter Mary from his post as Fort Snelling Indian agent. Mary seemed to redeem her father's hopes by adapting. She married a white man, raised children and lived in

The houses of Henry Sibley, foreground, and Jean Baptiste Faribault were part of the American Fur Company's trading base at Mendota.

white society at Mendota and St. Paul, even after becoming a widow. Yet late in life she decided to take her remaining daughter and move with her mixed-blood son to Nebraska's Santee Indian Reservation. Mary lived there until her death, at age 88, in 1916.

Seth Eastman's military transfer soon after his daughter Nancy's birth broke a developing bond. His unpredictable travels as a military officer made any intervention in Nancy's future almost impossible. Nancy Eastman/Great Spirit Woman led a Mdewakanton existence, but some of her children adopted Anglo-American ways. Following the Minnesota Dakota War, Nancy's husband, Many Lightnings, converted to Christianity, a faith he insisted his offspring adopt. He

also assumed the name Jacob Eastman, using the surname of his wife's father. Two sons from this marriage decided, at their father's urging, to get formal schooling. Both became significant leaders. John Eastman, the eldest, worked as a Presbyterian clergyman at Flandreau, South Dakota, and later as overseer of the Dakota band there. Charles Eastman became a physician and noted American author, sought after for his experience and knowledge of Dakota culture.

Daniel Lamont wasn't around long enough to exert much influence on the future of his daughter Jane. The decision of Hushes the Night, her mother, to send Jane to live with Anglo missionaries resulted in a clear cultural choice by her daughter. Jane taught at Indian schools, married a white man and, with him, chose the life of a settler. When the Dakota members of her family joined the 1853 exodus to the Minnesota River reserve, Jane stayed behind.

Helen Sibley, the daughter of fur trader and future governor Henry Sibley and Red Blanket Woman, whom he married in the winter of 1840–41, is not considered in this account, but deserves mention. Sibley arranged for Helen's adoption by an Anglo-American family and assisted her financially. He remained in regular contact with Helen, sent her to an eastern boarding school when she was a teenager, and saw her develop into an accomplished woman. In 1859, at age 20, she married Sylvester Sawyer, an Anglo-American doctor. They chose a Methodist ceremony. Helen gave birth to a daughter less than a year after her marriage but, sadly, the young mother died of scarlet fever soon after the delivery. The infant perished a few days later.[27]

ANGLO-DAKOTA MARRIAGE

As the case of Cloud Man's daughters illustrates, interracial and intercultural marriage during Minnesota's pre-territorial period—roughly 1820–1849—presented some predictable challenges.

When committing to marriages with Dakota women, Anglo-Americans of the 1820s followed the practices established by French, British and mixed-blood French-Indians in the 18th century. For early traders, such unions typically stemmed from romantic love, sexual attraction and/or the prospect of improving their standing in the native community. Suitors forging marital links with Cloud Man's daughters were leaders in the new American community around Fort Snelling. Such matrimony, at that time, made cultural and business sense to both Indian and white.[1]

In the 1820s and 1830s, racial diversity in the immediate Fort Snelling area was the rule, not the exception. A clergyman writing about this integrated culture in June 1838 noted, "These traders (on Fort Snelling reservation) brought into the country with them men of different bloods, some white, some half & quarter bloods, some French & some Americans [etc.]. The most of these men married women of whole, half & quarter blood Indians of the Sioux (Dakota) & Chippewa (Ojibwe) nations."[2] A traveler at Lac qui Parle mission on the upper Minnesota River saw a similar mix of races "consisting of Yankies, French, Scotch, Irish, Half-breeds and Sioux (Dakota) Indians...." He called it a "higgledy-piggledy" assembly.[3]

Although some visitors to the region found racial mixing distasteful, Anglo-Americans manning this remote frontier outpost embraced the long and successful tradition of intermarriage begun by the French nearly 200 years earlier. A "country marriage" proved acceptable to both Indian and white, but was not binding under American law.

U-SE-DO-HA.
Dakota (Sioux) Belle.

Following the 1862 Dakota War, Minnesota photographers typically labeled images of the Dakota with their names and perceived status. U-se-do-ha is called a "Dakota (Sioux) Belle."

While some Anglo-Dakota marriages lasted for life, others were ended quickly, even carelessly, and almost always by the white partner. It is unlikely the well-born trio of Lawrence Taliaferro, Seth Eastman and Henry Sibley considered their marriages

Henry Lewis oil painting, *Fort Snelling*, about 1850

to Mdewakanton women as life-long commitments. As a career officer and gentleman, Eastman would not have been able to travel with a Native wife in the social circles he would frequent. Virginia-born, slave owning Taliaferro came from a distinguished family with American roots dating back to about 1637. They would have expected him to marry within his class and racial group. The fact that he traveled back East to marry an Anglo-American at a time when his Mdewakanton wife was expecting their child is telling.

Sibley's English forebears reached America in 1629 and produced noted descendants including his father, the chief justice of the Michigan Territorial Court. It would have been difficult for Sibley to present a Native wife to the society from whence he came. The brevity of his country marriage also speaks of his commitment to it.[4]

Joel Whitney's 1863 photo of Can-ku was-te win (Good Road Woman) carries the words "A Sioux Beauty."

Marriage between Native women and Anglo-American men could, and sometimes did, overcome the cultural-racial divide. This more often proved the case with early trappers, traders and government farmers whose lives intertwined with Indians. Such was the example of Philander Prescott, a founder of Richfield, and his union with his wife, Mary. Their relationship weathered difficult times, surviving until Prescott's untimely death at the onset of the Minnesota Dakota War.

In marrying an Anglo-American, Native women were likely to see a reduction of heavy labor, along with a substantial increase in material things. Nonetheless, they were confronted by the standards of white society in which the husband held nearly absolute authority over his wife and children. "Under Anglo-American law, women literally ceased to exist legally once married," wrote historian Jane Lamm Carroll.[5]

At the 1855 marriage of early feminist Lucy Stone, both bride and groom joined in reading a statement protesting a husband's control over a wife's person, ownership of her property and income, their children, and the "whole system by which the legal existence of the wife is suspended during marriage."[6] One Dakota man commented on the position of white women, "We have seen that the white man makes his women like toys, like pets. Now we see they are possessions, without names of their own."[7]

Dakota husbands also took the lead in marriage, but women in that tribal society held some standing. Samuel Pond, who once lived with Cloud Man's people, produced this firsthand observation regarding Dakota women circa 1834: "...but a slight acquaintance" with the Santee (eastern Dakota) would show "the

Fort Snelling's sutler sold goods not provided by the army and also traded with the Dakota and Ojibwe.

PUBLISHED BY WHITNEY'S GALLERY, ST. PAUL, MINN.

SIOUX SQUAW AND PAPPOOSE,

Whitney applied what became the racially-charged epithets of "squaw and pappoose" to this Dakota mother and infant.

women were not afraid of their husbands [and] are not the right material to be made slaves." [8]

Mary Henderson Eastman took issue with such assessments. Mary, the Anglo-American wife of Fort Snelling commander Seth Eastman, became interested in the Dakota during her late 1840s stay at the military base. She believed, from a point of view based upon New England propriety, Dakota society "degraded" women. Mary Eastman saw tribal culture as overwhelmingly "male dominated." She wrote of a woman's status, "…when she is a wife there is little sympathy for her condition," she "must bear the burdens of the family," and "her work is never done." [9]

Tribal tradition afforded Native women some control over their lives. Generally, after marriage a Dakota man became a member of the wife's family and band. In that society, matriarchal in nature, women owned the home and all inside it, retained control of their children regardless of marital status, held authority to control the food they raised and gathered, worked together and relied upon each other. Women could also count upon kinship networks for assistance—a critically important component in any Dakota community. Some, perhaps all, of this traditional support network could be lost after marriage to an Anglo-American. [10]

As he made his way to Fort Snelling in 1820, Philander Prescott, Cloud Man's future government farmer, took note of attractive Menomonee women living in eastern Wisconsin. He learned they were often sought for marriage. To Prescott's way of thinking, there were good reasons for this: "I found this tribe had furnished about all the women for the trader's wives, for they are generally good looking, and their children were as white as many of the white children." Prescott would marry Spirit of the Moon, a member of Cloud Man's band. She took the Anglo name Mary. [11]

Whites new to the area found the eastern Dakota people to be fit, strong and attractive. Missionary Samuel Pond wrote that the Indians on average were taller than Anglo-Americans and more uniform in height. A New Englander visiting a Dakota hunting camp southwest of Fort Snelling asserted in a letter home, "The men were all young & most of them really fine looking fellows & and the girls rather handsome." Mary Henderson Eastman agreed, writing about the males, "They are, as a race, tall, fine-looking men." [12]

Replica of Dakota moccasins

Commemorative brass door knocker, Henry Sibley house

Prescott later wrote of the Dakota custom of a bride's price—obtaining a wife by purchase. He paid a "pony and some goods" for his. Prescott believed it "...frequently happens that there is not much love in the case, and sometimes the woman never expects to marry the man that she is sometimes compelled to marry." He claimed that suicide is a "not uncommon thing among the women...."[13]

The final words of Henry Sibley's unfinished autobiography illustrate his belief that both Dakota and white held conservative views on chastity. "...female virtue was held in as high estimation among the Sioux (Dakota) bands in their wild state, as by the whites, and the line between the chaste, and the demimonde, quite as well defined."[14]

A biographer provides a caveat for this statement, noting these words were chosen for "readers that worshipped propriety."[15] Had Sibley finished his life story, he might have told about his country marriage to Red Blanket Woman during the winter of 1840–41. His wife, a member of the Black Dog Mdewakanton

band, subsequently gave birth in August 1841 to their child Wahkiyee (Bird), later known as Helen Hastings Sibley.[16]

Overt ethnic stereotyping and racism came to the region hand in hand with the advance of Anglo-American civilization.

As early as 1853, one writer characterized the Minnesota of "a very few years ago" as "uninhabited save by the different hordes of savage tribes...."[17] Such phrasing was now becoming common, even to people who knew Indian history and culture. In 1851, Indian agent Nathaniel McLean advised the Dakota through the English-Dakota newspaper *The Dakota Friend*, "Other savage tribes have listened to the words of civilized men and are well off...if you do as they have done[,] the Great American Chief...would rejoice in your elevation."[18]

The Dakota also noticed a hardening of white attitudes towards them during the territorial period, 1849–1858. "They seemed to say," recalled Big Eagle, a Mdewakanton chief, "I am much better than you." He added, "...some white men abused Indian women in a certain way and disgraced them, and surely there was no excuse for that."[19]

By the turn of the 20th century, racial intermarriage in the United States was banned by law or greatly restrained by emerging social conventions. White ethnocentrism and racism in American society would become a dominant and menacing factor in the lives of Native people and other minorities. This cultural evolution would have surprised those racially and ethnically diverse citizens living around Fort Snelling during the 19th century's first decades.

Henry Sibley's Mendota home

A Missionary's Mission and "The Dakota Friend"

In the winter of 1850–51, Gideon Pond, working from his Oak Grove mission in the future Bloomington, published a newspaper written for the Dakota people in their language and English. After long years of arduous, largely unsuccessful efforts to bring the Dakota to Christianity, the dedicated Presbyterian missionary hoped this new method would make a familiar message more meaningful.

"Oh give me wisdom and discretion that I may conduct this difficult and responsible work to thy name and to thy glory. What am I that I should perform such a service!" So wrote Gideon Pond in his November 4, 1850, diary entry. He had just delivered the first issue of *The Dakota Friend* to a printer.

With this fervent prayer on his lips, Gideon Pond hopefully embarked upon a fresh approach in his ardent campaign to persuade the Dakota people to adopt Euro-American society and the Christian belief system fundamental to it. The determined missionary, now 40 and entering his 17th year with the Indians, was still searching for a way to make clear the benefits of American culture and the word of his God to a skeptical audience.

Stephen Return Riggs, a fellow missionary, later wrote with insight, "Mr. Pond had long been yearning to see the inside of an Indian. He (Pond) sometimes said he wanted to be an Indian, if only for half an hour, that he might know how an Indian felt and by what motives he could be moved." By 1850, his Minnesota experience may have cooled the "heaven-kindled flame" that, according to his nephew and biographer, once burned bright and pure in Gideon Pond's heart. But he continued his work.[1]

Gideon now planned to reach to the Dakota by publishing a newspaper written in both their language and English. He sought and received permission from his superiors at the American Board of Commissioners for Foreign Missions (ABCFM) to proceed.

Gideon Pond

Pond called the modest monthly *Dakota Tawaxitka Kin*, or *The Dakota Friend*.[2]

On page four of the first issue, Pond made no direct mention of religious instruction in a description of the newspaper's objectives: "…to bring before the Indian mind such items of news as will interest them, and any such matter…will be calculated to improve their physical, mental and moral condition." Nonetheless, each issue would carry Christian tracts, parables and lessons.[3]

Gideon Pond and his older brother Samuel, inspired in 1831 by religious reawakening, decided to travel to the Fort Snelling area where they expected to work with the Dakota. Samuel recognized the challenge of going to that nation, which he characterized as "...the most savage and warlike of all the northwestern Indians." Nevertheless, Samuel believed their prospects to serve were good, observing, "If God is with us, it will be enough." They would begin their service as lay ministers and instructors of agricultural technique before their ordinations.[4]

The Pond House at Oak Grove mission

The Ponds and fellow ABCFM missionaries, after long, challenging work among the Dakota, managed to build friendships and a level of trust, but had little success in converting them to Christianity. There had been some early success in the mid-1830s at Lac qui Parle mission, eight miles northwest of present-day Montevideo. About 40 people, mostly women from mixed-blood Joseph Renville's large extended family, attended church services. Rev. Thomas Williamson and Alexander Huggins founded this mission in 1835. Gideon

Pond was also stationed there (1836-1839) before returning to the future Bloomington, eventually to found the Oak Grove mission.[5]

Steven R. Riggs warned the Ponds, in December 1839, about becoming disheartened with their work, "Don't be discouraged. I am afraid you will, and therefore I always say this when I write you." It appears they needed support.

Gideon, in particular, proved sensitive. Rev. Robert Hopkins wrote in 1849, "It is almost a proverb with some of us that Bro. G.H. Pond looks at the dark side of things."[6]

Missionaries found Dakota men particularly reluctant to join their church. At Lac qui Parle, six years passed before a man became a member. In 1848, Orpe, an ailing Mdewakanton man living near Oak Grove, called Pond to his lodge and appeared ready to reject his traditional beliefs. He "...gave me his gods [likely a 'medicine sack'] saying they were no good for nothing," reported Pond. Orpe's was a "death bed" conversion. He died a week after his meeting with Pond, his passing unobserved by the Dakota. Only his wife was present at his burial.[7]

At Lac qui Parle, meanwhile, just 18 Dakota remained as active members in good standing at the mission church by 1849, despite the fact 54 had enrolled since 1835. Increased resistance during the 1840s to the missionaries and their work stemmed, in significant part, from Indian complaints about payments due them from the Treaty of 1837. The Dakota believed churchmen intercepted some of the funds designated for "education and civilization"—cash, the Indians maintained, that should have been theirs to control. Fourteen years later during new land negotiations, Indian leaders still complained about the misuse of their 1837 treaty funds. Said eastern Dakota spokesman Little Crow, "We will talk of nothing else but that money, if it is until next spring."[8]

After nearly two decades of largely unsuccessful crusading for Christianity, Gideon Pond opened a new front in his campaign to gain from the Dakota increased acceptance of the Christian religion along with the new American civilization that came with it. He would publish his message in Minnesota's first religious periodical.

"The Dakota Friend" as Propaganda

There is no doubt that Gideon Pond hoped to bring the Christian religion to the Indians who read or heard the news from *The Dakota Friend*. It is equally certain that he and his brother Samuel believed that increased Euro-American settlement would provide what small-scale missionary demonstration programs could not—an example of the well-ordered efficient American way of life. The organization of Minnesota Territory in 1849 promised Americanization sooner, rather than later.

One critic called *The Dakota Friend* "the official propaganda organ of the Dakota mission,"[9] an apt description that is open to expansion. Editor Pond also allowed Indian agent Nathaniel McLean access to readers. McLean saw the newspaper as an effective vehicle for bringing to Indians all the news he wanted them to hear. Excerpts from Pond's monthly show a consistent advocacy for the missionary and government positions, which typically were squarely aligned.

The Dakota learned in late 1850 that the United States government wanted to buy their remaining Minnesota Territory land.[10]

The Dakota Friend, Gideon Pond's Dakota and English language newspaper

When Samuel Pond heard Dakota complaints about the land proposal, he defended the government position in *The Dakota Friend*. He claimed charges that the Americans wanted to "rob them of their lands and drive them off the prairie" were not true. Pond said the United States would pay for Indian property and explained that the government offered Indians a choice. "The Americans wish to have them (the Dakota) live and for that reason will gather them in some place by themselves. Indians and white men cannot dwell together." Samuel Pond did see an option whereby Indian and white could live side by side: "[If the Dakota] would all...turn their attention to planting and make an earnest effort to adopt the habits of civilized people, they could dwell in the neighborhood of the Americans."[11]

Free advice continued to be offered by *The Dakota Friend*. The third issue, in January 1851, mentioned the value of hard work: "He who learns to work, accustom himself to it, and holds out, will dwell in a good house and will not be poor, while he who conducts himself shiftlessly, refuses to work, and is ashamed of work, it is said, will be poor and destitute and a beggar."[12]

In this same edition agent Nathaniel McLean praised *The Dakota Friend* in an article written for "My Dakota Children." McLean wrote, "Because white men who reside among you, have kind feelings toward you, and desire your welfare, they are publishing a newspaper. This pleases me. Now I can speak to you through the paper...."

McLean offered advice and important news. "Your Great Father (the American President) is anxious that his Dakota grand children, and all other savage tribes learn to read—adopt the manners of civilized men...." He noted their Great Father "heartily approves of the operations of your Missionaries, and wishes you listen to their

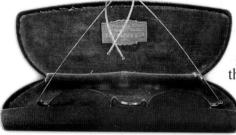

Nineteenth century spectacles in their case
Bloomington Historical Society collection

words." McLean then informed his newspaper audience that the government planned to buy their land.

McLean's letter in the February *The Dakota Friend* advised his Indian readers to turn in some young men reported to be stealing from whites. "I have heard that some of the young men have stolen from the white men. If these reports are true those of you...who desire to live in peace with the white men must assist me [and] expose those who are guilty. I shall expect this of you." The Indian agent implied he was looking out for the Dakota since, "If they molest the white men, I fear that they will bring great evil on themselves...."[13]

Although he was uncharacteristically oblique in the opening of his March

Gideon Pond's "Betty Lamp" burned fat or oil in its bowl.
Bloomington Historical Society collection

message "To my Dakota children," Indian and white alike understood McLean's words. "The great Council (Congress) at Washington has adjourned, and...when Mr. Sibley returns we shall hear some of the words of the Great Father, the President." The federal government was about to summon the Dakota to meetings regarding the sale of "Suland," the vast expanse of southern Minnesota Territory that still remained under Indian control.[14]

McLean then informed readers of starvation among the Wahpeton and Sisseton along the upper Minnesota River. "[I]t makes me sad to learn that some of my children...have suffered sorely from famine," said the sympathetic agent. He then pointed out there were lessons to be learned from such suffering. "White men don't depend upon the chase for their subsistence. Foreseeing the cold of winter, they, in summer build warm houses, raise large quantities of corn, wheat, potatoes and turnips...they also keep domestic animals...." Indians could learn to escape famine, he added, if "they would imitate the white man."[15]

In September 1851 Pond printed a summary of the land treaty agreed to by the Dakota the month before. In all, the Indians ceded an empire of some 24 million acres for $1,665,000 in cash and annuities. In reporting on the treaty-signing ceremony, Pond observed

A closer look at *The Dakota Friend's* masthead

that government negotiators Luke Lea and Gov. Alexander Ramsey gave the Dakota leaders "…a few words of very appropriate, and healthful advice, on various subjects connected with their future…."[16]

The Missionary Role

Both Gideon and Samuel Pond seemed to accept the apparent cultural imperative at work in Minnesota Territory during the early 1850s. Euro-American control of Dakota lands meant a wave of white immigration was about to break over the former Indian domain, sweeping Native inhabitants out of the way. Such had been the pattern of American growth since Congress opened, in 1787, Indian lands north of the Ohio River and east of the Mississippi.

The Pond brothers believed it proper to meld Christian theology to the lofty ideals and standards of a youthful democracy in order to lead the Dakota to salvation and a place in the superior American civilization. In later years missionaries have been criticized for an unquestioning presumption that their race and culture were superior to all others.

Illustrating the charge of missionary ethnocentrism is an excerpt from an 1846 speech by J.B. Ramsey, another Presbyterian missionary. Addressing an Indian audience, he pointed to places shown on a large map where people lived in "ignorance and misery" and "destitute of the Bible." Reported Ramsey, "I showed them people who speak the English language…held the great power of the world, and possessed the greater part of its wisdom and knowledge…." He told his listeners, "…power was to be obtained by Christianity alone."[17]

Members of the 1858 Dakota treaty delegation traveled to Washington, D.C. Big Eagle stands at the left.

Nineteenth century farmers used split-rail fences, such as this one next to the Pond House, because of their simple construction and durability.

In 1849 Alexander Reid asserted missionaries should focus upon Indian males as they attempted to bring Native people into the fold. "We must teach [boys] to think, feel, act and work. We must form their whole character—all their religious, moral, intellectual, social and industrial habits. This is the work to be done."[18]

The Presbyterian ABCFM board, the supervisors who had governed Minnesota missionaries, heard M.J. Hichock proudly proclaim in 1865, "Over half the heathen world already has been steamrolled, washing the bloody temples of Paganism, quenching the fires of horrid altars...[Missionary work] has lifted whole nations from debasement of the brute to the dignity of the sons of God."[19]

Gary Cavender offered, from a late 20th century perspective, a Dakota view of mission work. "The missionaries were the vanguard of the government. [They] would go in and prepare for the government to come in after them." Cavender also noted, "I believe the missionaries' hearts were in the right place." [20]

The words of Ramsey, Reid, Hichock and Cavender would not have surprised Big Eagle (Wamditanka), a Mdewakanton chieftain born near Mendota in 1827. Big Eagle spoke about Dakota dissatisfaction with the missionaries and other whites attempting to change Indian ways. He summed up the case against their Euro-American mindset: "There was great dissatisfaction among the Indians over many things the whites did.... The whites were always trying to make the Indians give up their life and live like white men—go to farming, work hard and do as they did—and the Indians did not know how to do that, and did not want to anyway. It seemed too sudden to make a change. If the Indians had tried to make the whites live like them, the whites would have resisted, and it was the same way with many Indians."[21]

The Dakota, according to Big Eagle, also chafed under the attitudes displayed by the Euro-Americans. "Then many of the white men often abused the Indians and treated them unkindly.... Many of the whites always seemed to say by their manner when they saw an Indian, 'I am much better than you,' and Indians did not like this."[22]

Minnesota missionaries received deserved praise for denying themselves the comforts provided by an increasingly wealthy American society in order to spend lives of service and hard labor in remote Indians villages. They predicated such lives on evangelicalism but, in most cases, did as much or more work improving the education, health care and agricultural production of the people with whom they lived.

The Pond brothers can serve as apt models of such dedication. They both chose their life's work under the influence of an American evangelical resurgence known as the Second Great Awakening. This movement echoed a similar American colonial era of religious revivalism in which enthusiastic adherents dedicated or rededicated their lives to God. Samuel and Gideon Pond became Connecticut converts of this movement.

Reading the letters and diaries written by the Ponds provides little evidence of backsliding from their original goal. But their lack of success in converting the Dakota continually frustrated the brothers, a factor that led them to finally leave their work, Samuel in 1852 and Gideon two years later. They stayed

Big Eagle, a Mdewakanton leader during the 1862 Minnesota Dakota War

behind to minister to white settlers when the Dakota moved to their Minnesota River Valley reservation following the 1851 treaty signings. Gideon remained in Bloomington and Samuel at Prairieville (Shakopee).[23]

It appears the discouraged brothers also thought that consolidating the Dakota bands on a small reservation would only increase Indian opposition to their work. Said Samuel, "We did not like to take our families among such a horde of lawless, reckless sons of Belial."[24]

Gideon Pond performed a final service to the Dakota people, one that clearly gratified him. Hundreds of Indian men had been imprisoned in Mankato following the Minnesota Dakota War of 1862, more than 300 under sentence of death. About 50 men of the Lake Calhoun band, men who for the most part knew Pond, asked that he baptize them.[25]

"They were before bound in the chains and confined in the prison of Paganism…" wrote Pond. The war proved to be "…like the earthquake to shake the foundations of their prison, and everyone's bonds have been loosed." Under the very real threat of impending death it is possible the prisoners underwent a "death row conversion." After a review ordered by President Lincoln, the number sentenced to die was reduced to 40, and finally 38. All but two on the final list of the condemned were baptized.[26]

As they awaited execution, the 38 Dakota chanted tribal death songs.

On December 27, 1862, Gen. Henry Sibley informed the president by telegraph that "…38 Indians and half-breeds ordered by you for execution were hung yesterday at Mankato, at 10:00 A.M. Everything went off quietly."[27]

"Many of the whites always seemed to say by their manner when they saw an Indian, 'I am much better than you,' and Indians did not like this."

Big Eagle

BET ON SIX: BALL-PLAY TOURNAMENT BRINGS HUNDREDS TO OAK GROVE

In July 1852, members of five Mdewakanton Dakota bands met at Oak Grove mission for "ball-play," the term their host, Gideon H. Pond, attached to a popular Indian pastime. The scenic venue, located in present-day Bloomington, provided splendid views of the Minnesota River Valley. The contest shaped up to be Minnesota Territory's largest in terms of participants since the games among the Sisseton and Wahpeton during the 1851 land treaty negotiations at Traverse des Sioux.

Indian Ball Players, George Catlin lithograph, about 1840

against a combined "home team" comprised of competitors from the Good Road, Sky Man (Cloud Man) and Grey Iron bands who lived closer to Oak Grove.

Excitement ran high as game day approached. Traditionally the competitors wagered heavily on the match's outcome before competition began. The ball-play set for Oak Grove produced remarkably large stakes. Six's men put up 16 guns (six with double-barrels), eight horses, blankets, cloth, belts and more, worth, according to Pond, "at least $800." The combined members of

Gideon Pond waited expectantly for Six ("Shakopee" in the Dakota language means six) and his Dakota ball players. Although representatives of five Mdewakanton bands had previously agreed to meet for ball-play (the Native American game that evolved into lacrosse), Pond couldn't be certain the event, scheduled for his Oak Grove mission on July 14, would take place until the contestants arrived.[1]

Six's band, one of the two largest Mdewakanton communities with about 500 members, moved into view as expected on Sunday the 13th. They traveled a longer distance and were comparative visitors when matched

Pond called ball-play a "severe game," reporting, "players receive knocks and bruises from which they do not recover for weeks or months; and sometimes they are knocked down by blows from the ball or club."

the Good Road, Sky Man and Grey Iron bands matched that amount. As the match started, Pond estimated the number of men and boys playing at close to 250, with between 200 to 300 spectators looking on.[2]

What Pond called "ball-play" originated in the eastern part on North America. Algonquian tribes are credited with its invention as early as the 1600s. It was a game of massive teams, seldom fewer than 100 players and sometimes more than 1,000, all in action at the same time. Playing fields used natural boundaries and were immense. Goals could be set several miles from each other but were typically 500 yards to a half-mile apart. Usually there were no side boundaries, so contestants could move over a large swath of land. Competitors carried a stick two to three feet long with one end bent into a palm-sized circle with crossed strips of rawhide forming a ball holder. Players could catch, carry or throw the ball using the pocket at the end of the stick. The object: move the ball over the opposing group's boundary, hit a designated target with the ball, or propel it between two posts.[3]

Pond called ball-play a "severe game," reporting, "players receive knocks and bruises from which they do not recover for weeks or months; and sometimes they are knocked down by blows from the ball or club." Explorer and writer Jonathan Carver said participants played the game "with much vehemence and they frequently wound each other." The contest also served as a kind of war game. Attributes of a great player matched those of a great warrior—strength, speed, endurance, agility, determination and courage. Cherokees viewed the sport as the "little brother of war."[4]

Philander Prescott, an early Minnesota and Richfield settler, reported on one game he witnessed. The field was a half-mile long with action starting at mid-field. When one team got the

Pictured is the entrance to the Pond house at Oak Grove mission in present-day south Bloomington. Gideon Pond wrote the description of the Dakota ball-play game referred to in this story.

ball across the opponent's goal, the competitors changed sides and play restarted. If the same team then moved the ball across the now-opposite goal, they collected the goods wagered. The match could then start over.[5]

Players tended to paint themselves for games of importance. Pond noted they "smeared" their bodies with assorted colors, "blue, white and yellow clay, charcoal, vermilion etc." Many wore ornaments in their hair and attached the tail of a fox, wolf or other animal to their belts. Pond observed that competitors he saw were generally naked except for a belt around the waist that held a breechcloth in place.[6]

As the Monday, July 14, match at Oak Grove opened, men and boys from Six's band gained an early advantage. They pressed on to a victory and excitedly claimed the sizeable prize package. Undeterred by the loss, the combined Good Road, Sky Man and Grey Iron team asked for a rematch. The amount wagered, however, shrunk in size. Six's team also won the second and a third match. One player, Visible Mouth, was knocked senseless but later recovered. The teams scheduled a rematch for Tuesday morning and then feasted on a post-game meal that included a barrel of pork, two kegs of lard and 10 sacks of corn.

Monday's losers became Tuesday's winners, and Six's men lost much of what they had already earned. The victors credited a time-worn game ball, made by a war prophet from Wabasha's band, with helping them triumph. Buoyed by their success, the Good Road, Sky Man and Grey Iron team challenged Six's men to

a Wednesday rematch. Six's athletes accepted.

Six's team lost the Wednesday opener and a prize stake that included guns, blankets, coats, cloth, tomahawks and pipes valued at about $350. Six's team then lost the second game, but readied for a third. Tempers flared when the winners insisted they had not received all of the promised goods. Grey Iron's men left the field in protest. Pond believed the ball-play ended because of the arrival of a contingent of Little Crow's men pledged to assist Six's team.

It appears this remarkable spectacle of able athletes was the last such match in the Fort Snelling vicinity, then the heart of the new Minnesota Territory. The eastern Dakota, including the Mdewakanton bands that played at Oak Grove mission, had reluctantly sold their land and would soon be moving west to their new Minnesota River Valley reservations.

The cheers of enthusiastic spectators witnessing that exciting, often bruising 1852 ball game echoed across the fields near Oak Grove. One hundred-nine years later sports enthusiasts traveled to Bloomington to watch athletes play another exciting, sometimes violent game. The Minnesota Vikings took over their new home, Metropolitan Stadium, a venue located about three miles from the Dakota's Oak Grove playing field.

Replica of a Dakota ball-play stick with strips of rawhide fashioned into a pocket

GEORGE QUINN'S DECISION:
"I WENT WITH MY PEOPLE AGAINST THE WHITES."

The August 1862 outbreak of fighting between the Dakota and whites presented part-white, part-Indian "mixed-bloods" with a potentially dangerous dilemma: Which side were they on? Anglo-Dakota, at the time, represented an estimated 15 percent of Dakotas living on reservations.[1] This quandary of race and culture confronted 19-year-old mixed-blood George Quinn, a resident of Bloomington. It is possible his father was Peter Quinn, most remembered today as a founder of Bloomington.[2]

"I am half white man and half Indian, and I learned to read and write the Sioux language at Lake Calhoun under the instruction of the Pond brothers. But I never learned to speak English and I was raised among the Indians as one of them." With these words, George Quinn, also known as George Ortley (Dakota name Wakandayamani, The Spirit that Rattles as It Walks), introduced himself during an 1898 interview with Return I. Holcombe, a St. Paul newspaperman and historian. Then age 55, Quinn recounted his part in the 1862 war.[3]

Peter Quinn, a prominent settler, Indian farmer and founder of Bloomington, may have been George Quinn's father. George's mother, Ineyahewin, was a member of Cloud Man's Lake Calhoun band at a time when Peter worked as government farmer for that group. As the Dakota War flared in August 1862, Peter Quinn joined a military expedition traveling to Redwood Ferry. The 73-year-old interpreter was shot and killed during an attack on this unit.[4]

In his interview with Holcombe, George Quinn said he took part in the attack at Redwood Ferry "and helped destroy that command." Twenty-four soldiers died in the fighting, including interpreter Peter Quinn and Capt. John Marsh, commander at nearby Fort Ridgely. George Quinn made no mention of the killing of Peter Quinn during that incident.[5]

George then joined a reconnaissance party sent to Fort Ridgely, home of

This 1865 studio portrait labels its subject, Te-na-ze-pa, a "Dakota warrior." Such Dakota soldiers and some mixed-bloods, including George Quinn (Wakandayamani), proved formidable opponents for U.S. forces that fought them during Minnesota's 1862 Dakota War.

Company B, U.S. Fifth Minnesota Infantry, to assess the base's vulnerability to attack. But before the Little Crow-led army could move against the fort, a 50-man element of Company B returned to Ridgely. On August 20, the Dakota launched the first of two unsuccessful assaults against the fort. George Quinn took part in the second. He and Good Thunder were attempting to capture horses near the stables when an artillery shell struck close by. The explosion panicked the horse Quinn was leading, and the frightened animal escaped. The Dakota did not press the attack because their leaders feared heavy losses.[6]

Upon learning of the fighting in the Minnesota River valley, Minnesota Gov. Alexander Ramsey ordered former governor and longtime Indian trader, Henry Sibley, to lead a contingent of four infantry units to the scene. Sibley thus began organizing a campaign against the Dakota.[7]

After just over a month of battle, Sibley's relief force numbering 1,619 men appeared to be closing in on the main body of Dakota fighters. Little Crow now readied a surprise for his pursuers—a carefully orchestrated ambush. The plan would allow Sibley's army to get under way and then be attacked when it was extended along the road and vulnerable.[8]

George Quinn, along with 13 Dakota led by Killing Hawk, was among those placed to the rear of Sibley's men who were encamped near Wood Lake (five miles north of present-day Echo). Killing Hawk's men would help cut off any retreat by the soldiers once the Dakota force was unleashed. Some soldiers leaving Sibley's camp early in the morning of September 23 encountered the waiting Dakota, prematurely springing the trap. The two armies collided violently and fought for about two hours before the Indians withdrew.

Third Infantry soldiers advancing toward Quinn's position killed Killing Hawk and wounded eight more in the group, forcing the Indians to pull back. Sibley did not pursue the retreating Dakota. Some of the most prominent Indian leaders then took their families

Gunpowder flask

and headed west out of Sibley's reach. The Minnesota Dakota War, at least the first part of it, was now over.

Large numbers of Dakota, including those who opposed the war and had not taken part in it, as well as some who did, met with Sibley on September 26 near today's Montevideo. Following the release of those taken prisoner during the war—162 mixed-bloods and 107 whites—Sibley's men assumed control of a camp of about 1,200 friendly Dakota. More Indians, facing starvation, came in under flags of truce. George Quinn surrendered, giving his weapon to mixed-blood Samuel J. Brown.[9]

Quinn expected a quick release. "Nothing was proved against me except that I was in some of the battles against the whites. I took no part in killing the settlers and was opposed to such work," stated Quinn. He spent four years in a Rock Island, Illinois, prison before being released. The former Bloomington resident eventually came back to Minnesota and lived in the Morton area where, as a 19-year-old, he had taken part in the Battle of Redwood Ferry, the curtain raiser on the war. In 1915 Quinn died in Morton.[10]

Mixed-blood George Quinn never second-guessed his decision to fight on the side of the Dakota, saying, in later years, "...I was raised among the Indians as one of them. So when the outbreak came I went with my people against the whites."[11]

Dakota war club

PARALLEL LIVES, PARALLEL DEATHS: PHILANDER PRESCOTT AND PETER QUINN

There is marked symmetry in the lives and deaths of Peter Quinn and Philander Prescott, most remembered in Bloomington and Richfield as founders of those communities. Their similarity of experience in south Hennepin County is worth noting.

Philander Prescott, left, and Peter Quinn were among the first permanent white settlers reaching what became Minnesota Territory. Prescott arrived in 1819, Quinn five years later.

Philander Prescott's 1819 wintertime introduction to the future state of Minnesota was far from auspicious. The 19-year-old Prescott and a small party of traders had traveled by sleigh up the frozen Mississippi. Their mission was to resupply a detachment of soldiers building a United States fortress at the confluence of the St. Peter's and Mississippi rivers. Upon reaching their goal, they found many at the camp desperately ill and suffering "…in a very unhealthy state with the scurvy" were already dead. Supplies brought by Prescott's party helped bring the epidemic under control, but not before another 10 men died.[1]

Subsequently, the fort builders were reinforced and completed construction of a limestone citadel that would become known as Fort Snelling. During the summer of 1823 Prescott married Spirit of the Moon (Mary), a member of Cloud

Man's small Mdewakanton band. The following year he began service as fort sutler, trading with soldiers and a growing number of Indians.[2]

At age 30, Prescott took a job as official interpreter at Fort Snelling and then later accepted a position as government farmer at Cloud Man's village. There, at the behest of Lawrence Taliaferro, Indian agent at Fort Snelling, Prescott taught modern agricultural techniques—plowing, use of tools—to the Mdewakanton, attempting to induce them to take up farming. He was working there in 1830 and financing the operation, in large part, out of his own pocket.[3]

In 1839, Cloud Man and his people moved to present-day Bloomington and the bluffs overlooking the Minnesota River. Gideon Pond established Oak Grove mission on that site in 1843, and Peter Quinn assumed Prescott's farming position. Quinn's decision to move to the future Bloomington and work with the Dakota earned him the distinction of being a founder of that community.[4]

Peter Quinn, born in Dublin, Ireland, around 1789, took a circuitous route to Minnesota. English sailors kidnapped Peter when he was a schoolboy and took him to North America and York Factory on Hudson's Bay. He later made his way to Fort Garry (today's Winnipeg). There he met and married Mary Louisa, the mixed-blood daughter of a "Rocky Mountain Indian woman" and a trader named Finley.[5]

In 1824, Hudson Bay Company sent Quinn to Lac qui Parle, in the future Minnesota. Once there, he accepted an offer from the powerful American Fur Company to be its representative at Fort Snelling. Peter and Mary settled near the fort, and he began a career working for the federal government.

Like his contemporary and acquaintance Philander Prescott, Quinn served as a sometime interpreter for government officials. He traveled to Washington, D.C., with a delegation of eastern Dakota leaders led by Lawrence Taliaferro, to conclude the Treaty of 1837. The Dakota and Ojibwe agreed to sell a wedge of land between the St. Croix and Mississippi rivers claimed by both Indian nations. This was America's first major land acquisition within future Minnesota borders.[6]

In 1854 Philander Prescott, joined by Eli Pettijohn and William Moffett, bought 12 acres of land bordering Little Falls Creek (the future Minnehaha

Philander Prescott was an early Fort Snelling sutler, first selling trade goods there in 1824.

Creek). The trio set about building Richland flour mill, situated at present-day Lyndale Avenue about West 53rd Street. A trading point grew up around the mill, and in 1858 the town of Richfield was organized at a schoolhouse meeting there. Philander's association with Richland Mill and his three earlier decades in the area qualify him as a founder of Richfield.[7]

Both Prescott and Quinn received similar honors in 1856 when John Stevens, an early settler himself, made an address before the Minneapolis Lyceum. Stevens proclaimed Prescott the "oldest resident in Hennepin County" and, with generous praise concluded, "It would be difficult for me to express the good deeds Mr. Prescott has done. Our country should be proud of having such a man for a citizen...."[8] Stevens also mentioned Quinn's contributions, including his long residency in the area and his years working with the Dakota.

The Deaths of Quinn and Prescott

The life experiences of Philander Prescott and Peter Quinn show marked similarity. They were among the first non-military, white American men to move to the Fort Snelling area and settle there. Prescott married Spirit of the Moon (Mary), a Mdewakanton from Cloud Man's band, and Quinn wedded Mary Louisa Findley, a Cree-Scot mixed-blood. Both couples stayed together for life. For most of their lives, Prescott and Quinn made their homes among Indians. Each man worked as a trader with the

Dakota and Ojibwe, both took jobs as government farmers, and each worked with Cloud Man's people. The two men served as government translators during negotiations with Indians. Even the manner of their deaths proved remarkably similar.

Both Quinn and Prescott looked on in the 1850s as the Dakota, particularly the young men, seethed over the government's bad faith in not living up to treaty obligations. Among their grievances were the corrupt trade practices, encroachment of settlers, and the ongoing assault on their way of life. Prescott complained to Gov. Ramsey in an 1860 letter, writing that the Dakota, "would not benefit in the least" by the sale of their remaining land.[9]

Minnesota River country exploded in violence on August 18, 1862, as the Dakota lashed out against Anglo-American traders, settlers and soldiers as well as mixed-bloods thought to be sympathetic with whites. Both Peter Quinn and Philander Prescott found themselves in the middle of the fray: Quinn stationed as interpreter at Fort Ridgely, and Prescott living at Lower Sioux, (Redwood) Indian Agency, site of the first fighting.

As the shooting began at Lower Sioux, a Dakota sister-in-law of Prescott went to the government warehouse where he lived. She wanted to take Prescott to her house, but he told her, "[I]f he had to be killed, he would be killed in his own house."[10] Wabasha, an

Sioux Indians Attacking a Camp, Minn., 1862. From Martin's Art Gallery, 264 Third St., St. Paul. Entered according to Act of Congress, in the year 1865, by J. E. Martin, in the Clerk's Office of the District Court of Minnesota.

Lurid depictions of the Minnesota Dakota War of 1862, such as this one from a St. Paul gallery, were sold to the public.

important Mdewakanton leader, also visited Prescott, asking for a letter that spelled out the chieftain's desire to side with the whites. Wabasha observed, "Mr. Prescott was very much frightened and did not write the letter well."[11] Dakota war parties, meanwhile, moved down to Redwood Ferry to prepare for a reaction from the Fort Ridgely garrison, 13 miles away. For the moment, Prescott was safe.

The first terrified refugees from the Lower Sioux Agency reached Fort Ridgely around 10:00 a.m. They reported to Capt. John B. Marsh, commander of the fort and Company B, a 78-man element of the Fifth Minnesota Regiment. The captain ordered Peter Quinn, his interpreter, and 46 enlisted men to prepare to advance to the scene of fighting.[12]

The fatalistic Quinn seemed to understand the Dakota's desperation and determination and told fort sutler, B.H. Randall, "I am sure we are going into great danger; I do not expect to return alive." Tearfully, Quinn then said, "Good bye, give my love to all." His wife, Mary, was visiting their daughter in Bloomington and thus not present at the fort to see her husband leave.[13]

Capt. Marsh and Quinn mounted mules, and the remainder of the men rode in wagons most of the way to Lower Sioux. They reached Redwood Ferry, a small boat and cable operation on the Minnesota River, just below the agency around noon. Marsh and Quinn saw White Dog, a former Indian farmer, standing across the river on the south agency side and began to talk with him.[14]

Quinn suddenly shouted a warning, and a shot rang out. Dakota warriors emerged from cover and fired a devastating volley that ripped into the surprised soldiers. At least a dozen of Marsh's men died from the gunfire, while interpreter Quinn slumped to the ground dead, his body riddled by 12 shots.

Only 15 survivors made it back to Fort Ridgely. Marsh was not among them.[15]

The following day Philander Prescott and other whites and mixed-bloods attempted to reach the fort. According to court testimony taken after the fighting, a group of Dakota saw Prescott near the Indian Agency, and two of these men shot him dead.[16]

Thus, two individuals who lived lives of great parallels were killed within a day of each other, mere miles from each other, and in almost identical fashion. It is probable that some or all of the men involved in Prescott's killing were among those who fired at Quinn the day before.

It is also likely that many of those attacking Quinn and Prescott knew their victims since, in the small world of the eastern Dakota, the two men had worked and often lived with the Indians. Philander Prescott's mixed-blood daughter, Lucy, believed the Dakota attackers recognized her father and argued about killing him. She had heard that one said Prescott "had always been a friend to the Indians."[17]

Prescott and Quinn would have agreed with the warning about Dakota discontent given government officials. Prior to the fighting, former Indian trader and future Minnesota governor Henry Sibley cautioned, "Your pioneers are encircling the last home of the red man, as with a wall of fire…. You must approach these [Indians] with terms of conciliation and friendship, or you must suffer the consequences of a bloody and remorseless Indian war…."[18]

Sibley's prediction almost perfectly describes what came to pass on the western Minnesota prairie in that late summer of 1862. Philander Prescott and Peter Quinn were only two victims of a truly "bloody and remorseless" war that consumed the lives of hundreds of Anglo-Americans, mixed-bloods and Dakota.

MEDICINE BOTTLE ON TRIAL

The tragic Dakota War of 1862 did not end with the victory of General Sibley's forces at Wood Lake on September 23 or the ensuing mass execution of 38 Dakota soldiers in Mankato on December 26. Some Indian leaders and their followers, mainly Mdewakanton, retreated onto the prairies of Dakota Territory and later to lands near the Canadian border. Among them were Little Six and Medicine Bottle, both accused by whites of being active leaders in the uprising and murderers of the innocent. Philander Prescott, a prominent founder of Richfield, was among Medicine Bottle's alleged victims.

In late summer 1862, distraught Canadian residents in the Red River settlement near Fort Garry (today's Winnipeg) worried that the desperate and destructive Indian war raging in Minnesota and on nearby northwest prairies would spill into their defenseless colony. One letter writer reminded officials in London that native troops in India had killed hundreds of British citizens in 1857 and warned that Indians might now try to annihilate all whites in the British Northwest.[1]

It took a year, but in December 1863 the Dakota began appearing at the Red River outpost. The Indians had moved north, seeking asylum in Canada after the pressure applied by three companies of mounted Minnesota volunteers at Pembina, near the Canadian frontier. The *Nor'Wester*, Fort Garry's newspaper, reported on the influx of Indians, "They are coming in multitudes—men, women and children—bag and baggage...."[2]

Alexander Dallas, British governor of Canada's Rupert's Land (today's southern Manitoba), attempted to maintain peace with the unwanted visitors, offering food and some ammunition to the Dakota in an attempt to convince them to leave the area. The Indians first declined the bribe, but when Dallas upped his ante they moved 20 miles away—still too close for the comfort of the governor and others in the settlement. The Canadians pressed their governor to ask the Minnesotans of Maj. Edwin A.C. Hatch's command at Pembina to forcibly remove the Dakota.

Little Six, left, and Medicine Bottle at Fort Snelling

Some went over the head of Dallas and personally wrote to the American major.[3]

Maj. Hatch, meanwhile, learned Medicine Bottle and Little Six, son of the recently deceased Six (Shakopee), were among the Dakota living near the Red River community, and he set in motion a plot to capture the Indian leaders. The Canadians informed the chiefs that their food supplies were about to be halted and arranged to transport the concerned Medicine Bottle and Little Six to Fort Garry for talks. Upon arrival, they were wined and dined by their hosts and later drugged. The two men were then delivered via dogsled to Minnesota and Hatch.[4]

The kidnapping seemed certain to trigger an international incident. The Toronto *Globe*, although professing sympathy for the suffering of Minnesota civilians during the war, called the capture a flagrant outrage "which cannot be overlooked." American officials, including Henry Sibley, Hatch's commander, responded by claiming British subjects had brought the two chiefs across the border. Sibley insisted he had no evidence that their actions were illegal. The British government, meanwhile, made no attempt to regain custody of the two Dakota leaders.[5]

Sibley's pursuit of other Dakota refugees from the Minnesota conflict delayed the trials of Medicine Bottle and Little Six. Finally, on November 25, a military commission arraigned Medicine Bottle at Fort Snelling and listed eight charges of alleged murder; the first item on the list—the shooting and killing of Philander Prescott. He was also accused of "the shooting of sundry white people" near New Ulm, and "the shooting and killing of sundry soldiers."[6]

Prescott's widow, Mary, became the first of five witnesses to testify. Known as Spirit of the Moon when a member of her father Cloud Man's Lake Calhoun farming village, Mary Prescott

The St. Paul *Pioneer*, November 12, 1865, reported on the conviction of Shakopee (Little Six) and Medicine Bottle.

MORE HANGING

Shakopee and Medicine Bottle Sentenced to Swing.

THEY RECEIVE THE NEWS WITH STOICAL COMPOSURE.

Yesterday Gen. Corse received orders from Washington approving the finding of the Military Commission which tried the two Indians Shakopee and Medicine Bottle, and an order from Major General Pope directing their execution at such time as Gen. Corse may fix. The order from Washington is as follows:

THE PRESIDENT APPROVES THE SENTENCE.

[General Court Martial, Orders No. 508.]

WAR DEPARTMENT, ADJ'T. GEN'S. OFFICE, } WASHINGTON, Sept. 7, 1865.

1. Before a Military Commission which convened at Fort Snelling, Minnesota, November 25, 1864, pursuant to special orders No. 244, dated November 18, 1864, and No. 248, dated November 23, 1864, Headquarters District of Minnesota, Department of the Northwest, St. Paul, Minnesota, and of which Capt. John R. Jones, 2d Minnesota Cavalry was President, were arraigned and tried.

1. *Tahta e-chash-nah-manne*, alias Medicine Bottle, a Sioux Indian.

CHARGE I.—"Murder."

CHARGE II.—"Participation in the murders, massacres and other outrages committed by the Sioux Indians upon the white settlers in the State of Minnesota," and their specifications the accused plead "not guilty."

---

ranked with her husband as a founder of Richfield. Mary, now approximately 60-years-old, testified she had known Medicine Bottle for about 10 years and had seen him at Lower Sioux Agency at the time of the first Dakota attack on August 18, 1862.

Mary Prescott said she had no personal knowledge of Medicine Bottle's possible part in the killing of her husband, but, while a prisoner of the Dakota, saw him "going on war parties many times." She also reported seeing the Indian leader returning with wagons containing goods taken from the whites. When asked if she knew if Medicine Bottle was in favor or opposed to killing whites, she replied, "I know he was in favor. ..." The defendant declined the opportunity to cross-examine Prescott.

The four others to corroborate the military's charges, all Dakota or mixed-bloods, added more detail to the prosecution's case, but only one provided eyewitness testimony. A 45-year-old woman said she saw Medicine Bottle during the opening attack at Lower Sioux's Forbes store and later saw him at Myrick's store. The woman's testimony was potentially damaging since she was an eyewitness. She then recalled that Dakota men involved in the assault told her "women had no business being with them (Indian men)" because they (the women) "were always meddling with their (the men's) business."[7]

After a two-day recess, the trial resumed. A Dakota man asserted he heard Medicine Bottle tell others that he had been to New Ulm. A second male witness claimed he had been told Medicine Bottle was involved in attacks against settlers in wagons near New Ulm.[8]

That second man also offered emotionally charged, albeit hearsay, testimony against Medicine Bottle. This witness said he heard the chief describe to others the attack on Philander Prescott.

Medicine Bottle allegedly said he and others overtook their victim not far from Lower Sioux Agency and that he and another Dakota fired at Prescott and saw him fall. At that point others in the party dismounted and severed Prescott's head. The witness also claimed Medicine Bottle bragged he had been among Indians who attacked and killed white men, women and children.

Medicine Bottle did not question any of his accusers or call his own witnesses, but he did offer a written statement in which he denied all allegations against him, asserting he was not present at the onset of fighting, that he never stated "he had killed or that he ever did kill or attempt to kill Prescott," or that he had ever admitted to the killing of men, women or children or "any white people."[9]

The chief also offered an opinion submitted by former governor, Willis A. Gorman, and a future governor, Cushman K. Davis. The attorneys supported the Indian leader's challenge to the court's jurisdiction, asserting, "he was kidnapped from the Territory of a foreign state...while living there and molesting no one." Gorman and Davis reminded the court of the notorious Trent Affair a year earlier when American naval officers boarded a British vessel near Cuba and captured two Confederate diplomats. The incident nearly ignited a war between Great Britain and the United States. Britain's Prime Minister Lord Palmerston thundered to his cabinet, "You may stand for this but damned if I will." An American apology defused the situation.[10]

"Not a muscle quivered—not a feature of their faces even moved. Blankly they stared into the distance, and with wonderful fortitude stood firmly up, though death was but a moment distant. It was impossible not to admire these sons of the forest."

Gorman and Davis asserted, "No state can reach over into the domain of a foreign or neutral power and drag any criminal by force." The tribunal, however, rejected the protest and found Medicine Bottle guilty of all charges, except for the killing of soldiers. On December 2 they sentenced the chieftain to death. The trial of Little Six followed and concluded with an identical result.[11]

After some delays, President Andrew Johnson agreed to the execution. When Little Six heard of the decision, he stoically declared, "I am no squaw—I can die whenever the white man wishes." Medicine Bottle then repeated those words. On November 11, 1865, the two waited impassively at the gallows as the order of execution was read. A reporter at the scene marveled, "Not a muscle quivered—not a feature of their faces even moved. Blankly they stared into the distance, and with wonderful fortitude stood firmly up, though death was but a moment distant. It was impossible not to admire these sons of the forest."[12]

Considering the virulent anti-Indian sentiments of a great majority of white Minnesotans in the wake of the 1862 war, the St. Paul *Pioneer* took a surprisingly broad view of the trial. The newspaper's editor observed, "no white man...would be executed upon the testimony..." that convicted Medicine Bottle and Little Six. The writer allowed that the two men were likely guilty, "but their execution will, nevertheless, establish the precedent of hanging without proving."[13]

THE EXTRAORDINARY LIFE OF CHARLES EASTMAN

Charles Alexander Eastman became the most famous descendant of Cloud Man. He was born in Minnesota, likely at Gideon Pond's Oak Grove mission in Bloomington, the sometime residence of his mother, Nancy (Winona) Eastman, and home of his aunt, The Day Sets (Anpetu Inajinwin). After a traditional Mdewakanton upbringing, he entered Indian school at age 15 in 1873 and embarked upon a different kind of journey through life.

The February 1858 birth of Cloud Man's latest great-grandson brought little joy to his Mdewakanton village. The infant's mother, Winona, better known to history as Nancy Eastman, was quite ill. Nancy, a famed beauty and high-spirited daughter of Capt. Seth Eastman, soldier and painter, and Cloud Man's youngest daughter, Stands Like a Spirit (Wakaninajinwin), died of tonsillitis and weakness from childbirth when her son was a few months old.[1]

Given the name Hakadah, The Pitiful Last, because of the circumstances of his birth, the boy was raised by his grandmother Uncheeda, mother of his father, Ite Wakandiota (Many Lightnings). At four years old Hakadah joined the exodus of Dakota families who refused to surrender to Col. Henry Sibley's forces in September 1862. They moved to the North Dakota and Canadian plains along with the followers and families of Shakopee and Medicine Bottle. During the following decade, the youngster grew to adolescence in a challenging and rewarding traditional Dakota environment.[2]

The boy assumed the name Ohiyesa (Winner) after men from his band came to believe he brought them good luck during ball-play. In the 1870s, his people roamed the northern prairies with a band of Wahpeton and became friendly with the Assiniboines and Cree. Ohiyesa believed his father had been killed during the Minnesota Dakota War. An uncle of the boy schooled him in revenge and advised, "never to spare a white man from the United States."[3]

> *"I was trained thoroughly for an all-round outdoor life and for all natural emergencies. I was a good rider and a good shot with the bow and arrow, alert and alive to everything that came within my ken."*
>
> Ohiyesa
> (Charles Eastman)

Dr. Charles A. Eastman

Still, Ohiyesa believed the Big Knives, as his people called whites, had power bordering on the supernatural. He heard of their "fireboat" (a locomotive) but couldn't grasp the concept. When told Big Knives had created a "fireboat-walks-on-mountains," it was too much to believe. He was amazed to hear that whites had bridged the Missouri and Mississippi rivers and built immense houses of wood and brick as high as the hills.

Recalling the days roaming the northwest, Ohiyesa later wrote, "I was trained thoroughly for an all-round outdoor life and for all natural emergencies. I was a good rider and a good shot with the bow and arrow, alert and alive to everything that came within my ken. I had never known nor ever expected to know any life but this." Then, when he was 15, Ohiyesa's grandmother gave him stunning news, "Your father has come."[4] Many Lightnings, he soon learned, had not been killed in the war but had been in prison.

For Ohiyesa, more shocking than the reappearance of his father was what he was saying. Many Lightnings had adopted the Christian faith while imprisoned and now talked to his son about rethinking his life. His father did say, "Our own life…is the best in a world of our own such as we have enjoyed for ages," but then talked about a new culture to which his son must adapt. Though skeptical, the son, because of a sense of duty to his father, agreed to join Many Lightnings, now calling himself Jacob Eastman, in returning to the United States.[5]

A reluctant and somewhat rebellious scholar, Ohiyesa began Indian school in Dakota Territory. His father's expectations and encouragement kept him in school at first, then his remarkable success created a thirst for knowledge.

He eventually earned his promotion to Beloit College in Wisconsin. To get to Beloit he boarded a train for the first time, but not without giving the

locomotive a "careful inspection." He felt a "stranger in a strange country and deep in a strange life from which I could not retreat." Ohiyesa, now known as Charles Eastman, settled in and began "absorbing knowledge through every pore."[6]

Eastman's academic achievements earned him an opportunity to study at Dartmouth College in New Hampshire. After excelling in that Ivy League school, he headed to Boston College where he earned a medical degree. He became the first Native American doctor in the Bureau of Indian Affairs, serving at Pine Ridge in today's South Dakota. Eastman and his future wife, Elaine Goodale, were there to tend to the dead and dying after the infamous 1890 attack on a Lakota encampment at Wounded Knee that killed some 300 men, women and children.[7]

Elaine was an acclaimed poet, but when meeting Charles at Pine Ridge she was working as a teacher. She came from a prominent New England family that paid for her lavish New York City wedding to Charles in June 1891. The couple raised six children, five girls— Dora Winona, Virginia, Irene, Eleanor and Florence—and one boy, Ohiyesa II.

Charles Eastman became a well-known and popular author who wrote 11 books detailing his life and telling of Dakota culture. A number were translated into other languages, and several are still in print. He also served two U.S. presidents as an expert on Native American-related issues and was an active supporter of the YMCA and Boy Scouts of America.

Eastman never forgot his Dakota origins, but he did believe it important that his people should adapt to white culture in order to survive within it. He hoped the young "…might at once take up the white man's way, and prepare themselves to hold office and wield influence in their native states."[8]

Seth Eastman, Fort Snelling's artist-soldier, married Stands Like a Spirit of Cloud Man's Mdewakanton band. They were Charles Eastman's grandparents.

From a Henry Lewis oil painting of Fort Snelling, about 1850

Thoughts From Charles Eastman[9]

◇◇◇◇◇◇◇◇◇◇◇◇◇◇◇◇◇◇◇◇◇◇◇

"What boy would not be an Indian for a while when he thinks of the freest life in the world? This life was mine. Every day there was a real hunt. There was real game…. We were close students of nature. We studied the habits of animals just as you study your books. We watched the men of our people and represented them in our play; then learned to emulate them in our lives."

◇◇◇◇◇◇◇◇◇◇◇◇◇◇◇◇◇◇◇◇◇◇◇

◇◇◇◇◇◇◇◇◇◇◇◇◇◇◇◇◇◇◇◇◇◇◇

"Is there not something worthy of a perpetuation in our Indian spirit of democracy, where Earth, our mother, was free to all, and no one sought to impoverish or enslave his neighbor?"

◇◇◇◇◇◇◇◇◇◇◇◇◇◇◇◇◇◇◇◇◇◇◇

Valley of the St. Peter's (Minnesota) River, gateway to the western reaches of the Dakota dominion, painted by Seth Eastman, Charles' grandfather, in 1848

◇◇◇◇◇◇◇◇◇◇◇◇◇◇◇◇◇◇◇◇◇

"Long before I heard of Christ or saw a white man…I knew God. I perceived what goodness is. I saw and loved what is really beautiful. Civilization has not taught me anything better."

◇◇◇◇◇◇◇◇◇◇◇◇◇◇◇◇◇◇◇◇◇

"In the old days, our mothers were single-eyed to the trust imposed upon them; and as a noted chief of our people was wont to say: "Men may slay one another, but they can never overcome the woman, for in the quietude of her lap lies the child! You may destroy him once and again, but he issues as often from that same gentle lap—a gift of the Great Good to the race, in which man is only an accomplice!"

◇◇◇◇◇◇◇◇◇◇◇◇◇◇◇◇◇◇◇◇◇

"The American Indian was an individualist in religion as in war. He had neither a national army nor an organized church. There was no priest to assume responsibility for another's soul. That is, we believed, the supreme duty of the parent, who only was permitted to claim in some degree the priestly office and function, since it is his creative and protecting power which alone approaches the solemn function of Deity."

◇◇◇◇◇◇◇◇◇◇◇◇◇◇◇◇◇◇◇◇◇

◇◇◇◇◇◇◇◇◇◇◇◇◇◇◇◇◇◇◇◇◇

"…even in those white men who professed religion we found much inconsistency of conduct. They spoke much of spiritual things, while seeking only the material. They bought and sold everything: time, labor, personal independence, the love of woman, and even the ministrations of their holy faith! The lust for money, power, and conquest so characteristic of the Anglo-Saxon race did not escape moral condemnation at the hands of his untutored judge, nor did he fail to contrast this conspicuous trait of the dominant race with the spirit of the meek and lowly Jesus."

◇◇◇◇◇◇◇◇◇◇◇◇◇◇◇◇◇◇◇◇◇

"If the child should chance to be fretful, the mother raises her hand. 'Hush! hush!' she cautions it tenderly, 'the spirits may be disturbed!' She bids it be still and listen—listen to the silver voice of the aspen, or the clashing cymbals of the birch; and at night she points to the heavenly, blazed trail, through nature's galaxy of splendor to nature's God. Silence, love, reverence,—this is the trinity of first lessons; and to these she later adds generosity, courage, and chastity."

◇◇◇◇◇◇◇◇◇◇◇◇◇◇◇◇◇◇◇◇◇

–Two–
Patrons of
Agriculture

During their first decades of existence, the townships of south Hennepin County were part of a rural agricultural district recognized largely for wheat and flour production. Small flouring hamlets grew along Minnehaha and Nine Mile creeks, including those around the mills of Richfield, Edina and Bloomington. By the close of the 19th century, however, a new era in south suburban agriculture had dawned. Area farmers shifted their focus to market gardening, supplying burgeoning Minneapolis with fresh produce.

SQUATTERS IN SOUTH HENNEPIN COUNTY

For three decades, whites had cast covetous eyes toward the west bank of the Mississippi River and the fertile but largely fallow lands of the Dakota people. And when the Dakota grudgingly sold their lands to the United States in 1851, some settlers didn't wait for the U.S. Senate to seal the deal. They became Minnesota "sooners," staking out the inviting fields of the future Richfield, Edina and Bloomington before the land was legally available. Then they prepared to defend their claims.

In 1852 Riley and Fanny Bartholomew claimed land in the future Richfield and soon built this house. It stands today near the Richfield Historical Society's headquarters at Lyndale Avenue and 69th Street.

Nineteenth century Americans knew a thing or two about claiming Indian lands. The system dated back to the 1787 Constitutional Convention that enacted the Northwest Ordinance, a plan to administer American-claimed territory north and west of the Ohio River. The United States pledged to the Indian nations occupying this vast expanse that it would not be taken from them without their consent. Impatient settlers soon found to their satisfaction that the government wasn't much interested in keeping that promise.

Hungry for land, Americans pushed up against the Ohio River border in the 1790s and faced resistance by a loosely knit assembly of tribes—Miami, Shawnee, Ojibwe, Delaware, Pottawatomie and Ottawa—determined to keep them out. The Battle of Fallen Timbers, fought near present-day Toledo in 1794, and a treaty that followed marked the end of major Indian resistance in the area and the opening of Ohio to white settlement.[1]

Of course there had been other Indian wars dating back to the colonial period as early as the 1600s, and more would follow the battle at Fallen Timbers. Notable among the later conflicts in the Old Northwest were Tecumseh's Rebellion in Indiana (1811–1813), Kickapoo Resistance in Illinois (1819–1824), Winnebago Uprising in southwest Wisconsin (1827) and the struggle against the Sauks and Foxes, known as the Black Hawk War, in Illinois and Wisconsin (1832). But it was the Northwest Ordinance that served as the template for America's expansion following the Revolutionary War. In almost every case the pattern persisted: war with Indian tribes, peace treaties through which Indians ceded their ancestral lands, and finally, the opening of former Indian territory to land seekers.[2]

Settlement of the Dakota lands in southern Minnesota Territory proved to be a somewhat different story. In 1851, the United States sought and finally obtained by treaty, a Dakota domain of nearly 24 million acres. Historian Roy W. Meyer aptly described the coercive negotiation process as "a thoroughly sordid affair, equal in infamy to anything else in the long history of injustice perpetrated upon the Indians."[3]

Upon learning of the treaty signing, land-hungry settlers charged across the Mississippi looking to establish claims. This movement was an early form of illegal immigration. The U.S. Senate changed the 1851 land sale agreement by simply removing a provision that reserved land for the Dakota. The politicians thus placed both the treaty and Indians in limbo. In the meantime, the Dakota still retained ownership of the land.[4]

The future Hennepin County held a healthy share of the squatters, people with little interest in legal complications and a strong attraction to the land. These newcomers continued claiming land throughout 1851 and saw their numbers boosted the following year by an even larger wave of settlers. By late summer 1852, Indian agent Nathaniel McLean estimated 5,000 whites were living illegally on Dakota land. Even the squatters' greatest supporter, Minnesota's Territorial Governor Alexander Ramsey, had to admit all such trespassers were liable to prosecution.[5]

You Say "Squatter," I Say "Preemptor"

Some of the most revered pioneering families of Minneapolis, Richfield and Bloomington thus began their years in Minnesota as law-breakers. They would have vigorously objected to such a characterization. They expected that Congress, thanks to efforts of Ramsey and the territorial legislature, would legitimize their squatter status by granting them the rank of "preemptor." The Preemption Act of 1841 had allowed people to claim government-owned land before it was put up for sale; they could "prove up" (legally purchase) their claim after it was surveyed.[6]

Congress did not accept Ramsey's florid appeals to make legal the status of newcomers living on Dakota lands. Still, the immigrants could take heart from the words of this governor who strongly endorsed their presence. He called them a "great army of peaceful progress" that "makes the country[,] its history, and its

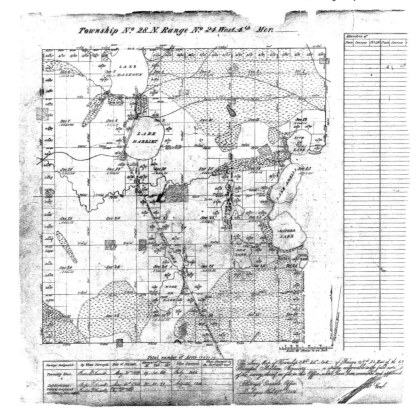

This 1854 survey map shows Richfield's northern border at present-day Lake Street and its western boundary at the future Highway 169.

glory." Ramsey proclaimed, "Extension to them of the preemption privilege would be an act of peace and repose"— rank hypocrisy to Dakota hearing those words.[7]

The 2,000 eastern Dakota concentrated in villages along the Mississippi and Minnesota rivers were the first Indians to face the immigrant wave. In Mdewakanton villages such as Oak Grove (Bloomington), Kaposia (South St. Paul), Red Wing and Wabasha, whites and Indians had coexisted for several decades. Missionaries, soldiers, traders, explorers and travelers passed through and even lived in the Indian communities. But the arrival of steamboat loads of settlers fundamentally changed the white-Dakota relationship. The small, scattered Mdewakanton bands awaiting U.S. Senate approval of their land treaties were in no position to resist swarms of settlers.

It didn't matter that white settlers who boldly ventured onto Dakota lands in 1851–52 believed their status would be formally approved. Legalities were completely immaterial. They understood the American frontier's fundamental rule for claiming Indian land: "Get there first." For American Indians, the corollary to this dictum was equally basic: "Get out of the way."

Riley Bartholomew, shown here in uniform as a general in the Ohio militia, was among the early settlers Territorial Gov. Ramsey called a "great army of peaceful progress."

about aggressive claim jumpers who would forcibly push them off the land. Committees of vigilance cropped up around the territory as the first land claimants organized for self-protection.

One of the territory's most powerful settler associations formed in what would become the southern sections of Hennepin County. The 1852 Equal Right and Impartial Protection Claim Association brought together a group of men, including some speculators, mostly from the city and township of Minneapolis, and from Richfield. The association, which eventually grew to 125 members, pledged to settle disputes among themselves and prevent new speculators from taking over member land claims.[8]

If a disagreement arose between claim association members, their constitution called for a hearing. Each party submitted a list of 18 association members; the disputants would then alternately strike out six names, with the remaining people to determine the outcome. Members received protection for just one claim not to exceed 160 acres, or a single preserve "no more than 40 acres on the banks of the Mississippi, or 80 acres back of or immediately adjoining said 40 acre lots."[9]

Vigilante Justice

Settlers of the future Minneapolis, Richfield, Bloomington and throughout the treaty land found they had little to fear from the Dakota, whether the Indians were in their villages or roaming in hunting parties. But squatters were anxious about speculators—those willing to gamble on the growth of the real estate market by outbidding settlers for claims. They also worried

Equipment like this Knox Pattern Horse Hoe made work easier for early farmers in south Hennepin County.

The names of some prominent early and future community leaders appear on the 1852 Equal Right and Impartial Protection Claim Association roster. Those living in what would become Richfield and Edina included Jesse A. Richardson, William P. Day, William P. Finch, John McCabe and Thomas W. Pierce. Among the group from Minneapolis city and township were Dr. Alfred E. Ames, Daniel M. Coolbaugh, Martin Layman, Robert Blaisdell, Sr., Hiram Burlingame and Waterman Stinson.[10]

In Article 7 of the group's constitution, the claim association boldly asserted the unfettered power to enforce its rulings. "[T]he association upon deliberation may enforce its execution by such means as they may deem propper [sic]."[11] With law enforcement on the Minnesota frontier spotty to non-existent, these early settlers made clear that they would fill the void.

Such power came in handy following the long-awaited decision by Congress on August 5, 1854, to give Minnesota squatters preemption status. That opened the territory to an 1855 tidal wave of immigration. The crew of *War Eagle*, the first steamer arriving that April, crammed some 814 passengers onto their vessel—the vanguard of 30,000 immigrants the packet company carried that season. In overcrowded St. Paul, people camped on the streets.[12]

Where vigilance committees were strong, claim jumping by newcomers

A portion of the Hennepin County Equal Right and Protection Claim Association membership roster, about 1852

was next to impossible. Speculators still presented a threat, however. Most territorial land sharks moved inland, laying out distant prairie town sites they preempted or held by murky claim, all in the hope that soaring land values and quick sales would make them rich. Still others with deep pockets looked to snap up the valuable claims of original settlers by outbidding them at the formal government auction. In Hennepin County's case, that's where the Equal Right and Impartial Protection Claim Association stepped in.[13]

Speculators, learning of the threat the claim association presented, appealed to Willis A. Gorman, the new territorial governor, asking for protection. Gorman believed it his duty to offer such security by supplying troops during the land sale, but he clearly sided with the original settlers. A suspicious speculator asked the governor how he would order his militia to load their weapons. "Blank, by God," came the emphatic reply.[14]

Claim association members chose Thomas W. Pierce, Richfield farmer and future Minnesota territorial legislator, to represent them when the government held the land sale. During the bidding, other members of the group patrolled the crowd looking for strangers, ready to discourage any competition. Not surprisingly, the association men found no challenges.

Eager to preserve the historical record of their county during Minnesota's pre-statehood days, residents formed the Hennepin County Territorial Pioneers Association in 1858. This group changed its name to Hennepin County Historical Society in 1938.

New England of the West

Family genealogies have become a significant part of county and city historical society collections. These studies, typically a combination of documentation and transcribed oral histories, can shed light on aspects of local history too specific for researchers looking for bigger game. In a similar way, genealogical analysis of an area's first residents can help later generations better understand its culture and traditions. South Hennepin County's early ethnic history is thus worth consideration.

In the early 1850s, New Englanders led the way into Hennepin County and its southern townships. Immigrants from Maine were in the forefront, their usual position during the settlement period of the Old Northwest. Traditionally, Maine loggers worked ahead of other settlers, chopping their way through massive forests of the region. But when confronted in Minnesota by the great grasslands of the northern prairie, many Mainers decided to stake claims and stay put.[1]

By 1860, New Englanders from Maine, along with New Yorkers, dominated Richfield and the future Edina. Of U.S.-born adults, settlers from Maine made up 35 percent of new residents in the town of Richfield, while "Yorkers" supplied 21 percent. Among future community leaders with Maine roots were Cornelius and Nancy Couillard, James and Almira Dunsmoor and Ard and Harriet Godfrey. New Yorkers included James and Mary Bull, William and Angeline Finch and George and Maria Gilmore.[2]

John G. Rice, an expert in historical demography, notes of immigrants to Minnesota, "It was settlers from the East, especially Yankees and Yorkers, who laid the groundwork for the future state of Minnesota. They built and managed towns, founded industries and established important institutions." The territorial legislature, during its first session, passed the Yankee-molded, common-school act (for publicly funded programs) with Richfield and Bloomington among towns establishing free education. The influential Northeasterners helped Minnesota gain the nickname, "New England of the West." Between 1850 and 1880, Richfield held one of the state's larger concentrations of New England-born citizens.[3]

Other settlers with New England and Northeastern roots chose to claim or buy land on the fertile, made-for-farming plains of Richfield. Twenty-two of the town's citizens came from Vermont. Sixteen migrated from Massachusetts, 14 from New Hampshire, five each

Cornelius Coulliard took his family from Frankfort, Maine, to St. Anthony in 1854 to work on a new suspension bridge. They claimed land in Richfield around 70th Street between the future Portland and Lyndale avenues.

from Rhode Island and Connecticut, and four from New Jersey. Among the more wealthy citizens by 1860 were Vermonters Robert and Mary Blaisdell, and Harley and Elvira Hopkins of Rhode Island; George and Elizabeth Odell, Connecticut; and Alonzo and Mary Sawtell, New Hampshire.[4]

Ohio and Pennsylvania ancestry also proved common among these new Minnesotans, including Riley and Fanny Bartholomew (Ohio), and Charles and Ann Hoag (Pennsylvania). The Hoag family's American roots were in New Hampshire, and the Bartholomew family originally came from New York.[5]

Minnesota Territory in the 1850s had not yet experienced the massive European immigration it would see during the remainder of the 19th century. The Irish proved an exception with considerable numbers reaching Minnesota before 1860. In the Richfield-Edina area they represented the largest European immigrant group. The 1860 U.S. census lists 58 natives of Ireland in Richfield, most in the town's southwest quadrant. Among early neighbors there were the families of Michael and Mary Delaney, Thomas and Catherine Moriarty, and Michael and Mary Ryan.[6]

Many of the first Irish Catholic immigrants, escaping failures of potato crops in 1845 and 1851 and famine that resulted, received anything but a warm American welcome. The 1850s were the heydays of the "Know-Nothings," an anti-Catholic, anti-immigration political party that sparked violence and, for a time, wielded considerable influence. In Minnesota, the *Daily Minnesotian* (St. Paul) offered a June 1857 slam against Irish voters, "We hope to gracious, none of the Paddies will hear where

St. Paul is…." A more direct insult to the Irish in Minneapolis produced a bloody St. Patrick's Day riot in 1858. A group of men hanged an effigy of St. Patrick, placing a necklace of potatoes around its neck.[7]

Bloomington's Early Arrivals

The Ponds and McLeods, two families important in Bloomington history, had a long head start on those settlers who arrived in the early 1850s. Connecticut Yankees Samuel and Gideon Pond reached the area in 1834, desiring to bring Christianity to the Dakota people. The ambitious French-speaking Martin McLeod, a man of Scottish extraction and a native of Quebec, traveled to Fort Snelling in 1837. The Ponds later became ordained missionaries, while the urbane McLeod, a devotee of Lord Byron's

Four generations of the pioneering Bartholomew family are shown around 1890. Family matriarch Fanny Bartholomew is seated at the far right. Others are Virginia Nash Bartholomew, seated left, Carrie Nash Wright, standing, and Florence Wright Brooks.

This Bloomington log cabin was located on the Chadwick farm near the Minnesota River.

Canada-born Martin McLeod, French-speaking of Scottish heritage, reached Fort Snelling in 1837. He went to work for the American Fur Company. Well-educated and adventurous, he moved to Bloomington in 1849 and was elected to the first territorial legislature.

poetry, was active in the fur trade. Gideon and Sarah Pond opened Oak Grove mission (Bloomington) during the winter of 1842–43, with McLeod, his wife, Mary Elizabeth, and three children settling nearby in 1849.[8]

French Canadians established the region's fur trade in the early 1800s, providing a foundation for the local economy. These traders and trappers subsequently reached the future Minnesota and sought to do business with Dakota and Ojibwe, the area's two principal Indian nations. As the fur industry faded, some French Canadians settled in the new territory, as evidenced by a notable statistic: By the 1980s, some 130 years later, more French Canadians lived in Minnesota than any state outside of New England.[9]

In 1860, 25 Bloomington citizens claimed Canada as their place of origin, specifying one of four areas: Canada East, Canada West, Red River or simply Canada. Another 16 listed France as their home. Not all were French Canadian, but the St. Martin brothers, Pascal, Pierre and Javier, and their large families were. They settled and farmed along Nine Mile Creek

not far from Jean Pascal Pierre Ballif and his wife, Victoria. Ballif migrated from Normandy in France and became a farmer and owner of a Bloomington inn.

Ireland and England each contributed 27 citizens to Bloomington's 1860 population. Joseph Dean and William Chambers arrived during the winter of 1851–52 holding a government charter to build and operate a ferry across the Minnesota River. Dean was born in Ireland but immigrated to Minnesota from Canada. He became Bloomington's postmaster in 1854 before moving to Minneapolis. Chambers, also a native of Ireland, and his wife, Martha, stayed on.[10]

Bloomington's first major wave of easterners surged into the area in spring 1853. By the end of the decade, New Yorkers topped the numbers list of American-born adult emigrants with 28, including town official E.B. Stanley, Robert and Frances Bunker, and J.D. Scofield and his Canadian-born wife, Sophia.[11]

R.B. and Margaret Gibson emigrated from New Hampshire, and Elijah Rich, the first town clerk, and his wife, Charlotte, were Vermonters. The U.S. Census showed 17 adults in the town were Vermont natives, with 11 from Maine and seven from Connecticut.

Minnesota's early immigration model gave added proof to a remarkable fact: By 1860, nearly half of all New Englanders then living had moved from New England.[12]

Joseph Dean's Bloomington cabin, built about 1852, is an early example of settler architecture.

JONATHAN AND ELIZA GRIMES: AN EDINA FIRST FAMILY

Jonathan and Eliza Grimes rank as an Edina first family for their early settlement in the community and because of their significant impact upon its development. They left an imprint upon Edina that remains visible.

Jonathan Taylor Grimes and Eliza Gordon Grimes moved to Minnesota Territory in 1856 and to west Richfield (the future Edina) in 1858.

On a late spring day in 1861, a hopeful Henry David Thoreau tramped toward Lake Harriet, following up on an important lead. The famed American essayist, philosopher and naturalist had heard that a wild apple tree, "same as they had in Vermont," grew near the lakeshore. To confirm this rare sighting, he was directed to a "... Mr. Grimes (Jonathan Taylor Grimes) as one who had found it." Thoreau located Grimes, and the two headed out to "quite a cluster" of the fruit trees.[1]

The men got along quite famously, sharing common interests and beliefs. Well-educated with inquiring minds, they discussed nature, horticulture and the just-begun Civil War. Thoreau, age 43 and 10 months older than his new friend, was a New Englander, while Grimes family roots reached back to Virginia, the political heart of the Southern Confederacy. But Jonathan Grimes and his family, members of the Society of Friends (Quakers), believed in the abolition of slavery, a leading factor in Jonathan's initial decision to leave home in 1839 and move to Indiana. Thus, Massachusetts-born Thoreau and Virginia-native Grimes held much the same political view. Jonathan and Eliza Grimes invited Thoreau to take meals with them while he was in the vicinity. In his memoirs Jonathan wrote of the enjoyment derived from his talks with Thoreau and of the warm friendship they developed.[2]

Moving to Minnesota

At the time of his 1861 meeting with Thoreau, Jonathan Grimes and his family had been living in Minnesota for six years. Moving to Minnesota, however, had not been in their original plans. The Grimes family led happy and comfortable lives in Indiana during the 1840s. Jonathan married Eliza Gordon there in 1843, and they soon built Clay County's first frame house in which they raised four children. They prospered until Indiana officials ran the new Erie and Wabash Canal right through their farm.

In its wake, the waterway left a stagnant lagoon—a source of serious family health concerns. Malarial fever struck Jonathan, and the Grimes's seven-month-old daughter, Anna, also became ill. In 1855 the family's first-born son drowned in the canal, and they immediately decided to travel to Minnesota Territory to see about moving there.[3]

Thus began an epic trip to Minnesota. Eliza placed Jonathan and the ailing infant on a mattress in the bed of their wagon. She then added their two sons, ages six and two, to the cargo and started the long 260-mile journey to Galena, Illinois. There, Eliza loaded the boys and invalids, both still dangerously unwell, onto a steamboat bound for St. Paul. Fortunately, Eliza noticed improvement in the health of her patients as their vessel steamed steadily up the Mississippi. The family spent the summer of 1855 recuperating in tiny Minneapolis and decided to move permanently to Minnesota.

The Grimes family returned to Indiana that fall to sell the farm and most of their belongings, traveling back to Minneapolis in spring 1856. A now-healthy Jonathan bought three-fourths of a city block, bordered by the future Marquette and 2nd avenues, South 4th and 5th streets, and then moved into a six-room house on the property. The neighborhood was questionable

> *"Fortunes seemed to be dropping from the skies, and those who would not reach and gather them were but stupids and sluggards."*
>
> William Watts Folwell

however. Eliza and Jonathan did not like the idea of their sons walking past A.A. Ames's saloon on their way to school. Ames kept a keg of beer tapped and offered a free drink to passers-by, including some children.[4]

Grimes learned in 1858 that a flour mill was for sale south of Minneapolis on present-day Minnehaha Creek. He considered buying the property. Four partners, including Richard Strout, one of the original commissioners of the new town of Richfield and a land speculator in the future Edina, owned the mill.

Strout had gambled and lost in what had been the profitable business of town site speculation. He and his partners had planned to establish the town of Waterville (on the future site of Edina) and surveyed lots near the new flour mill they were building. Such land development in Minnesota by early summer 1857 had created a tremendous economic boom. "Fortunes seemed to

The Grimes family bought the future Edina Mill and, in 1859, hired John Baird to operate it. The photo shows Edina Mill in the early 1890s.

be dropping from the skies, and those who would not reach and gather them were but stupids and sluggards," wrote historian William Folwell about "easy" profits from speculation. One politician complained Minnesotans were "so engrossed in speculating" that they forgot about politics.[5]

This millstone is found on Edina Mill's historic site at West 50th and Browndale. It is within the city's heritage preservation district.

But the August failure of a leading New York financial firm created a devastating nationwide economic implosion. In Minnesota, Waterville and other once valuable Minnesota town sites became next to worthless overnight, and the value of city lots plummeted. Land speculators who had happily signed up for boom time interest rates of 5 percent *per month* were wiped out. Jobs vanished. Money in the territory practically disappeared. Steamboats carried meat and flour into Minnesota, but locals too often had no cash to pay for the goods. Some merchants printed their own scrip to be used in place of money. Observed Folwell, "Thousands who had believed themselves wealthy soon found themselves in actual bodily need."[6]

Jonathan and Eliza Grimes, however, held ready cash from the 1856 sale of their Indiana property. The Grimeses and partner William C. Rheem could and did strike a hard bargain with the Strout group. Grimes, who knew nothing of milling, had enlisted Rheem to run the idle Waterville Mill once the purchase was complete. For just $300, they arranged for the Strout partnership to "quit-claim" their interest in the west Richfield Mill and the southwest quarter of section 18 surrounding it. At the same time, the financially strapped Strout accepted Grimes's $100 offer to quit claim another 160 acres in nearby section seven.[7]

Waterville Mill

Rheem soon left the partnership. In fall 1859, Grimes hired John Allen Baird, 44 years old, and his son James, 21, to operate a new, improved flour mill. The senior Baird lived with his nephew, George W. Baird, on a 120-acre farmstead near the mill. The Waterville Mill had just been geared up to supply flour for troops at Fort Snelling about the time Henry Thoreau arrived for his June 1861 Minnesota visit in search of Jonathan Grimes and apple trees.[8]

The advent of the Civil War brought soldier recruits to Fort Snelling for muster and training before their deployment. The Grimes-owned mill, the only one in operation near the fort, swung into a busy routine of what Jonathan described as round-the-clock operations. Grimes wrote of harvest time, "...it was not uncommon to see 25 yoke of oxen at the mill all at one time" waiting for wheat to be unloaded. Grimes introduced the Marsh Harvester in Hennepin County, using the machine to gather freshly cut grain and drop it in piles for binding. The versatile farmer also sold butter and fresh vegetables to the military, delivering them himself twice weekly using his own team of horses.[9]

Because the war was on, Grimes wrote his horses were among "...the few left in the county." Following an

This image was used on the life membership form of the Minnesota Horticultural Society. Jonathan Grimes played a critical role in the Society. He was present at its founding and was twice elected president.

eight-mile one-way trip and unloading, the tired farmer reclined in the wagon bottom and let his team "find their way home." Winter made the trip more difficult, even though Eli Pettijohn, who lived along Lake Harriet's south shore, kept that part of the route free of snow out of a "sense of patriotic duty." During one notable blizzard, Grimes and his team became lost when blowing snow obscured the road. They sheltered that night in a ravine near Lake Calhoun.[10]

Peter Wolford, a Minneapolis investor, muddied the Waterville millpond waters in November 1861 when he produced a mortgage on the property signed by Richard Strout. Wolford then filed for the mill's foreclosure. Grimes and his partner Rheem had no knowledge of this encumbrance at the time they bought the land. It was lost to Wolford following a January 6, 1862, sheriff's sale. Three weeks later Jonathan lost his section seven land after Edwin S. Jones, also a holder of a Strout mortgage, foreclosed.[11]

Eliza Grimes now became a player and trader in this game of mortgages in motion. John Gordon, Eliza's father, died in summer 1862 and left his daughter $1,600. She first used that cash to get Edwin Jones to re-assign the original Strout mortgage to her, and on April 3, 1863, Eliza Grimes purchased the section seven farm from Edwin Jones. Then, in August 1865, Jonathan Grimes bought 160 acres of unimproved and uncultivated land for $1,600. Three-fourths of the property lay between today's France and Beard avenues from 50th to Morningside Road, and the remainder between Grimes and France avenues from Morningside Road to 46th Street.

Jonathan Grimes now embarked upon a new career. In 1866 he founded Lake Calhoun Nursery and began a career in horticulture that brought him prominence in Minnesota and the nation. As a Hennepin County representative that year, Grimes was present when the Minnesota Horticultural Society was organized in Rochester. In the years following, Grimes was twice elected president of the Minnesota organization and was its five-time treasurer.[12]

National recognition for Grimes was still in the future as he started his Lake Calhoun Nursery. He immediately began planting fruits, with an early specialization in small-sized varieties including currants, strawberries and raspberries. Grimes found little competition for his products, leading a *Minnesota Horticulturist* biography to report he "...obtained good prices for several years and his venture proved a

Jonathan and Eliza Grimes's Gothic Revival home, built on their farm in 1869

grand success." He tested new varieties of fruit, flowers and shrubbery and became the well-known supplier of plants, trees and shrubs for nearly all the first residences in Minneapolis.[13]

Near the end of their lives the respected Edina residents, Jonathan and Eliza Grimes, decided to move from the community. They had built a handsome Gothic Revival-style home on their farm in 1869, but 14 years later moved to southeast Minneapolis to make attendance at the University of Minnesota easier for their children. Eliza died in November 1902. Jonathan survived her by only three months.[14]

Three years after their deaths, the Grimes's heirs decided to plat a housing development on their land they called "Morningside." The children had previously laid out Waveland Park but now incorporated that acreage into Morningside, thus bringing a change to a street first known as Highland Avenue, later named Coburn Avenue.[15]

This road ran through the development and dead-ended at the streetcar tracks on 44th Street. They called the thoroughfare France Avenue.

THE SPLIT: EDINA DIVORCES RICHFIELD

From its beginnings in May 1858, the frontier town of Richfield faced difficulties holding onto its assigned 63 square miles. In its first three decades the community lost land to Minneapolis, Fort Snelling and St. Louis Park. When the western part of the town asserted its independence in 1888, nearly half of what remained of Richfield was subtracted.

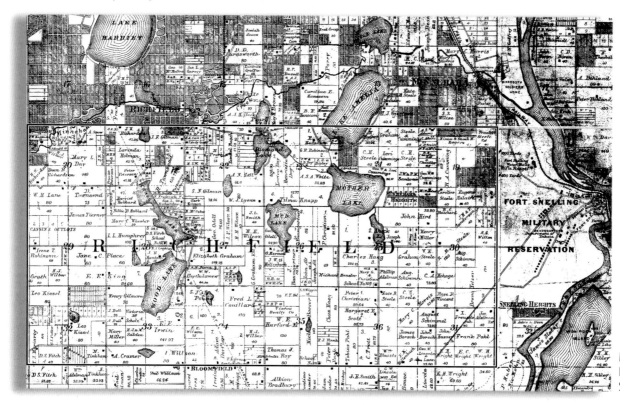

Map of 1890 Richfield including South Minneapolis

Forty settlers living west of Fort Snelling gathered in a humble schoolhouse at Richland Mill on May 11, 1858, to undertake important business. In April, the Hennepin County Board of Commissioners had directed them to organize their small part of Minnesota Territory into a town. It appeared the U.S. Congress was finally going to approve Minnesota as the nation's 32nd state, thus governmental units needed to be in place. As part of their business, these citizens decided by acclamation that their town would "hereafter be known by the name of Richfield."[1]

Two miles almost directly to the west of Richland Mill, now known as Richfield Mill, lay Waterville Mill, the eventual political center of the future Edina. Waterville, Richfield's other flour producer, had been idled by America's financial Panic of 1857. When Jonathan Grimes and William C. Rheem re-opened this mill in 1859, farmers in Richfield's western sections had a more convenient place to bring their wheat and to socialize. Waterville Mill, at present-day West 50th Street and Browndale, became west Richfield's most important trading point.[2]

Waterville Mill's opening created a natural division between the eastern and western portions of Richfield. This small fissure did not arise from political or economic pressure, and it certainly was not cultural. The town was a loosely knit confederation of farmers working to establish themselves. They relied on wheat as their main crop and patronized nearby mills that could convert their grain to flour. It was this process that put cash in farmers' pockets.[3]

In Richfield, those living west of the future France Avenue gravitated to Waterville Mill, while those in sections to the east, roughly from Penn Avenue to the Mississippi, typically headed to Richfield Mill.[4] Harley H. Hopkins, whose name was later applied to the village formed near his land, settled on Richfield's distant northwestern border and found Waterville handy. Hopkins would assert with pride, in December 1860, that he had a higher than average wheat yield of 27 bushels per acre. Like other area farmers, he could expect about 50 cents per bushel.[5]

By fall 1861 America's Civil War brought on a national mobilization that turned citizens into soldiers. Fort Snelling became headquarters for Minnesota's prospective soldiers. Waterville Mill, now owned by Jonathan Grimes and operated by the father and son team of John and James Baird, was the fort's principal supplier of flour. This critically important commodity steadily increased in cost. When Pvt. James Pratt, a west Richfield farmer turned soldier, returned home in November 1864, he noticed the soaring grain prices. He also reported that Richfield farmers, made more prosperous by wartime increases in crop prices, were "ready to set by the fire and toast their shines [shins] and injoy [sic] life."[6]

During the post-war years, Richfield, a self-governing, sparsely-settled farming community, faced few political problems. Citizens conducted most of their business at the well-attended annual town meeting. They taxed themselves for road and bridge construction, schools, modest government costs and emergencies. Town supervisors shared governmental duties.

In microcosm, the Richfield of this era served as an example of American democracy and society as Thomas Jefferson had envisioned it.[7]

In 1867, Minneapolis, through an act of the state legislature, absorbed a large swath of north Richfield ranging between 30th (Lake Street) and 46th Street, and from present-day France Avenue in the west to the Mississippi River in the east. The southern portion of Lake Harriet remained in Richfield until 1883 when the legislature approved pushing the Minneapolis city limit from 46th to 48th streets, between Xerxes and Lyndale.[8]

A small trading center grew up around Richfield Mill during the 1850s and formed the city's economic core.

These events caused no alarm in Richfield. To community residents, the fact that their agrarian peers wished to sell their farmsteads to others was none of their business. Its citizens understood the practical and political reasons for the existence of Richfield, but their allegiance to it as a rural hometown had limits. Barring the few scattered trading points within town borders, there was not much community identity.[9]

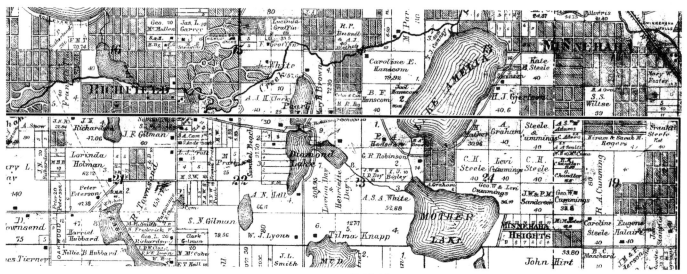

Richfield's new northern border emerges in this 1890 map. Edina, to the immediate west (not shown) seceded from Richfield two years before. At center, 54th Street, Richfield's new northern boundary, runs through southern Lake Amelia.

Land losses continued in 1886 and 1887. A group of citizens living in the northwest sections of Richfield and land further north successfully petitioned the Hennepin County Board of Commissioners in November 1886 to incorporate that area into the village of St. Louis Park. A few months later, the Minnesota legislature approved a move of Richfield land to Minneapolis between 48th and 54th streets, and from Xerxes to the Mississippi River. This annexation brought nearly all of Minnehaha Creek, along with its falls, within Minneapolis borders while removing from Richfield the original town center at Richfield Mill.[10]

Becoming Edina

In 1888, citizens in west Richfield still viewed the area around the old Waterville Mill— renamed Edina Mill by Andrew Craik after he assumed ownership in 1869—as the community center. But by this time the new Grange Hall at 50th Street and Wooddale Avenue, not the nearby mill, had become the local meeting place. Leading residents in the area had joined Oliver Kelley's nationwide farmer's organization, commonly known as the Grange, in December 1873. Six years later, local Grangers put up a building that would serve as Edina village hall until 1942.[11]

The Grange initially advertised itself as a social and educational organization for farmers, and its members often formed close friendships. Local Minnehaha Grange members met at the Grange Hall and at each other's homes. The natural east-west geographic divide in Richfield seemed to be widened by changing views held by many living in the town's western section. They began seeing themselves as residents of the place called Edina Mills.

These westerners took notice when people living in Richfield's northwest corner formed St. Louis Park in 1886 and when Minneapolis took another chunk of the town in 1887. For those in Edina Mills, creating a new community seemed an evolutionary, not revolutionary, step. It appeared both logical and convenient that the two agricultural districts and their residents split into separate communities.

Thus, when west Richfield's residents held a town meeting in 1888 and took action to form the community of Edina, they found little resistance.

A March 12, 1889, town meeting formalized the secession and "laid on the table" a process for equitably dividing with Edina the town's property. A few weeks later the Board of Supervisors met to examine and divide the town's papers and delivered to James A. Bull, a former Richfield board member, all documents belonging to Edina.[12]

The suburbanization that transformed the area remained decades away and played no part in the decision to divide. In the early 1920s, a Richfield promotional booklet still focused upon its truck farms and cattle, while a group of urban pioneers in the small residential district of Morningside broke free of Edina because they were fed up with being governed by farmers.

Richfield lost more of its domain to Minneapolis in 1927. The creation of a small airfield that eventually grew into Minneapolis-St. Paul International Airport took more community land. After experiencing more than a century of annexation and territory lost to its neighbors, Richfield's original 63 square miles had been reduced to a mere seven.

The Edina Grange building was headquarters for the local Minnehaha Grange, #398. This structure became a de facto city hall for Edina from the village's founding in 1888 through 1942.

Sarah Gates Baird and the Grangers

Historians tend to overlook contributions made by American women, particularly those who lived during the first 200 years of the nation's history. Sarah Gates Baird serves as an example of such unrepresented women. Her contributions to the founding of Edina and her leadership role in America's first farmers reform movement, known as the Grange, are little remembered today.

For 21-year-old school teacher Sarah Gates, marriage to an up-and-coming farmer like George W. Baird held many advantages. Baird, eight years Sarah's senior, owned nearly all of the northeast quarter of section 18 in west Richfield. It encompassed 120 acres of well-sited land just west of the Waterville Mill (later Edina Mill). George had moved to Minnesota Territory in 1857 and was the first to introduce sheep to the Fort Snelling area. He impressed Sarah and others with his intelligence and drive—attributes important to the observant young bride. They wed on October 11, 1865.[1]

Sarah Gates Baird

During their 51 years together in the prosperous agricultural enclave of Edina, the Bairds quietly assumed leadership positions in community and state affairs. George drew notice for his work in establishing the Minnesota Agricultural Society, the organization that would run the annual State Fair, and was the longtime president of the Hennepin County Agricultural Society. Together, they served prominently in Edina's Minnehaha Grange #398, an important affiliate of the National Grange of the Order of Patrons of Husbandry, initiators of America's first agrarian reform movement. Sarah's service on behalf of the local Grange was significant, but her 30 years of dedicated service as leader of the Minnesota Grange was remarkable.

In a move highly unusual for its time, the Grange admitted women as members. When Minnesota farmer Oliver H. Kelley founded the national organization 1869, he believed that women, acting as full members in the organization, would increase its chances of success. Thus, the Grange became an outlet for Sarah Baird's natural talents—organizing, writing and lecturing—that might otherwise have remained hidden on an Edina farm.[2]

Move to Minnesota

Eleven-year-old Sarah Gates had traveled with her parents, William and Miriam, from Vermont to Minnesota Territory in 1854. They lived in St. Anthony where her father worked as a blacksmith. Sarah, one of four Gates children, completed her education and on April 26, 1862, at age 18, she became a certified teacher in Richfield. The growing school district had expanded from two, one-room schools in 1855 to six in 1861. W.W. Woodward, Superintendent of Richfield Schools, personally tested Sarah Gates and

George W. Baird

presented her with a handwritten teaching license.[3]

Another teacher introduced Sarah to George Baird, a Pennsylvania-born bachelor who had purchased his property in west Richfield, later Edina, from the original settler. The two married and created a union that lasted 51 years until George's death. The couple did not have children.

Oliver Kelley's Grange grew slowly at first, and without the Bairds or other Edina members. He had originally organized his group as a secret society based on the rituals of Masonry, but Midwesterners generally distrusted such closeted orders and kept their distance. As 1870 began, Minnesota was home to 40 of America's 49 Granges. In January 1873, the Grange reconstituted itself and expanded membership by allowing "any person interested in agricultural pursuits" to join. They also advertised themselves as a social fraternity of farmers dedicated to educating themselves about modern progressive agriculture. Five months later, Minnesota alone had more than 200 affiliates.[4]

The collapse of the railroad boom gutted the value of high-flying stocks and bonds. Most rail firms could not pay their debts. The Panic of 1873 ensued and caused an economic depression that lasted six years. Banks cut credit, foreign trade faltered and prices fell sharply. Stunned farmers watched the price of wheat wither to half its normal price and saw their livelihood threatened. Already organized, the Grangers were ready to demand change.[5]

The Bairds weathered the financial crisis. They proved adept at produce gardening, raised prize-winning Merino sheep and made a very good living. In running the Baird household, Sarah could

be both frugal and lavish. People said she never bought common pins, but instead picked up strays. She heavily patched George's clothes and repaired her own shoes. She made butter, canned fruits and baked her own bread. But Sarah found fine linens and beautiful clothes enticing, and she did occasionally give in to those temptations. During a trip to New York for a Grange meeting—the Bairds enjoyed travel—she bought a dress pattern on sale at 16 percent off its hefty $51 price tag.[6]

Edina's Minnehaha Grange #398 organized on December 9, 1873. The small assembly at Waterville Mill elected

In 1862, W.W. Woodward, Richfield Superintendent of Schools, found Sarah Gates qualified to teach in Richfield.

James A. Bull, a neighbor and friend of the Bairds and a leading member of the community, as master of the Grange. Other well-known residents became officers: J.W. Griswold, overseer; William Finch, lecturer; Martin V. Pratt, steward; Mrs. M.C. Griswold, chaplain; B.C. Yancey, treasurer; Joseph Hamilton, secretary; and James Hawkes, gate keeper. The group initiated the Bairds and Hawkes's wife at their next meeting. Men paid a two-dollar initiation fee, women one dollar.[7]

Granger Impact

Late 19th century American farmers saw agriculture, once the unquestioned

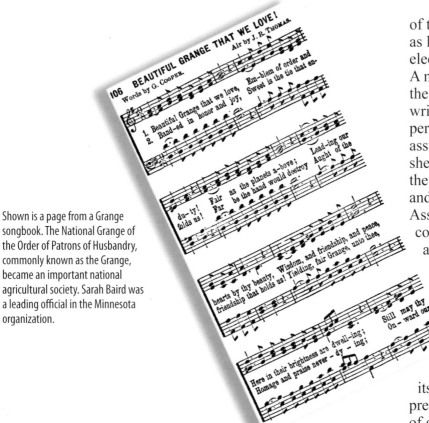

Shown is a page from a Grange songbook. The National Grange of the Order of Patrons of Husbandry, commonly known as the Grange, became an important national agricultural society. Sarah Baird was a leading official in the Minnesota organization.

bedrock of the American economic system, being overshadowed by a robust and growing industrial sector. Even during the hard economic times, frustrated farmers nursed a belief that railroads, grain buyers, bankers and factory owners were harvesting bumper crops of cash while they struggled to survive.

Minnesota Grangers believed America's farmers needed to fight for their political and economic goals. Although their constitution prohibited political discussions during Grange meetings, members took part in "county councils" that dealt with matters important to the agrarian reformers. They proved their power in the state by passing a so-called 1874 Minnesota "Granger Law" that brought regulation to railroads.[8]

Edina Grangers continued to focus upon the social and educational traditions of the order. They chose Sarah Baird as lecturer in December 1875, her first elected position in the organization. A month later they appointed her to the editorial board where she helped write and publish *Minnehaha Spray*, a periodical of the Grange. In 1878 she assumed the treasurer's office. Before she moved on to her 30-year service to the state Grange, Sarah became a founder and shareholder in the Edina Hall Association, a Granger-related group committed to building a community hall at Edina Mills.[9]

Creation of the Edina Hall Association in March 1879 illustrates a growing sense of community around Edina Mills, at that time still well within the confines of Richfield. When Richfield was organized in 1858, its western border was established at present-day Highway 169. After 20 years of growth, two town centers had grown up along Minnehaha Creek—the original political base at Richfield Mill (near today's 53rd and Lyndale) and Edina Mills (near the future 50th and Wooddale Avenue).[10]

Sarah and George Baird would be among those who contributed money to build the community center. The secretary's book of the Edina Hall Association reported a "considerable number of persons" gathered on March 7, 1879, at the home of B.C. and Ellen Yancey, a pioneering black couple in the area, to discuss building a Grange Hall near Edina Mills. They elected E.J. Woodward president and William Bryant

secretary. George Baird, James Hawkes, James Bull and Bryant agreed to purchase three shares for the building effort, while M.V. Pratt, A.P. Stanchfield and B.C. Yancey bought one each. Sarah Baird, with one share, became the only woman to buy into the program. The association completed the building, and less than 10 years later west Richfield residents, led by Bull, George Baird and Patrick Ryan, decided to incorporate their own village. Their Grange Hall doubled as headquarters for the village until 1942.[11]

George made a special 20th wedding anniversary present to Sarah; the promise of a new house. They moved into their handsome red brick Victorian home in January 1887. Sarah ran her household and kept current with Grange-related social and business responsibilities. Her personal diaries covered more than 30 years, detailing daily life on the farm and in Edina, as well as her Grange activity. Her diaries also tell of the Bairds' travel to seven national Grange meetings. A good neighbor and friend, Sarah made social calls, visited shut-ins, and would stay all night with the ill. Her description of the terrible winter of 1888 and the toll it took on the community brought home the power of Minnesota weather at its worst.[12]

Sarah Baird continued to be a deeply involved member of Edina's Minnehaha Grange and earned election as the group's first female Master in 1894. But by that time, she had established herself as treasurer of the Minnesota State Grange. She would later assume the office of Master of the state organization.[13]

Viewed from a 21st century perspective, Sarah Baird's ascension in 1901 to the commanding position in the Minnesota State Grange might not seem

remarkable. Having amply demonstrated the ability to handle the job, Baird was well qualified to lead. But smothering societal attitudes regarding the role of women continued to limit the ambitions of those with interests wider than family and home. The Grange, with its tradition of men and women working together, was that rare place where a woman could serve as a leader of men.

In her final speech to members of the Minnesota Grange, Sarah Baird declared their organization, "national in scope

George and Sarah Baird moved into their red brick Victorian-style home in 1887. It was George's gift on their 20th wedding anniversary.

[and] the most important and influential of all farmers' organizations because it combines all agricultural interests…in a common effort for general welfare."[14] Baird explained that assertion, noting Granger perspective on education, parcel post service, migratory birds ("who stand guard…against insect pests"), the Good Roads Movement, and the threat of oleomargine as a butter substitute. She believed the Granger movement to be relevant, while acknowledging the national decline of the organization she loved, declaring, "[W]hile many of the original granges became dormant, the sacred fire of faith was kept burning on many a farm hearthstone…."[15]

Few would have agreed with Baird's assessment of Grange strength. As a national movement, the Grange took a backseat to other farm organizations—Greenbackers, the Farmers' Alliance and the People's (or Populist) Party—that took their successive turns as the voice of American farmers. Nevertheless, the Grange had first brought to the American people what farmers believed to be the case against the conniving capitalists who repressed them. Even though a shadow of its former self, the Grange remained the organization in which Sarah Baird could still believe.[16]

As she relinquished her title of Master of the Grange, Baird offered some personal remarks. "This closes a period of 30 years of continuous service as an official in the State Grange, 12 as Treasurer and 18 as Master. I have spent the best years of my life in Grange work…No one can hold our Order in higher regard and affection than I do, and no one can be more ambitious for its further growth and advancement…."

She closed with a suitable benediction to the membership. "And now Patrons…let our deliberations be characterized by wisdom, calmness, and justice that the work may make us stronger as an order, more prosperous as producers, dearer friends and better citizens." [17]

Upon Sarah Baird's death on April 3, 1923, the Minnehaha Grange ordered its hall draped in mourning for 90 days as a sign of respect for the life of a great leader.

This weather vane stood atop Edina's Grange Hall, headquarters of the Minnehaha Grange #398.

BOOM, BANKRUPTCY, BUST—STEELE, KING AND MENAGE

Since territorial days, speculators in what became south Hennepin County hoped to strike it rich by exploiting the area's most precious commodity—land. Hundreds of investors mingled with the first settlers of the area, ready to gamble their money, talent and nerve in the potentially lucrative enterprise of land speculation. A few of these 19th century capitalists nurtured hopes of creating their own land empires south of Minneapolis. The stories of three such men illustrate the risks and rewards of these endeavors.

The United States House of Representatives investigated one; another crumpled from wealth to utter bankruptcy and soared back; a third accumulated immense wealth before fleeing to Central America to avoid creditors. Franklin Steele, William S. King and Louis Menage, the three ambitious and enterprising men in question, cast imposing shadows in south Hennepin County during the last half of the 19th century. They owned or controlled thousands of acres of land in south Minneapolis, Richfield and Edina, and were renowned throughout Minnesota.

Franklin Steele

Frank Steele became known in Minnesota for an ability to get the jump on potential rivals by boldly and brazenly pulling off land grabs. Born in 1813 to a leading Pennsylvania family, Steele migrated to Fort Snelling at age 24 carrying $1,000 in capital. He arrived at an opportune time to speculate.[1]

Steele was at the fort when the United States completed an 1837 treaty with the Dakota and Ojibwe that opened a wedge of land west of the St. Croix River that ranged to the Mississippi. To Steele, the treaty meant land near the falls along the St. Croix would be available for claiming. He moved immediately. "I started from Fort Snelling in a bark canoe accompanied by a scow loaded with tools, supplies and laborers," he later recalled. The aggressive speculator staked two claims around the now-available waterfalls.[2]

The following spring, Steele and some fellow investors established St. Croix Lumbering Company. That business floundered, but Steele was able to sell his share in the operation for $1,300. Using that capital, he became a sutler at Fort Snelling. He sold trade goods to officers, lumbermen, Indians and traders, often by credit, and soon was something of a banker.[3]

Steele's next land coup added to his reputation as an opportunistic land claimant, or claim jumper, depending upon who was telling the story. Important news in the late mail reached Fort Snelling's commander during a winter day in 1838. The exact date is unknown. A letter informed Maj. John Plympton that land around St. Anthony Falls, the famous landmark and hugely valuable source of waterpower, would be opened for settlement. Plympton had seen fit to leave the falls *outside* the fort's boundaries when, in March 1838, he mapped the military reservation. Now, St. Anthony land was up for grabs. The story goes that

Franklin Steele is pictured about 1856. Steele audaciously offered to buy the Fort Snelling Military Reservation from the federal government. He failed, but continued to pursue the valuable tract of land.

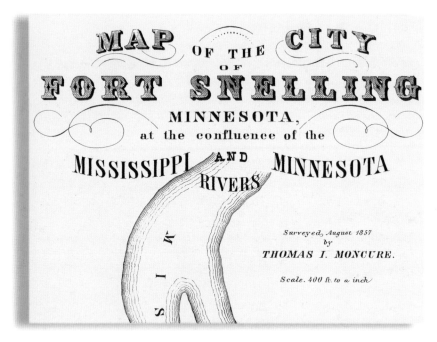

Frank Steele received the news about St. Anthony at the same time as Plympton.[4]

An eager Maj. Plympton prepared to head for the falls at first light the following morning. Steele, meanwhile, lined up some assistance and made a night march to St. Anthony. When the major arrived the following morning, he found Steele enjoying breakfast in a shack he had built on his claim. Other versions of this incident use different names, time frames and claim jumping charges, but the fact remains that Steele outsmarted his rival for the St. Anthony Falls land.[5]

Frank Steele's next scheme to acquire Minnesota land dwarfed his earlier moves. It occurred to Steele and others that, with the removal of the Dakota to a western Minnesota reserve in the early 1850s, Fort Snelling no longer provided important military service. Its entire 12-square-mile site could be sold, and speculators anxiously awaited word of the fort's availability. Steele had no intention of letting matters go that far. In April 1856, he made an offer to the U.S. Secretary of War, Jefferson Davis, to buy the *entire* Snelling tract for $15 an acre. Davis scuttled the idea.[6]

In April 1857, Virginia land speculator Dr. Archibald Graham met with John B. Floyd, the new secretary of war. The doctor learned of the possible sale of now-available Fort Snelling lands and enlisted John C. Mather, a New York politician, and an investor named Richard Schell to get their hands on fort land. First, they had to deal with Steele, the insider still working on the project. Mather traveled to Minnesota for a meeting.[7]

The fledgling cabal developed a scheme to get the fort site appraised and sold privately to Franklin Steele, with the others along as silent partners. On May 31 in Washington, D.C., Graham and Mather, by happy coincidence, bumped into William K. Heiskell, the just-appointed Fort Snelling land commissioner. Soon, Graham was making a cross country trip to Minnesota with his new friend. Graham, Heiskell

This portion of the City of Fort Snelling map shows the proposed street plan near the fort itself.

The depiction of Fort Snelling is found on Franklin Steele's 1857 "Map of the City of Fort Snelling."

and Maj. Seth Eastman, the other Snelling land commissioner, soon met and concluded the government could get a better price for the fort land by arranging a private sale. They offered the land to Steele, who agreed to the appraiser's price of $90,000. Steele, with the aid of Mather and Schell, paid $30,000 down on July 25.[8]

The odor emanating from the land deal resulted in an 1858 investigation by the U.S. House of Representatives. This inquiry evolved into a political struggle of one-upmanship between Democrats and Republicans and fizzled. The effects of the financial Panic of 1857 and the House investigation left ownership of the base undecided. Steele had been given possession of the Fort on July 19, 1858, but soon saw the bad economy halt expected land sales. He and his partners defaulted, and an ensuing government lawsuit was brought. It was later suspended. When the Civil War broke out in April 1861, the military arbitrarily assumed control of Fort Snelling.[9]

The audacious Steele reasserted his right to the fort lands after the war, asking the army to pay $162,000 for use of his citadel. The military examined the issue and decided the Fort Snelling sale was a fraud, of which Steele was *not* a part. Leading officers suggested an agreement

In 1857 Steele, aided by well-connected political insiders, secured an agreement to buy the Fort Snelling reserve. The national economic collapse, known as the Panic of 1857, dried up the money supply, and Steele defaulted, as this letter from the Secretary of War confirmed.

Franklin Steele papers, Minnesota Historical Society

between the United States and Steele could be reached. The canny Minnesotan offered the military a deal: He would forget the debt if he got the Snelling land back.

The army retained land equal to the $38,030 it said Steele still owed and drew up papers granting him ownership of the remainder of the Fort Snelling reservation. He received a deed for 6,394.80 acres of prime Minnesota real estate.

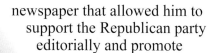

William S. King,
about 1888

William S. King

New York-born William S. King liked to claim he founded the Republican party in the United States when, in 1853, he organized the Young Men's Republican Club in his home state. And indeed, his affinity and talent for politics would serve him in well in Minnesota and Washington, D.C. In the "political galaxy of Minnesota" following the Civil War, wrote leading Minnesota historian William Watts Folwell, there were "lustrous wandering stars, few of which, if any among them, were more brilliant than William Smith King."[10]

King moved to Minneapolis in 1854 and founded the *State Atlas*, a weekly newspaper that allowed him to support the Republican party editorially and promote his adopted Minneapolis. His efforts to champion Minneapolis at the expense of rival St. Paul became Minnesota legend. King's efforts to hijack the State Fair from the capital city to Minneapolis and his actions during the famed 1890 census war between the two cities made his name poison in St. Paul.

A hearty, friendly, but no-nonsense man, King plucked a political plum when he was elected postmaster for the House of Representatives in 1861. His position in Washington, D.C., along with a growing network of friends, provided him with information on investment options that greatly increased his wealth. In 1868 he bought a farm in northwest Richfield, eventually owning 1,400 acres east of Lake Harriet and Lake Calhoun.

He specialized in breeding registered cattle on his Lyndale Farm, named for his Methodist minister father, Lyndon King. By 1870 King had invested $248,000 in the property, with stock costing $120,000, the farm $100,000 and the barn and house $28,000. Wheat, corn and oats raised on

Bill King's Lyndale Farm, at today's Bryant Avenue South and 38th Street, was located on the 14 acres he owned east of Lake Calhoun and Lake Harriet.

650 acres furnished food for the family and stock. The Minneapolis *Tribune* noted King's cattle were so well known that "the names of his great animals are familiar to almost every stock breeder in the country...."[11]

Baronial Bill King had borrowed lavishly to finance Lyndale Farm and his purebred stock. Heavily leveraged, King soon found himself in trouble. He had invested in the massive Northern Pacific Railroad project backed by banker Jay Cooke, the prominent "financier of the Civil War." In September 1870 King received a handwritten letter from Cooke calling for the balance of his $17,333.34 "Nthn Pac subsc" [Northern Pacific subscription]. King also lost money through investments in the Minneapolis Street Railway Company during the financial Panic of 1873, triggered by the failure of Cooke's bank.[12]

The collapse of Jay Cooke and Co. Bankers put King in a deeper hole. Cash poor, King and his wife, Caroline, understood the value of their land, encumbered as it was, and in June 1875 sought help from New York friend Philo Remington. The Minnesotan later recalled in court his predicament: "...everybody I owed was clamorous and insisted upon immediate payment...I was liable to be wiped out of every dollar of property I had in the world."[13] Remington agreed to assist the Kings with an immediate advance of $53,000, and $70,000 at a later time, as long as they granted him total control and management of their property.[14]

Then, on Halloween 1877, a Minnesota court declared King bankrupt. Robert C. Innes, acting on Remington's behalf, took control of the King estate, but the Kings still believed they remained the *actual* owners, thanks to friend Remington. Innes, possibly assisted by Remington, allowed the Kings to believe this fiction.

Jay Cooke, the famed "financier of the Civil War" and prominent American banker, had problems funding the mammoth Northern Pacific Railroad project as early as 1870. With this letter Cooke called in the balance of William King's subscription for that railroad. Three years later financial backing for the Northern Pacific collapsed, causing Cooke's firm to fail, bringing on the Panic of 1873.

William S. King papers, Minnesota Historical Society

The New Yorkers had their eyes fixed on the crown jewel of the King estate— the property along Lake Harriet and Lake Calhoun lying directly in the path of booming Minneapolis's growth. Innes and Remington now made a deal with the ambitious Louis Menage—in Minneapolis for less than 10 years, but clearly a man on the rise. They agreed to sell King's land to Menage.

Louis Menage and Bill King

Menage seemed a perfect partner for the New Yorkers. He had been buying farmland in south Minneapolis, platting it, and then putting residential lots on the market. His early developments would include Prospect Park, Bloomington Avenue, Cottage City and, on the west side of Lake Calhoun, Menage's Lake Side Park. Louis Menage agreed to pay Innes and Remington $496,000 for the Kings' remaining 1,057 acres. In a separate side contract, Menage made a deal with Innes to divide proceeds from the development of the land— Menage getting two-thirds, Innes the remainder.[15]

Although not an official party to the sale, King expected to receive the lion's share of the proceeds once his debts had been cleared. Remington sent him nothing. King sued Remington, Innes and Menage for the return of his properties or the proceeds derived from them. The Kings won their case in Hennepin County District Court, a decision upheld on October 19, 1886, in the Minnesota Supreme Court. Menage handed over to the Kings cash and other assets totaling near $2,000,000—a massive sum for that time. The courts ruled Remington and Innes not liable for damages but wrote, with disgust, that the men were guilty of a breach of trust.[16]

Bill King, a wealthy man once again, joined the Minneapolis Board of Park Commissioners and made generous contributions of land to the city from the property returned to him by Minnesota courts. In the early 1890s he bequeathed 51 acres along Lake Harriet's east shore for Lyndale Park and gave the Board title

The words "Northwestern" and "Guaranty Loan Co." stood out on the building's red Lake Superior sandstone exterior walls.

Louis Menage's Northwestern Guaranty Loan Building was Minneapolis's largest and tallest office building when completed in 1890. It stood at the southwest corner of Third Street and Second Avenue.

to adjacent tracts. In effect, he secured possession of the lake for the city.[17]

Menage sustained the court's heaviest wallop. He had asserted no knowledge of claims against King's land, a declaration Loring Staples, an attorney and historian of the case, rates as "pure nonsense." Staples wrote, "Menage should have smelled not one, but two rats. As found by the courts, he was *not* a *bona fide* purchaser." Staggered, but far from leveled by the legal blow, Louis Menage moved forward. [18]

His Northwest Guaranty Loan Company continued to thrive as a money source for those wanting to buy Menage-owned property. In 1888, Menage poured more than $1,000,000 into what became Minneapolis's tallest office building, a 12-story structure named after his company. Colorfully and extravagantly clad on all four sides in red Lake Superior sandstone, it held 400 sought-after offices arranged around a soaring open light atrium, accessible by six elevators or a marble staircase.[19]

Menage expanded his reach far beyond south Minneapolis, controlling large pieces of desirable land in Madison, Wisconsin; North Galveston, Texas; Gary, Indiana; and Bozeman and Great Falls, Montana. He saw huge potential in Washington state's Puget Sound and invested heavily in that area, purchasing 1,700 acres of land and founding several companies there.

The aggressive investor also created a New Jersey firm that sold securities in eastern states.[20]

Louis Menage

Like his south Hennepin County predecessor Bill King, Louis Menage was brought down by a nationwide financial meltdown. The 1893 collapse of the Reading Railroad depressed other rail firms and soon shattered banks and other businesses. Home mortgage failures stabbed at the heart of Menage's empire, and Guaranty Loan crumpled into insolvency.

Receivers charged with liquidating Menage-run firms soon uncovered a startling fact—many of the mortgages endorsed and sold by Guaranty were phony. Mortgage holders didn't exist or, if they did, it was because their names had apparently been taken at random from Minneapolis phone directories and forged onto documents. Menage had also prepared, for fictitious buyers, deeds and

mortgages to Puget Sound properties. Guaranty Loan then "guaranteed" their loans. Menage later lugged bunches of the bogus documents to his New Jersey firm and proceeded to sell them. Local investors in Menage's loan company lost their investment, and more, in the meltdown. Under Minnesota law at the time, they had to pay cash to the firm's creditors, up to the par value of their shares.[21]

The one-time land investment wizard and lion of Minneapolis real estate learned that a grand jury had convened to investigate his dealings. Menage briskly departed the country, heading to Guatemala. Investigators discovered his location but, since that country had no extradition treaty with the United States, he could not be brought back to Minnesota.

In 1895, Menage wrote a letter to a Minneapolis friend that pointed to the Bill King lawsuit as the source of his business problems. He suggested he would return to the city and clear up his financial affairs if charges lodged against him were dropped. Officials offered no deals. Menage did get off the hook, however, on December 11, 1899. Four key witnesses from his trial had died, and another five were reluctant to testify, so a court dismissed all charges against him.

Louis Menage returned to the United States and lived in New Brunswick, New Jersey, until his death on March 15, 1924. He spent his final 25 years selling real estate.

Minneapolis Tribune, March 18, 1924

Louis F. Menage, Once Figure Here in Finance, Dies

Flight to Gautemala After Guaranty Loan Company Failure Recalled.

When dispatches arrived in Minneapolis telling of the death in New Jersey of Louis F. Menage, old-time business men Monday recalled his flight to Guatemala after the panic of 1893 had leveled the financial structures which he had reared in the Northwest.

Forty years ago Mr. Menage was one of the romantic figures of Minneapolis. He co-operated in the formation of the Guaranty Loan company and became its president. Then, in the financial upheaval of 1893, the Guaranty company failed for more than $4,000,000 and Mr. Menage fled to Guatemala at the time criminal proceedings were instituted against him. Feeling ran high. A reward of $5,000 was offered for his capture, and the Populist party made political capital of his flight.

After 10 years, however, the feeling subsided and there was no protest when the indictments were nolled. Some time later he returned to the United States, but never to Minneapolis.

He was 72 years old when he died at his home in New Brunswick, N. J.

The Poet and the Park

Upon its 1855 publication, Henry Wadsworth Longfellow's powerful narrative poem, The Song of Hiawatha, *captured the nation's attention and imagination. Longfellow based his tribute to the traditions of North American Indians largely on Henry Rowe Schoolcraft's Minnesota research. From a famed local waterfall, Longfellow adopted the name "Minnehaha" for use in his poem. Both Longfellow and the mythic Minnehaha came to be identified with one of the state's most popular parks.*

To those mid-19th-century Americans who even recognized the name, Minnesota Territory on the upper Mississippi River was a distant backwater on the nation's northwest frontier. Then, two significant events combined to bring Minnesota to the public's attention: the Grand Excursion of 1854 and the 1855 release of Henry Wadsworth Longfellow's narrative poem, *The Song of Hiawatha.*

About 1,000 influential Americans traveled by rail and river to Minnesota during the 1854 excursion to bear witness to yet another notable advance made by their ever-expanding republic: The nation's railroad system now reached the Mississippi River. The guests, including former President Millard Fillmore, received free rail passage to where the new tracks ended at Rock Island, Illinois. Then came the real adventure. They boarded five steamboats and headed upriver to the wilds of Minnesota Territory. The New York *Times* called the trip "perhaps the most magnificent ever projected." Its rival, the *Weekly Mirror*, considered the famed passengers, distance covered and the "wildness, richness and beauty" of the region and concluded, "…the world has never witnessed a more remarkable achievement."[1]

Once in St. Paul the visitors scattered, enjoying excellent weather as they took site-seeing trips. St. Anthony Falls and the Fort Snelling area attracted much interest. Little Falls (some used the name Minnehaha Falls) charmed many. Writers told of the hidden cascade that might be missed except for the noise of "its merry music," and how the creek "pours itself in one gush…into a softly beautiful pool sixty feet below."[2]

Indeed, Little Falls captivated the interest of most who saw it. Missionary Samuel Pond described the "beautiful cataract" in 1835 and wrote, "I seldom pass without going to see it." Visitor Mary Jones had heard the falls rivaled those at Niagara and was pleased with her 1855 visit. She wrote of the beauty of the area and of standing beneath the falls "under whare [sic] they went over us." Six years later, Horace Mann, Jr., noted the now-accepted name for the cascade, "Minne-ha-ha," and explained the word meant "water laughing or laughing water."[3]

Longfellow, The Poet

Henry Wadsworth Longfellow, a talented 47-year-old Harvard professor, decided to leave the classroom in 1854 and pursue a writing career. The Maine

---

Song of Hiawatha

Excerpt

By the shores of Gitche Gumee,
By the shining Big-Sea-Water,
Stood the wigwam of Nokomis,
Daughter of the Moon, Nokomis.
Dark behind it rose the forest,
Rose the black and gloomy pine-trees,
Rose the firs with cones upon them;
Bright before it beat the water,
Beat the clear and sunny water,
Beat the shining Big-Sea-Water.

There the wrinkled old Nokomis
Nursed the little Hiawatha,
Rocked him in his linden cradle,
Bedded soft in moss and rushes,
Safely bound with reindeer sinews;
Stilled his fretful wail by saying,
Hush! the Naked Bear will hear thee!

native excelled as a linguist and educator but had also published *Evangeline*, a narrative poem that found a small but loyal audience. Longfellow, inspired by the work of Henry Schoolcraft, the explorer who discovered the source of the Mississippi River and wrote about his Minnesota experiences, now began work on an ambitious new poem.[4]

Schoolcraft seized Longfellow's imagination with an 1839 study regarding characteristics of North American Indians that carried a subtitle, "Indian Tales and Legends." The explorer later updated that volume using the title *The Myth of Hiawatha*. Longfellow began work on *The Song of Hiawatha* in summer 1854 and completed it in November 1855.

The epic poem created a sensation in American literary circles. For the first time, a noted author used Indian themes as the basis for a narrative, with the noble, magical, Hiawatha as a leading character. Readers learned of Native traditions, customs and myths and of the Ojibwe and Dakota who lived in the northland's forests and on its prairies. Written with an introduction and in 22 parts, *The Song of Hiawatha* reached audiences in America and Europe. It would be read and recited in American classrooms for generations.[5]

It is difficult to overstate Longfellow's status in the America of the late 19th century. Dana Gioia, a future chair of the National Endowment for the Arts, wrote in 1993, "Longfellow was not merely the most popular American poet who ever lived but enjoyed a type of fame almost impossible to imagine by contemporary standards. His books not only sold well enough to make him rich; they sold so consistently that he eventually became the most popular living author in any genre in 19th century America."

"He is," Gioia observed, "as much a part of our history as of our literature."[6]

Robert "Fish" Jones erected this statue of Henry Wadsworth Longfellow on what were the grounds of Jones's Longfellow Gardens, part of today's Minnehaha Park.

Longfellow's features deteriorated by a century of weathering

Given Longfellow's remarkable popularity, it is little wonder that Minnesotans felt honored when its Minnehaha Falls became identified with the poet's *The Song of Hiawatha*.[7]

Establishing Minnehaha Park

Forward-thinking Minneapolis and St. Paul civic leaders talked seriously about creating a public park at Minnehaha Falls as early as 1875. The fact that the scenic falls still flowed within Richfield's borders did not deter the notables, but the lack of St. Paul support did. Visionaries, however, still saw public parks in their future. They hoped to stretch Minneapolis's southern border into Richfield and acquire Minnehaha

The card of Charles M. Loring, the "Father of the Minneapolis Park System" and supporter of a park at Minnehaha Falls
Charles M. Loring scrapbooks, MHS

Falls, as well as the remainder of Lake Harriet.[8]

In 1883 the state legislature annexed to Minneapolis a strip of Richfield land between 46th and 48th streets from Xerxes to the Mississippi. Against strong opposition, park proponents won voter approval to create a supervisory commission. The board chose as its leader the visionary Charles M. Loring, later known as the "Father of the Minneapolis Park System." Prominent landscape architect H[orace] W.S. Cleveland was signed on to develop a comprehensive park plan for the city. This Cleveland did, but without including Minnehaha—too far from the city— in the scheme. Nonetheless, Cleveland, seeing the area's potential, recommended its future purchase.[9]

Within two years the Minneapolis Board of Trade had wheedled $1,000 from the legislature to be used in selecting lands suitable for a park in the area surrounding Minnehaha Falls. The exploratory committee recommended the state of Minnesota buy 173 acres for $88,736.58. St. Paul leaders, busy working on acquiring the State Fair grounds for their city, did not object. When the legislature couldn't come up with the cash, Minneapolis produced the money and Minnehaha became a city park. Loring later called that purchase the park system's "most important."[10]

Minneapolis real estate developers saw Minnehaha Park as an invaluable drawing card for prospective home buyers. An 1891 syndicate opened a housing tract, wisely named "Minnehaha Park," near the parkland and proclaimed the area's natural beauty and easy accessibility to Minneapolis and St. Paul. Their advertising booklet claimed it took just five cents and 20 minutes to reach downtown Minneapolis. The publication also noted, "It is doubtful if the most diligent search would reveal another…area where Nature has been so prodigal of her favors…."[11]

Although home building got underway, the nationwide financial meltdown of 1893 slowed development. Minnehaha Park itself developed a questionable reputation. When a 1905 scandal involving Park Superintendent John O'Brien broke, a *Journal* editorial noted the "investigation tends to show why Minnehaha has always been a disappointment to the better element in the community."[12]

Indeed, the Minnehaha scandal reminded Minneapolitans of the corrupt administration of Mayor A.A. Ames and its eventual collapse just three years earlier. Superintendent O'Brien faced seven charges ranging from lying in wait to catch and blackmail young lovers found in compromising positions, to hosting a "beer and woman party" in the historic Stevens House. Debauchery in the venerable Stevens home, the "birthplace of Minneapolis," was an outrage that could not stand. O'Brien resigned.

Longfellow to the Rescue

At this disgraceful low point, the park began a rebound. In 1906, Robert Fremont Jones opened his Longfellow Gardens and zoo adjacent to Minnehaha. The elegant and diminutive Jones, with his ever-present silk top hat, Prince Albert suit, Van-Dyke beard and high-heeled shoes, had operated a fish market upon arrival in Minneapolis in 1876, hence his nickname, "Fish" Jones. By 1885 he owned a menagerie of animals on the future site of the Basilica of St. Mary, but complaints about the noises and smells emanating from his Hennepin Avenue zoo forced him to sell the property. He then purchased a pond and land from the Franklin Steele estate and created a new home for his animals near Minnehaha Park.[13]

Longfellow's mythical characters Hiawatha and Minnehaha were the subjects of this Jacob Fjelde bronze statue that was moved to Minnehaha Park in 1912.

"Fish" Jones enjoyed posing with his animal stars, in this case a sloth.

Fish Jones, a natural showman, helped make the park and gardens a must-see Twin Cities destination. His exotic menagerie included lions, leopards, jaguars, camels, a young elephant, ostrich, bears, "orange-utan" and nearly "100 head of monkeys." Jones could often be found on the grounds, "topper" (top hat) in place, feeding the animals. A series of formal gardens were perfect for strolling and talking. Everything was easily accessible, thanks to the park's own rail stop. Charles Loring reported, "...many thousands visited during the summer months and on Sundays and holidays, the visitors frequently number over 10,000."[14]

In 1906 Jones built, on the garden's grounds, a two-thirds scale replica of Longfellow's Massachusetts home and then lived in it. Two years later Jones

Robert "Fish" Jones built and then lived in this two-thirds replica of Longfellow's house. It has been restored and placed near the site of Jones's Longfellow Gardens in Minnehaha Park.

Visitors to Robert "Fish" Jones's Longfellow Gardens enjoyed his menagerie. Jones is shown here, in his ever-present top hat, preparing customers for a camel ride.

placed a statue of the great poet nearby. In 1912, following a long fund drive during which Minnesota schoolchildren donated pennies, a most appropriate bronze arrived at Minnehaha Park. It showed Longfellow's mythic Hiawatha about to carry his love, Minnehaha, across the creek. [15]

As more housing developments approached the park and gardens, Fish Jones began hearing complaints about excessive noise from his Longfellow operations. In 1922 the Park Board started condemnation action. Two years later Jones responded with a counter-offer. The aging showman agreed to donate his property to Minneapolis if he was allowed to operate Longfellow Gardens for 10 more years, until November 1934. The city agreed.

Fish Jones lived for just six more years before dying, on October 15, 1930, at age 79, in his beloved Longfellow-replica home at Longfellow Gardens.

–Three–
LOOKING SOUTH

Advances in transportation technology slowly drew the rural towns of south Hennepin County into the orbit of an expanding Minneapolis. Interurban trains and streetcars had reduced travel time to the city, but the advent of the auto in the first decades of the 20th century gradually erased lines separating city folk from country cousins. Meanwhile, the development of the airplane and the beginnings of an airport in Richfield during the 1920s introduced a new concept—air travel across America and, to the far-sighted, air travel across the world.

STREETCAR SUBURB: EDINA'S RAIL LINKS TO THE TWIN CITIES

Without quick, efficient means of transportation, rural areas surrounding America's young metropolises were, at the 20th century's dawn, far from convenient reach. Farm products flowed easily by wagon and train from the fields surrounding budding big cities, but moving people was another matter. Trains made cities more accessible, but weren't designed for the numerous and short stops mass transit required. The introduction of the streetcar brought on a new age in transportation that made suburban living more practicable.[1]

Bridge Square, about 1890, was the site of the first Minneapolis city hall, and key junction for Thomas Lowry's street railway system. William McCrory's "Motor Line" ran from here to Edina and Lake Minnetonka.

Minneapolis Illustrated

By the 1880s, most large American cities, including Minneapolis and St. Paul, featured horse car transport. New York City began experimenting with horse-drawn railways as early as the 1830s, a process updated by the 1852 invention of a grooved rail that lay flush with a street's surface. But the slick New York system couldn't be used on Minnesota's unpaved and winter-susceptible streets.

St. Paul investors founded a street railway in 1872, and three years later Minneapolis opened a similarly constructed line. Workers for Minneapolis Street Railway Company built the track system to conform with the city's unpaved streets by bolting wooden stringers (5x5s about 16 feet long) to rail ties. They then spiked yard-long bent iron plates weighing 23 pounds to the stringers. As a result of rail line imperfections, derailments were common, and passengers were expected to assist in getting the car back on the track. Riders also hopped off on occasion to assist the horses in getting cars up steep grades.[3]

Until railroads liberated frontier Minnesota from its dependence upon the Mississippi River for transportation and communication, the arrival of the first steamboat of spring ranked with the territory's most important days of the year. Then, in 1867, Minnesotans forged steel links between their 32nd state and the rest of America. Chicago was a mere 25 hours away and the East just a few days travel. Clearly, Americans had mastered the challenge of transporting people en masse between their great cities. Now, they set about planning to move the populace *within* those ever-expanding metropolises.[2]

From the beginning, horse cars in the Twin Cities were popular with passengers. The St. Paul *Pioneer* viewed the new system a "success," adding, [horse cars] have "already become a necessity." But horses were expensive to buy and feed. Winter forced them to become sleigh-pullers. Spring thaws in March 1873 resulted in a track buried so deep in mud that the *Pioneer* reported, "…many doubt if it will be found."[4]

St. Paul Street Railway suffered from the financial Panic of 1873, and its lingering effects forced foreclosure. A New York group bought what remained of the assets in 1877, but the rail firm failed four years later. Thomas

Thomas Lowry, about 1890
Minneapolis Illustrated

quintet quickly voted themselves $35,000 each for their time and trouble—about what they had already invested. This maneuver aligned neatly with Lowry's avowed goal in life—being "all even." That meant, Lowry joked, he'd be even when he owed money to as many people as he didn't owe money to.[6]

Debt didn't bother Tom Lowry. His grandson later offered two examples to prove the point. Tom mortgaged his handsome Lowry Hill mansion early in his career and then defaulted. Word got out about his insolvency, but when friends came to the home to console him, they found Lowry and his two daughters racing around the halls in a game of tag. He had redeemed his home the day before. About a year later his wife, Beatrice, returned from a

Lowry, a former Illinois lawyer and Minneapolis resident since 1867, joined four St. Paulites in purchasing the firm in February 1882. Affable, capable and confident, the lanky six-foot-two Lowry was a land speculator and developer who saw good public transportation as great for business. And he was already president of the Minneapolis Street Railway Company.[5]

Tom Lowry immediately squeezed cash out of the failed St. Paul operation. Two days after paying the New Yorkers $175,000 for the line, Lowry, representing the partnership, managed to convince investors to loan their firm $200,000. The

This bronze and stone 1915 monument to Thomas Lowry originally stood at the Lyndale and Hennepin "narrows." As a result of the construction of Interstate 94 it was moved to 24th Street West and Hennepin Avenue.

TRAIN STOPS

WESTBOUND—Lake Minnetonka or Deephaven Trains stop only to receive passengers for points west of Hopkins at—
Sixth Street
Seventh Street
Twelfth Street
Groveland Ave.
Douglas Ave.
29th Street
Lake Street
A   Lake Harriet Station
Lake Harriet Loop
City Limits
Grimes
Browndale
Brookside
Mendelssohn
Hopkins Sub Station

A—Westbound only.

EASTBOUND—Stop at points west of Lake St. only to discharge passengers from west of Hopkins.   East of Lake St. make all local stops to 6th St.

LAKE MINNETONKA Trains stop at—
9th Ave. (Hopkins)
Deephaven Junction
Glen Lake
Clearspring
Vine Hill
Christmas Lake
Excelsior—Dock Station
"   1st Street
"   2nd Street
"   3rd Street
Manitou
Crescent Beach
Tonka Bay

DEEPHAVEN Trains stop at 9th Ave. (Hopkins)
Deephaven Junction
Baker
Boulevard
Groveland
Breezy Point
Northome
Deephaven

shopping trip to find the living room completely emptied of its expensive furnishings. Tom had traded it all away to purchase potentially valuable real estate. He told his flabbergasted spouse to go downtown and buy anything she wanted to replace the loss and to charge everything to his account.[7]

Lowry ran both the St. Paul and Minneapolis street railways and, to keep them on track, borrowed lavishly. Customers paid a nickel to ride the cars, an affordable if not cheap rate that they accepted. The horses clopped along carrying up to 14 riders on the half-ton cars, losing money every step of the way. By 1888 Lowry was still president of the St. Paul line, but because of a weakened financial situation, no longer owner.[8]

Reaching toward Edina

While entrepreneurs like Tom Lowry struggled to make money by moving people from place to place in downtown business districts, forward-looking thinkers in other cities were laying tracks to outlying districts, increasing population and real estate values of those areas. The more distant

rural-suburban sectors were within a few miles of crowded urban centers but too far from most jobs to support housing developments.[9]

In 1878, William S. King persuaded a group of investors led by Col. William McCrory of Columbus, Ohio, to form Lyndale Railway Company, a suburban railroad. King, the renowned and highly successful Minneapolis businessman, had teamed with Tom Lowry in 1875 to reorganize the city's street railway system. McCrory's steam-powered trains would eventually run from Minneapolis to Lake Harriet, Lake Calhoun and Lake Minnetonka, with branch lines serving Minnehaha Falls and Fort Snelling. It was no surprise that the line included a stop at Bill King's popular Lake Calhoun pavilion. The McCrory group reached agreement with Lowry and Minneapolis Street Railway to lease their tracks and began operating in 1879.[10]

To make the railway's steam-powered trains more palatable to city customers, owners of the Lyndale Line, also known as the McCrory Line, built housings around the locomotives to disguise and quiet their workings. These engines took on the name "Steam Motors," later simply "Motors," hence the name most commonly applied to the Lyndale

The Minneapolis, Northfield and Southern Railroad, better known as the Dan Patch Line, also served south suburban customers in Bloomington, Edina and Richfield. This train is shown at 54th Street and Nicollet Avenue where the line reached the Twin Cities streetcar system.

railway—the "Motor Line." But a locomotive by any other name is still a locomotive and, reports Atwater's history of Minneapolis, "...there was bitter opposition on the part of many residents along the line, to steam being used as a motive power for street transit."[11]

The Motor Line had two small, underpowered motors and two passenger coaches as original equipment. These early trains struggled with Nicollet Avenue hill between 18th and 22nd streets. If passengers called for a stop on the slope, the small locomotives did not have enough power to continue and had to be backed down the incline to begin another ascent. The company gradually grew to own 12 motors and 25 coaches. Trains ran on a single, narrow gauge track, starting their day at 6:45 a.m. in Bridge Square (where Hennepin and Nicollet met) with departures every 45 minutes until 10:45 p.m. It took 35 minutes to reach Lake Calhoun.[12]

McCrory changed his railroad's name to Minneapolis, Lyndale & Minnetonka Railway in 1881 after extending its reach to Excelsior on the shores of Lake Minnetonka. The railroad ran four to six trains daily to its new stops, but only two during winter. Cost for the 80-minute ride was 75 cents in summer and a dollar during the cooler seasons. Its owners continued to feed capital into the Motor Line, but it never paid off. Like the city-only horse car operations, this suburban route was a money loser.

The expansion of the railway provided prominent Edina landowners Henry and Susan Brown reason to celebrate. Village historian Elvira H. Vinson reported, "When the McCrory's Motor was extended from Lake Harriet to Excelsior, the Browns gave a party and all the guests came by 'Motor.'"[13]

McCrory's Motor Line did have an impact on Edina and the suburbanization of south Hennepin County. The railway cut through the future northern edge of the community, skirting the Baird farm and sliding south to 44th Street and Motor Way before continuing west. Besides passengers, the trains brought increased land values to the areas it reached. In Edina's case, the Motor Line's arrival led to the platting of West Minneapolis Heights and Emma Abbott Park. Trains stopped at Grimes (Jonathan and Eliza Grimes's property in the future Morningside), Emma Abbott Park (at 44th and Brookside) and Mendelssohn (West Minneapolis Heights), the first stop after Morningside.[14]

An "Electrifying" Idea

Electrification transformed America's street railways, and in the Twin Cities was critical to securing the future of urban mass transport. The nation's first electric streetcar system opened in Richmond, Virginia, during the summer of 1888. Big city politicians, promoters and pedestrians learned electrified lines could quickly and safely move streetcars almost anywhere in a community. Electric cars rolled along their tracks in almost any weather. They were cheaper and more reliable than horse cars, more adaptable than cable cars and boasted a higher power-to-weight ratio than steam. Speedy and comparatively quiet, these electric cars, commonly known as "trolleys," were also pollution free.[15]

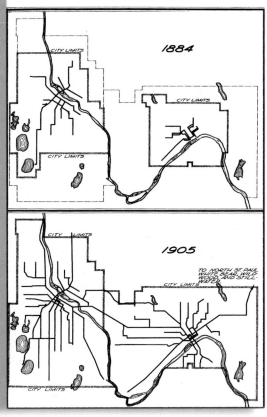

The early expansion of Twin Cities' street railways is illustrated on these maps.

Calvin Schmid, *Social Saga of Two Cities*, 1937

In September 1889 the St. Paul city council passed an ordinance authorizing Lowry's firm to electrify its entire system. Not to be outdone, the Minneapolis council followed suit, approving electric lines while proposing a new inter-urban line to link the business districts of the two cities. Lowry, perpetually short on cash and weighed down by a $4,000,000 debt on his two firms, had no cash for the job.[16]

Persuasive and persistent Tom Lowry convinced Henry Villard, the man behind the powerful Northern Pacific Railroad, into backing him. St. Paul's first electric trolley line was open and rolling on February 22, 1890. Then a stunning series of financial setbacks rocked Villard's empire and wiped him out, once again leaving Lowry in limbo. The Minnesotan soon found himself in New York City "trudging up and down Wall Street trying to get a loan" to cover the estimated $5.8 million required for his two electric rail systems. When Lowry discovered the easterners preferred the prospects of the Minneapolis line to that of St. Paul's, he merged the two. It had taken him six months in New York, but Tom Lowry now had the money he needed.[17]

By November 1891, Lowry's merged lines served both of Minnesota's leading cities. Atwater's history called it a "complete electrical system of urban cars, suburban and inter-urban cars which transport passengers from the

A Place For New Brooms
THOMAS TO JOHN—Here, John, you've got to get a move on you earlier in the morning. The Board of Health says these cars have got to be cleaned every morning and I can't do it alone.
Minneapolis Journal, November 30, 1895.

An 1895 Minneapolis *Journal* cartoon chides Thomas Lowry and the need to keep streetcars clean.

Minneapolis Journal, November 30, 1895

The western portion of this streetcar map shows the route of the McCrory "Motor" Line that ran through northern Edina to Lake Minnetonka. When the Minneapolis Street Railway took over the route, service past Lake Calhoun was halted.

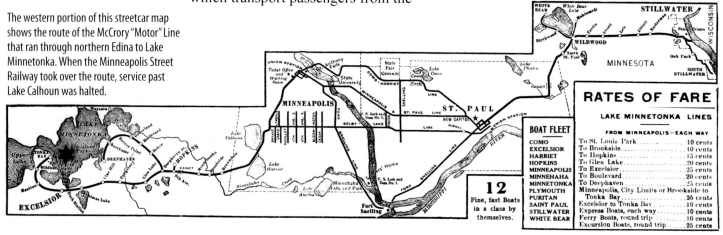

WM McCRORY, PRESIDENT
ROBERT S. INNES, GEN. PASS'R & TICKET AGT.
SAM'L E. NEILER, TREASURER

The Lyndale Railway Company.

Minneapolis, Minn. Oct 29th 1879

The letterhead of William McCrory's first "motor line"

furthermost limits of Minneapolis to the outmost limits of St. Paul for the pittance of ten cents." Streetcar tracks linked but did not, in any other way, unite the two cities. Their bitter rivalry approached a boiling point in 1890 and would continue to percolate for decades. Nevertheless, Tom Lowry figuratively brought the adversaries together when he named his rail network Twin Cities Rapid Transit Company.[18]

For those living in Minneapolis, affordable trolley lines now stretched into every district, bringing with them fundamental change. Developers built and sold houses to buyers in areas once believed too far from the city's center. In its southern environs, housing tracts made accessible by the railways reached 54th Street and the Richfield border. This became a factor in Minneapolis's eventual expansion to 62nd Street and brought the first stirrings of urbanization to Richfield.

Edina's Morningside neighborhood can trace its 1905 origins to the extension and electrification of Twin City Rapid Transit's Lake Harriet line. Residents of a citified Morningside engineered a successful 1920 secession from the then-agricultural enclave of Edina.

Streetcar access figured in the planning of Edina's Country Club District later in the 1920s. Three Country Club trolley stops—Grimes, Wooddale and Browndale—guaranteed homeowners quick access to the reliable electric railway.[19]

Later, automobiles would create the Twin Cities' suburbia of the 20th century, but trolleys deserve credit for bringing the first stages of urbanization to "streetcar suburbs" such as Edina.

Thomas and Beatrice Lowry built this mansion on the Devil's Backbone, later called Lowry Hill. It commanded an excellent view of Minneapolis from its location on the corner of Hennepin and Groveland avenues.

THE GREATEST RACE COURSE IN THE WORLD

Promoters of America's new sports venues happily lavish extravagant praise when describing the latest cutting-edge arenas, stadiums, tracks and ballparks. But in 1915, when the new Twin Cities Motor Speedway opened in Richfield, its builders actually had a factual basis for advertising it as "The Greatest Race Course in the World."

BIRDSEYE VIEW OF THE GREATEST RACE COURSE IN THE WORLD
SAINT PAUL **TWIN CITY MOTOR SPEEDWAY CO.** MINNEAPOLIS

NEW MILLION DOLLAR **SPEEDWAY** NEAR MINNEHAHA AND FORT SNELLING

Dario Resta is shown in 1916 behind the wheel of a Peugeot, the same kind of vehicle he used at the Twin City Motor Speedway.

Frank H. Wheeler, a major figure in Indiana's emerging automotive industry, entrained for Minneapolis in summer 1914, looking for Minnesota allies willing to help construct a massive auto speedway. He needed no letter of introduction. Wheeler's well-known automobile world resumé included the words, "builder of the Indianapolis Motor Speedway."[1]

Wheeler now planned to eclipse the five-year-old Indy track with a speedway unsurpassed "in all the world." At the meeting in Minneapolis, Wheeler enlisted physician Charles Dutton, auto enthusiast and prominent local surgeon, to coordinate his moves in Minnesota, and later signed up James F. Sperry, a St. Paul real estate and investment firm operator, to assist. He looked to Dutton to acquire land for the track, and in September was impatiently asking, "What have you done to secure more ground? We have to have at least 400 feet back of the grandstands on the west side…in order to make turns."[2]

Dutton, at Wheeler's behest, had been purchasing land in south Richfield, a site with numerous advantages. Comparatively flat farm fields could be easily graded to conform to the racetrack's planned layout. Cost of acreage in the rural south metropolitan area was reasonable, and its location, south of Minneapolis and near the St. Paul border, made it accessible to both cities. For some of these same reasons, developers of future sports, shopping and entertainment venues would find this area enticing.

In all, the Minneapolis men bought 342 acres of land and laid plans to have Twin City Motor Speedway open and operating by Labor Day 1915. Wheeler planned for a two-and-one-quarter-mile, banked, concrete roadway that promised both high speeds and safety to drivers and spectators. Safety emerged as a critical issue after track breakup during the 1909 Indianapolis speedway inaugural caused an accident that killed two drivers, two mechanics and two spectators.[3]

By almost any measure, construction of Twin City Motor Speedway—St. Paul newspapers preferred to call it "Snelling Speedway," while the name "Richfield" is not mentioned in any news reports— proved to be a remarkable achievement. Ground breaking commenced May 20, with track and seating construction not underway until July 8. Some 3,000

DETAILED DIAGRAMS OF STANDS

Location of stands shown in Speedway Diagram on other side of sheet.

PURCHASERS SHOULD SPECIFY FIRST, SECOND AND THIRD CHOICE OF SEATS.

GRAND STANDS "A" and "B"

Located on North Turns offering Splendid View of Entire Grounds
Grand Stand A, Sections 1 to 23.   Grand Stand B, Sections 23 to 46

Numbered spaces in front indicate boxes which contain six arm chairs. It is not necessary to order an entire box to obtain box seats. Small square spaces in back indicate reserved seats not in boxes. Each section is numbered. Rows are lettered as appear in aisle spaces. Seat Prices:—Stand A, Boxes, Front Row, $48.00; Single Seats, $8.00: Second and Third Row, $36.00; Single Seats $6.00: Fourth Row, $30.00; Single Seats, $5.00; Stand A, Reserved Seats $2.00. Stand B, Boxes, Front Row, $60.00; Single Seats, $10.00: Second and Third Row, $48.00; Single Seats, $8.00: Fourth Row, $36.00; Single Seats, $6.00; Stand B, Reserved Seats $2.50. These seat prices do not include $2.00 General Admission charge for each person. Each row is well elevated above the others so that every seat offers a clear view of the course. All Reserved seats have comfortable backs.

GRAND STAND "D"

Located on West Side of Course across from Judge's and Timer's Stand, and interesting work at the Pits
Sec.76   75   74   73   72   71   70   69   68   67   66   65   64   63   62

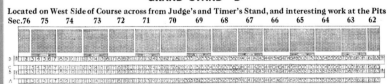

Numbered spaces in front indicate boxes which contain six arm chairs. It is not necessary to order an entire box to obtain box seats. Small square spaces in back indicate reserved seats not in boxes. Each section is numbered. Rows are lettered as appear in aisle spaces. Seat Prices—Boxes, Front Row, $60.00; Single Seats, $10.00: Second and Third Row, $48.00; Single Seats $8.00: Fourth Row, $36.00; Single Seats, $6.00. Reserved Seats in stands $3.00. Seat prices do not include $2.00 General Admission for each person, Each Row is well elevated above the others, so that every seat offers a clear view of the course. All Reserved seats have comfortable backs.

Race promoters used this chart to illustrate the Speedway's seat availability.

THE TWIN CITY MOTOR SPEEDWAY UNDER CONSTRUCTION IN 1915

workers redistributed 300,000 cubic yards of earth and poured 18,000 barrels of cement to create the track. In their rush to complete the oval, crews of 200–300 worked day and night to pour concrete at a daily rate of 2,000 square yards at a depth of six inches. Workers dug three tunnels under the track to provide infield access for up to 25,000 fans. Other crews, meanwhile, hammered together five grandstands made of 3.5 million feet of Ingvoldstad Company-supplied lumber.[4]

The Minneapolis *Journal* called

Ralph DePalma and his Mercedes are shown in 1913. DePalma was among the favorites to win at the new Minnesota track.

the track "a fitting tribute to the progressiveness and up-and-coming spirit of the twin cities." That article overstated seating capacity at 120,000. The track could hold 75,000 people in grandstands and boxes and 25,000 in the bleachers. To get fans to the track, streetcar tracks were extended to the northern edge of

the speedway. They were completed just three days before the race.[5]

Minneapolis and St. Paul newspaper sports pages gave heavy coverage of the run-up to the Saturday, September 4, 1915, race. The sport's leading drivers appeared at the track for mid-week time trials. That group included international star Dario Resta in a Peugeot and Indy 500-winning Ralph DePalma in his Mercedes, both hoping to claim the $50,000 purse. American driving legend Barney Oldfield and his co-driver Eddie Rickenbacker operated a Delage. Stutz drivers Gil Anderson and Earl Cooper were also competing. Rickenbacker, who in three year's time would become the nation's leading World War I pilot and ace, set the first track record, buzzing around the oval during a practice run at 114 miles per hour.[6]

A breathless *Journal* report on the eve of the race offered a suitable send-off for the illustrious new track: "This two mile concrete ultra modern shrine of King Speed on which in elimination trials the rubbertired [sic] projectiles have hurtled through space at a rate in excess of 100 miles per hour, is a triumph in construction and engineering skill." The writer of that tribute would soon eat his words.[7]

Race Day

A fashionable but disappointingly small Labor Day crowd of 25,000 turned out for the action. Conditions described as hot, sunny, windy and dusty combined to disturb the crowd. The outfits of some well-dressed women suffered from wind-driven clouds of dust, oil and smoke that "settled like a coating upon prized dresses." Advertisements that claimed, "The speedway is for everybody, not merely the rich, but all," lured only a "sprinkling" of race fans to the one dollar bleacher seats. Front row box seats, each holding six, went for $60, while boxes in rows two and three cost $48.[8]

Racing began at noon. Drivers rolled around the track on a slow approach lap and then gunned their engines as Fred J. Wagner, auto racing's top starter, gave them the green flag. Dario Resta charged past 13 other cars to the front. As the race progressed, drivers wrestled with mechanical problems that steered them

Drivers and their cars before the start of the Twin City Motor Speedway's first auto race

Earl Cooper steered his gleaming white Stutz past competitors and won the Speedway's inaugural 500-mile race by 30 feet.

broke out their lunch boxes while race cars broke down. Eight of the 14 drivers who began the race would finish. Those remaining offered a cheer when Earl Cooper capped a late duel with Gil Anderson by hurtling past his fellow Stutz driver to win the race by 30 feet.[9]

Drivers complained about the uneven concrete track and irritating vibration that shook them and

to the pits. Relief drivers took over for some of the stars, and the leaders slowed the pace to ease the strain on their autos. Some spectators settled in and watched with "apathy," according to one reporter, while others chose to escape the heat by exiting. Around one o'clock, fans

their autos. Said O.H. Hable to a St. Paul reporter, "That's the roughest ride I ever took." Breakdowns attributed to the track made the race less interesting—a major concern for track promoters. The *Journal* rated spectator reaction: those, "...who declared it a frost; those who thought it mildly interesting and then the over-enthusiastic."[10]

Frank Wheeler disguised his disappointment with the tepid fan support by publicly praising the efforts of the track builders and race organizers. But gate receipts provided a discouraging fact: only $27,000 in paid admissions. Still, Wheeler offered a bold prediction, "The time will come when there will be 100,000 people at the Minneapolis Speedway."[11]

Within a week, the future of the Twin Cities Auto Speedway appeared grim. On the Tuesday following the race, scores of laborers stormed the St. Paul office of James Sperry, the track's managing director, demanding their wages. They

Drivers line up for a pre-race photo in front of the Speedway's grandstand. Barney Oldfield is in the white coat.

angrily protested when told payday "would be next Friday." Contractors and building supply people met separately with both Wheeler and Sperry at the St. Paul Hotel. The following day Ralph Capron, a former University of Minnesota football and baseball star, now in advertising, got into a scuffle with Sperry over unpaid ad bills. "He got abusive and hit me a few times," reported Sperry.[12]

Hoping to scare up some quick cash, Wheeler tried to sign on drivers, including Resta and DePalma, for a race on September 10. That deal had no chance, leading the battered Jim Sperry to a Friday announcement. He admitted "lack of attendance" during the race had caused problems, then pleaded, "…if everybody will keep quiet for a few days we will have everybody taken care of nicely…." The speedway actually owed Sperry $75,000, an amount second only to lumber contractor Walter Ingvolstad's claim of $100,000. Wheeler retreated to Indianapolis where he launched a $350,000 bond issue.[13]

Talk of more races soon waned,

Racing legend Barney Oldfield raced at the Twin City Speedway's 1915 opening. Oldfield and his pit crew are shown a year later during the Indianapolis 500.

and by 1916 the partnership between the speedway's Twin Cities and Indianapolis leadership shattered. Wheeler wrote to Dutton, warning that "Sperry and his crowd" could not be trusted. Foreclosure of the track loomed that spring, prompting Wheeler to see receivership as the best way to "get rid of Sperry and his gang."[14]

The speedway track itself suffered through two Minnesota winters before getting a final reprieve. The American Red Cross scheduled a 100-mile derby for July 15, 1917, two months after the United States formally entered the Great War (First World War) in Europe. Earl Cooper returned to defend his championship won at the speedway's opening, but Ira Vail drove to victory. Drivers had financed the race themselves, but with just 4,000 looking on, it didn't appear they would make expenses. The low turnout, a "huge disappointment," was blamed in part on the track's "bad reputation."[15]

Return to Richfield?

Although the Twin Cities Motor Speedway lay entirely within the boundaries of Richfield, most observers considered the racetrack to be a kind of rural Minneapolis province. Despite this de facto loss of territory, Richfield residents offered no complaint. But when the Hennepin County sheriff sold the failed speedway in 1917, it seemed appropriate that a local farmer, Gus Hohag, was the buyer.[16]

The Hohags had been a leading Richfield family since settlement days, and now Hohag brothers Art, Gus and John (Jack) operated farms neighboring the speedway. To Gus and his wife, Lottie, the land buy seemed logical,

but they held it for less than two years. The Minneapolis Trust Company and agents of Guy A. Thomas paid Gus Hohag $56,300 for the former racetrack. On November 19, 1918, three days after getting the deed, Thomas sold the property for $100,000 to Snelling Field Corporation, an outfit with plans to convert the land to an airfield. Thomas happened to be an official of this new airport consortium. [17]

With auto racing halted, airplane pilots had been using the old racetrack and its easy-to-find concrete oval as an airbase. The pilots shied away from the unpredictable track

Driver Rene Thomas and his Delage in 1914

surface and landed on the grassy area inside. In December 1919 the Minneapolis Aero Club corralled enough money to purchase the field. The base ranged north to 60th Street, south to 66th Street, west to 34th Avenue and east to 46th Avenue. The state legislature passed a bill in 1927 giving the city of Minneapolis the right to equip and operate the airfield; a year later Minneapolis assumed control of all former speedway land and gave to it the name "Minneapolis Municipal Airport." Workers broke up and buried the old concrete racetrack.[18]

Although Richfield no longer exercised control over its former territory, the people of the village accepted the placement of the airport. Residents worked at the air base and the small businesses that supported it. The Jack Hohag family truly signed on for the air age. Jack built the Air-O-Inn at 34th Avenue and 66th Street on his land across the street from the airfield. Sons Robert and Earl became pilots for Northwest Airways. Another son, Bill, became chief mechanic at NWA, and daughter Mary worked as a flight hostess.[19]

Gus and Lottie Hohag showed no interest in the airport or in leaving their farm. Over the years, the airfield continued to encroach upon their land, but they stayed put. The Metropolitan Airports Commission (MAC), formed in 1943, wanted to buy them out but met stout resistance until the Hohags accepted a MAC compromise in 1949. "[They] said my wife and I could stay here until we died," laughed Gus in 1960. "Well we're still going strong, both of us are 85 and staring right back at the planes." Gus died a year later, but Lottie lived on to 1970 and age 92.[20] Soon after, MAC bulldozers made the old Hohag farm disappear as well.

Autos can be seen on the banked track of the former Twin City Speedway, following the site's conversion to an airfield. The large building in the foreground is a hangar for the 109th Observation Squadron.
Photo date approximately 1922

A Disastrous Inaugural: The Arrival of Airmail Service

In the mid-1920s the federal government felt ready to turn over its fledgling airmail operation to privately owned air services and, in the process, laid the foundation for the nation's commercial aviation industry. Flyers at Wold-Chamberlain Field in south Richfield were ready on June 7, 1926, to assume control of the Twin Cities to Chicago airmail route.

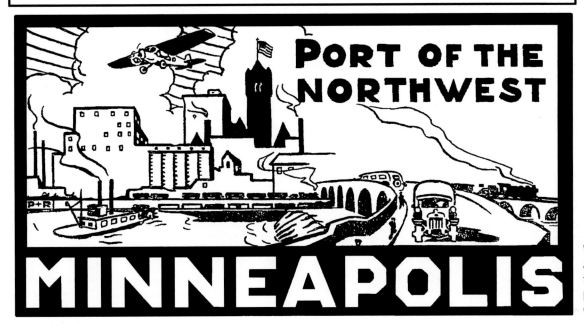

CITY'S BADGE AS "PORT OF NORTHWEST"

PORT OF THE NORTHWEST

MINNEAPOLIS

With the opening of civilian airmail service in June 1926, the Minneapolis *Journal* proclaimed the city the "Port of the Northwest."

To most Twin Citians in spring 1926, the buzz of airplanes flying overhead remained a novelty. Though advances in technology had improved the dependability of aircraft, the public continued to see flyers as barnstormers—stunt men and women—not the early ambassadors of a new form of American mass transportation. Midwest aviation leaders now prepared to prove they could handle more important matters. They had secured government contracts to carry mail speedily and dependably through the air.

The U.S. government had begun experimenting with airmail service in 1911. Postal pilots proved the concept viable, and Congress, encouraged by this success and improved ground support and aircraft, passed laws in 1925 and 1926 that allowed for the creation of investor-owned airmail service.

The idea of scheduled airmail flights to Chicago and beyond caught the attention of a Twin Cities populace not yet aware of even more exciting plans. Early airmail operators wanted to add passengers to their airplane manifests as soon as practicable. For the moment, however, they continued to build public interest in the June 7, 1926, inauguration of scheduled airmail flights between Chicago and Minneapolis and St. Paul.

But a predictable sub-plot to this new airmail delivery program brewed as the unfailingly competitive leadership in

Montgomery Ward & Co's Retail Store

At 1400 University Avenue—Away From the Downtown Traffic Jam.

Our Whole Hearted Congratulations To Those Whose Vision, Persistence and Faith in Air Mail Made Possible This New Epoch and Boon to Saint Paul And the Northwest Empire : : : : :

Facts About Saint Paul Air Mail Service Starting Today

Montgomery Ward cheered the beginning of air mail service with this June 7, 1926, St. Paul *Pioneer Press* advertisement.

Minnesota's twin towns found something new to fight about. Minneapolis business interests expected that their Wold-Chamberlain Field, originally established in 1919 as Speedway Field in south Richfield, would continue to serve as the Twin Cities most important air link to the nation. St. Paul leaders believed their newly opened airfield, across the Mississippi from downtown, should become the major regional air base.[1]

Airmail operators made certain that the airports of both communities would see flights on the first day of service. The Minneapolis *Journal* explained the airmail route would link "…Minneapolis to the nation [and] this city will become in actuality the 'Port of the Northwest.'"

The St. Paul *Pioneer Press* drummed up excitement by backing a one-hour June 7 parade scheduled to weave through the heart of downtown and cross the river to the new St. Paul Airport. City leaders filmed and distributed a "picturization" of their community, showing it at the heart of America's air system, and sent locally made candies to important public figures.[2]

Dangerous Weather

The Minneapolis Civic and Commerce Association invited business leaders and the public to the June 7 airmail kickoff ceremonies at Wold-Chamberlain. But gusty winds and dust scoured the field and forced guest speakers to forego their oratory. The dignitaries simply shook hands with pilots as mail pouches were loaded into the planes. In St. Paul, two bands and military units led a crowd of 20,000 (by newspaper estimate) that braved winds, dust and debris during their hour-long parade to the airport.

Air mail pilot Elmer Partridge (inset) prepares to take off from windy Wold-Chamberlain Field on Monday June 7, 1926. His plane had been forced down earlier in the day, damaging the right wheel on its landing gear.

Arriving at 1:30, they awaited the mail planes.[3]

Miserable flying weather confronted the pilots. A large, low-pressure cell covered the Upper Midwest and produced northwest winds that the National Weather Service clocked at 35–38 miles per hour. Dust clouds obscured the sun while pilots already in the air encountered snow, sleet and hail. Errol Stiff, at the

St. Paul Airport, remembered the day as "just like a storm without the thunder and lightning."[4]

Expected heavy loads of mail forced route operator Charles Dickinson to schedule four planes to travel each way on the Chicago-Twin Cities CAM

(Contract Air Mail) Route 9. The colorful 68-year-old "Pop" Dickinson, son of a wealthy Chicago merchant, had gathered aircraft and pilots after securing the airmail contract. Wealthier investors managed to snatch the most lucrative airmail contracts, while small operators like Dickinson got CAMs for the "more dangerous, less lucrative routes." CAM 9 would soon prove to be treacherous.[5]

Dickinson's lead pilot, Billy Brock, left Chicago in a new Laird Swallow biplane and met headwinds that, at times, slowed his progress to 35 miles per hour. He took off on Saturday, June 5, and hoped to make Minneapolis the next day. Pilot Merrill K. Riddick left Chicago before Brock and struggled mightily with the conditions before becoming so airsick he could not continue. He landed at Watertown in southeast Wisconsin and wired Chicago for help.[6]

Riddick flew a rebuilt, closed-cabin monoplane designed by 38-year old Elmer Lee Partridge, a Dickinson substitute pilot. Their boss sent the relief pilot to take over for the ailing Riddick. Partridge had been a flyer since 1913. The experienced airman literally knew this plane inside and out, having built it.

A fatigued Elmer Partridge is shown just before takeoff. His trousers had been torn following a forced landing earlier in the day. Despite dangerous flying conditions, he was about to fly to Chicago.

Wold-Chamberlain field in August 1927 as crowds awaited the arrival of famed pilot Charles A. Lindbergh and his airplane, *Spirit of St. Louis*

He had also worked as a civilian flight instructor for the U.S. Army Air Service during World War I.[7]

Partridge flew to La Crosse, Wisconsin, on Sunday. He took off on Monday morning, with Riddick as a passenger, and quickly confronted a dangerous dust storm with heavy winds. Trying to recline in the back, Riddick soon found himself flying around *inside* the aircraft. The plane ran low on gas near Hastings, Minnesota, forcing Partridge to land and refuel. A shaken Riddick had had enough. Calling the flight "the worst experience I have ever had," he opted to rest up before rejoining Partridge at Wold-Chamberlain.[8]

Merrill Riddick was far from being a nervous, novice pilot. He graduated with the Army Air Corps' first pilot class in 1917 and flew combat missions during World War I. He became an instructor at America's first flight school and also

toured the nation as a daredevil flying barnstormer. If a veteran like Riddick couldn't stomach the flight, the flying conditions must have been appalling.[9]

The route from Hastings to Wold-Chamberlain Field, some 15 air miles away, couldn't have been easier. All Partridge had to do was follow the Mississippi River. But swirling dust clouds obscured the river route, and the confused flyer continued past the airfield and on to Elk River before realizing his mistake. Upon his return around noon, Partridge flew over Wold-Chamberlain and spotted the old concrete Twin Cities Speedway track that still encircled the field. Partridge believed he was over a lake and kept flying until he ran low on fuel and had to make a forced landing in a cornfield near Robbinsdale. He damaged the plane's right wheel on his landing gear and tore his pants on barbed wire.[10]

Tired and frustrated, Partridge gassed up his airplane and made his way back to Wold-Chamberlain where he landed just before one p.m. He met Billy Brock and told his colleague the flight was the bumpiest he had ever experienced. Partridge also admitted to being "just about all in." He would have about 90 minutes to rest before embarking upon the return trip to Chicago.

A Minneapolis *Journal* photograph of Partridge taken at this time shows him in torn trousers standing next to his aircraft. He did not look the part of a dashing, resolute pilot. Partridge appears tired, perhaps pensive. He then climbed back into his airplane that carried the words "U.S. Airmail, Partridge, Cabin 3, Partridge Inc. Chicago, Ill." painted near the cabin. At approximately three p.m., he took off for a short hop to St. Paul Airport.[11]

The Crash

Strong winds still whistled across Wold-Chamberlain from the northwest, and Partridge headed directly into them. The plane almost jumped into the air, assisted by a set of lower wings added for extra lift. He headed west where dust clouds hid him from view. The plane circled before the pilot took it south and into more dust. A farmer south of the Minnesota River spotted Partridge overhead, flying to the northeast toward St. Paul.[12]

Louis DesLauriers saw the plane from his viewpoint in a field near Minnesota Highway 13. At first Partridge seemed to be having no difficulty, but then the eyewitness saw the plane "quiver" and start to "plunge from side to side." Everest A. Tousignant, another witness, believed the plane to be about 1,000 feet high, and yet another, S.J. Letendre, said

Witnesses saw Partridge struggling to keep his plane aloft in heavy winds before it crashed in Mendota. The pilot died in the accident.

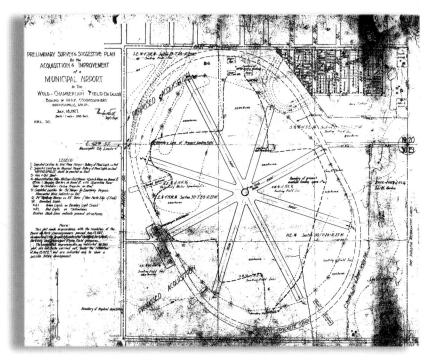

The Twin City Motor Speedway track still encircled Wold-Chamberlain Field in this 1927 "Preliminary Survey & Suggestive Plan" for airport development.

This formal 1929 plan for airport improvement shows Wold-Chamberlain Field between 60th and 66th streets and 34th Avenue on its western border. What remained of the old race track was scheduled for removal.

far from the crash scene and discovered later.[14]

Stevens could see Partridge in the cockpit struggling with the controls and "working frantically with the levers." The plane then seemed to shoot upward for a few minutes before beginning a downward plunge. Witnesses Stevens and DesLauriers believed the pilot was accelerating as it continued to dive. "I could hear the motor roaring and in an instant he had plunged into the sidebank near the roadway." The flight from Wold-Chamberlain had lasted just 15 minutes.[15]

After the crash both Letendre and Stevens ran to their nearby homes, jumped into their autos and raced to the accident scene. Partridge could not immediately be seen, so Stevens and Letendre lifted the wing that covered the cabin area. They saw Partridge's head on his knees with his legs bent under his body. Letendre cut the pilot's safety belt free and leaned toward Partridge's

the winds appeared to make the aircraft stand still.[13]

Martin J. Stevens, who lived south of the Minnesota River, had been looking for the airmail plane when he spotted Partridge's craft approach. "It was so dusty and the wind was blowing with such force that it was difficult to see," Stevens reported. He believed the plane to be flying at about 1,000 feet, but the wind was forcing changes in elevation. He and other witnesses said they saw a white, square object fall from the plane just as it began to wobble from side to side. The object proved to be a piece of wing fabric blown

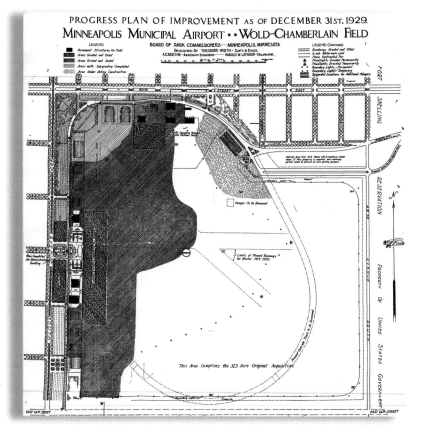

chest. He detected a faint heartbeat even though he could now see the flyer's skull had been partially crushed and his face lacerated. They summoned an ambulance from St. Paul, but the gravely injured pilot died before medical help could arrive.[16]

William A. Kidder, in charge of Dickinson's airmail operations at Wold-Chamberlain, arrived on the scene and surveyed the wreckage. He theorized the accident might have been caused by pilot airsickness or the challenging weather conditions. Kidder said Partridge was tired from his difficult morning trip, but he had time to eat before his next flight. Kidder ordered the plane's motor removed for shipment to Chicago and then ordered the wreck, which had been leaking fuel, burned.[17]

In all, weather forced down five airplanes in the area that day, but Elmer Partridge's was the only one to be lost. Pop Dickinson ordered CAM 9 operations to continue as soon as flying conditions improved. In the weeks that followed, Dickinson's bad luck with the air route continued as more accidents cut into the profitability of his operation. He held on until October 1 when he ceased operations.[18]

The new firm taking over CAM 9 service appeared even weaker than Dickinson's outfit. Its owners, a group of Detroit and St. Paul business people, including Col. Lewis H. Britten, managed to rent just two open cockpit biplanes, a Thomas Morse Scout and a Curtiss Oriole, to get started. But under the command of Britten, this new flying service, called Northwest Airways, gathered strength. The Minnesota firm grew into a leading international carrier as Northwest Airlines before its 2009 purchase by Delta Air Lines.[19]

There is a fitting postscript to this account. A Chicago resident owns a letter postmarked "Minneapolis, MN, 1:00 PM, June 7, 1926." It carries an imprint that reads "First Flight Inauguration, Contract Air Mail, Chicago-Twin Cities. Minneapolis, Minn., 2:10 PM, June 7, 1926." More significant is the information stamped on back:

A Northwest Airways Ford Tri-Motor, with the words "U.S. Mail" painted on its wing, flies CAM 9 (Contract Air Mail route 9) between Minneapolis-St. Paul and Chicago.

"Chicago, IL, June 8, - 8:30 AM, 1926" and "June 8, 10:30 AM, Logan Square Station."[20]

The letter came from the airmail bags carried by Elmer Partridge on the day his plane crashed. It, along with the other mail, was taken from the wreckage of Partridge's aircraft, re-stamped by postal officials and forwarded to Chicago by train.

FLY NORTHWEST AIRLINES, CIRCA 1932

Comparing air travel in 1932 to present-day flying is akin to relating a jaunt by Model T Ford to a high-speed journey in a modern luxury vehicle. In both cases, the difference is in the comfort, convenience and speed. The following account relates what a passenger could experience during a 1932 trip on Northwest Airlines from Wold-Chamberlain Field in south Richfield to Chicago. The aircraft would be a different Ford, not a Model T, but a Tri-Motor.

The Minneapolis Terminal of Northwest Airways, predecessor of Northwest Airlines, with a Ford Tri-Motor receiving a pre-flight check

Passengers looking to fortify themselves for the nearly four-hour flight to Chicago found Jack Hohag's Air-O-Inn at 34th Avenue and 66th Street quite handy. You could see Wold-Chamberlain Field's small passenger terminal from Hohag's place, where you could get lunch or dinner and hot and cold beverages before takeoff. But veteran flyers knew to eat lightly. Air trips to Chicago were notoriously rough, and keeping a heavy meal down could be difficult.[1]

By 1932, more Minnesotans proved willing to try air travel. Northwest Airways started as an airmail service in 1926, but the company planned to begin carrying paying passengers as soon as possible. Thus, few were surprised when Northwest purchased four Stinson Detroiters in 1927 and began flying people as well as mail. A single-engine Stinson SB-1 that could carry three passengers flew the Minneapolis to Chicago route, making Wisconsin stops at La Crosse, Madison and Milwaukee before reaching its destination. The one-way fare was $40. The airline added service to Canada, Illinois, South Dakota and Nebraska by 1930.[2]

Most passengers booked their Northwest flights early, but it was possible to get tickets at the airport from the company's flight stewards. These busy young men dealt with a number of pre-flight issues. Along with last minute ticket sales, they signed for registered mail and loaded it into the plane, then gathered passenger luggage, hauled it through the door and up the cabin aisle to stow it in back of the cabin and in overhead bins located in the wing sections. They sometimes assisted in fueling the aircraft.[3]

Bobby Johnston, Joe Kimm, Bobby Hohag and Bert Richie became Northwest's first stewards and worked the Chicago run. Kimm got his start at age 17 as a replacement for Johnston, injured in June 1929 when a Northwest Ford Tri-Motor crashed in St. Paul. Johnston's misfortune opened the door to flying for Kimm. The eager teenager had been pestering a Northwest pilot he knew for a chance to fly, and now received an invitation to become a substitute steward. He recalled, "I went home and said, 'Mom, can I fly to Chicago tomorrow with Walter Bullock?' She said 'ask your Father.' So I went to dad.

Dad said to go ask your ma. So I knew I had them." He went to the hospital, got Johnston's uniform, cleaned it up and made the flight.[4]

St. Paul newspapers had praised the 18-year-old Johnston as a hero during the terrifying 1929 Tri-Motor crash in St. Paul's Mounds Park neighborhood. Pilot Eddie Middagh steered the plane off the St. Paul Airport runway, but a loss of power quickly forced a desperate attempt to clear a row of river bluff houses. The three-engine airliner grazed the roof of 52 Mounds Boulevard, struck a tree, fell to earth and burst into flames. Middagh died in the wreck, but 13 others on the plane survived. Johnston ran back into the burning cabin to help passengers and the pilot. The young steward suffered burns in the process.[5]

Steward Bobby Hohag came from a well-known Richfield family whose descendants, Arthur, Fred, Gus and Jack

Ford Tri-Motors were a mainstay of Northwest Airways in the late 1920s. This plane is being fueled. Its duralumin "skin" gave the aircraft the nickname "Tin Goose."

Hohag, happened to own some of the land Wold-Chamberlain Airport would later occupy. In fact, Bobby's Uncle Gus purchased the entire acreage of the future airfield during a 1917 sheriff's sale and sold it to the Speedway Airfield developers a year later. Bobby lived next door to the airport, a plus in his effort to become a steward. His father Jack's ownership of the Air-O-Inn didn't hurt Bobby's chances either.[6]

Clearly, the training regimen for the first Northwest stewards was less than rigorous, so the young men learned on the job. They had to be able to think on their feet and become calming influences during minor or major emergencies.

The airplane's corrugated "skin" often captured a first-time viewer's eye. It was made of duralumin that gave all Tri-Motors the nickname "Tin Goose."[7]

Passengers entered the aircraft through a cabin door at the rear of the fuselage. They walked up the narrow inclined aisle—the airplane's two-wheel landing gear produced this slant—and to their seats. Lightweight cane-backed chairs featuring adjustable positioning lined the aisle, six to each side, front to back. Seat belts attached to each chair were used during takeoff, landing and in heavy weather.

Each seat had its own rectangular draped window, a reading lamp and an electric cigar lighter with ashtray. Passengers were able to watch the pilot and copilot at the controls through a half-partition door. Windows could be slid open to provide fresh air but were kept closed during takeoff, mainly to keep out mud and water. At higher altitudes heaters in the floor provided warmth. A toilet was a convenient feature.

Northwest's Stinson Detroiters could carry three passengers.

Both Kimm and Bobby Hohag harbored ambitions to become pilots, and within a few years found themselves flying for the airline.

After checking in with the stewards, passengers walked to the plane, getting a close-up view of the Ford Tri-Motor. It spanned 74 feet, wing tip to wing tip, was 50 feet long and stood nearly 13 feet high; its three 450-horsepower Pratt and Whitney engines, one on the nose and one under each wing, comforted those nervous about engine failure.

Experienced passengers understood that forced landings were not that unusual and not necessarily a dangerous event. When the pilot or copilot briefed passengers about the flight, mention typically was made of the Tri-Motor's safety. It could fly on two engines and, if only one functioned, the pilot would begin a slow gliding descent and look for any suitable landing spot. Unpredictable weather plagued the Minneapolis to

Jack Hohag's Air-O-Inn was adjacent to Wold-Chamberlain field, across 34th Avenue South at 66th. The Hohag family was prominent in Richfield history, producing civic leaders and farmers.

Chicago route. If wind, snow, rain, lack of visibility or other issues made continuing the flight hazardous, the pilot would merely land the sturdy Tri-Motor.[8]

Joe Kimm, who piloted Ford Tri-Motors for Northwest after leaving his steward's post, made a forced landing sound routine. "We'd pick out a good pasture or hayfield and we would land. The first thing we would do is shut the aircraft down and get it tied down. The farmers would all come gathering around the aircraft, naturally, so we would get some of them to bring their cars over. The passengers, we'd take them to town and put them on a train…." Radios became commonplace on Northwest in 1931, greatly improving communication with company headquarters. Until that time, pilots found a railroad station, wired their location, and then went looking for a hotel.[9]

Passengers, first time flyers in particular, found takeoff to be both frightening and exhilarating. As mechanics hand-cranked them, the engines coughed, clanked and then sputtered to life with a rumble that gradually increased to a full-throated roar. Just a thin sheet of aluminum and a light sidewall stood between the air traveler

Bobby Hohag, right, started with Northwest as one of the airline's three stewards. Shown here in October, 1929, Hohag soon learned to fly and became NWA's youngest pilot.

Ken Hohag collection

and the loud throbbing of the three powerful Pratt & Whitneys as each motor was tested at high power. After being cleared to depart, the pilot steered the Tri-Motor into position and commenced takeoff, bumping across the field and into the air. The engines continued to run at full power until the plane leveled off at about 2,500 feet. The pilot then eased the throttle back, reducing noise in the cabin somewhat, and cruised on at about 100 miles per hour.[10]

Pilots liked the ease with which a Ford Tri-Motor lifted off the ground. Leon (Deke) Delong flew for Northwest in the 1930s and was one of the airline's first pilots. Delong flew many different aircraft, but the Ford was his favorite. "It could go up like an elevator," he remembered. "It was safe, maneuverable and fun to fly." Charles (Speed) Holman was believed to be the first to fly a Tri-Motor through an inside loop (on its back).[11]

Pilots navigated using visual flight rules (VFR), which meant the crew used ground references below and in front of them during their flight. Clear views could be a problem on the Minneapolis-Chicago run. Joe Kimm noted that a

Tri-Motors could be configured to carry 12 passengers. Seats had windows that could be slid open and had overhead reading lights.

low ceiling didn't bother flyers until they were down to about 200 feet with a quarter-mile window ahead. Said Kimm, "If you can imagine flying from Minneapolis to Chicago, for almost four hours and at 200 feet, having to know where the high-tension wires were so we could get up and over them, and [without] knowing enough about your ground points…this gives you a pretty good idea of how strenuous these flights could be." It was no picnic for passengers either.[12]

During Kimm's years flying Tri-Motors, weather conditions kept the ceiling for an average Chicago trip at about 500 feet. Pilots flew low because of wind conditions and VFR requirements. Low and slow meant bumpy flights and uncomfortable passengers who often became airsick. The result was a mess on the plane's sidewall, floor and on the air travelers. Northwest stewards Johnston, Hohag and Kimm came up with a partial solution—brown bags they bought at grocery stores.

Working the paper bag patrol was unpopular duty. First, the brown bags "were only efficient for a very few seconds," meaning leakage could be a major issue. In rough weather the steward stood ready, brown bags in hand, studying with a practiced eye the faces of his passengers. He was a teenaged apparition that no doubt provided scant comfort to the uncomfortable. Said Joe Kimm, "…if we saw someone in trouble, we'd whip one out, you know, like they used to do in grocery stores, snap it open and put it in the passenger's face."

The steward now contended with a new problem—removal of the bag and its offensive contents in the only way possible. "As soon as they used it we'd whip another one out [for the passenger] and madly run with the first one to the back door, and we'd kick it open and throw the bag out. If we were fast enough the bottom wouldn't come open before we got there. This sounds like a bunch of malarkey but it's true."

Eventually the creative stewards convinced Northwest to install linoleum on the sidewalls and floor. The stewards obtained "little rubber squeegees" about a half-foot long. Kimm asserted, "We got so we could squeegee everything down off the walls onto the floor and into the dustpan…. There was no such thing as a waterproof burp bag as they have today." Clearly, present-day air travelers owe a debt of gratitude to those first Tri-Motor stewards.

But what about paper bags and other objects heaved out of the aircraft's door? Kimm answered, "Anything we didn't [want] on that airplane—we threw it out…I think this is rather interesting because we gave the passengers Cokes to drink and when the bottles were empty we opened the door and threw them out. Everybody had the idea that traveling at these tremendous speeds everything was blown to bits long before it got to earth. This was a misconception of that day. I like to think we never beanballed anybody, but I really don't know."

INDESTRUCTIBLE MAL FREEBURG

The legacy of Northwest Airlines pilot Mal Freeburg languishes in the shadows of "Speed" Holman, a more famous Minnesota and Northwest flyer. But Freeburg, who later became mayor of Richfield and a Bloomington resident, regularly proved his bravery and skill while flying for the airline. President Franklin D. Roosevelt personally decorated this outstanding pilot for heroism.

Northwest Airways needed pilots in the late 1920s as the slowly developing company hustled to expand its passenger service. The airline opened operations in October 1926 as a contract airmail delivery line but nourished hopes of adding passengers to its flights.

Northwest first flew passengers in 1927 when it occasionally managed to cram a few, along with the mail, into its Stinson SB-1 single-engine biplanes. The Stinson could hold up to three passengers looking for a ride to Chicago. By 1929, Northwest was buying 12-passenger Ford Tri-Motors for its air fleet and adding pilots as well.[1]

Northwest hired the dashing and dauntless Charles "Speed" Holman as its chief pilot even though the new air boss was still determined to build on his national reputation as a crack stunt pilot and air racer. Born on the Richfield-Minneapolis border in 1898 and raised in Bloomington, Holman owned a

Mal Freeburg , early in his career with Northwest Airlines

reputation as a top American flying ace. On December 5, 1928, Mal Bryan Freeburg became one of the first flyers to join Holman at Northwest.[2]

During the mid-1920s Freeburg piled up hours in his own aircraft, barnstorming throughout the summer and fall and then repairing his plane in the winter. His wife, Ruth, told her children that she and Mal flew across the country with their suitcases lashed to the wings, a story later confirmed by family photos. When Freeburg heard Northwest was hiring, he signed up and was quickly hired.[3]

In May 1931, Holman entertained spectators at the Omaha Air Races with some daring stunt flying but was killed in the horrific crash of his Laird biplane. Freeburg, after building an impressive resumé as a pilot, became Northwest's chief pilot two years later.[4]

Before joining Northwest, Freeburg used his own airplane to "barnstorm." His wife, Ruth, flew with him during his travels in the mid-1920s, their suitcases lashed to the wings.

Freeburg's first brush with fame occurred in summer 1930 while the 24-year-old flew his WACO biplane along the Minneapolis-Chicago night airmail route. As the pilot traced the tracks of the Burlington & Quincy Railroad, he observed a rail trestle on fire. The Northwest pilot, knowing a speedy Burlington Blackhawk express passenger train would soon reach the burning bridge, flew watchfully along the rail route. Upon meeting the onrushing train, Freeburg dove repeatedly at the locomotive while blinking his plane's landing lights. The engineer saw the aircraft hurtling down at him, but figured the pilot was hot-dogging. Freeburg went into another dive and dropped his landing flares on the Blackhawk. The train stopped, and a possible disaster was avoided.

Prominent among those saved by Freeburg was Bobby Jones, already a legend in the golfing world of the day. He was en route to Edina's Interlachen Golf Course and a victory in 1930 U.S. Open. The Burlington & Quincy Railroad presented the Minnesota pilot with a gold watch, and the Chicago *Tribune* kicked in a $100 reward for his actions.[5]

Amelia Earhart gained international fame as a pioneering woman pilot. In January 1933 she joined Freeburg and other Northwest personnel in the first passenger aircraft to cross the Rocky Mountains in winter.

An accident on April 12, 1932, threatened the lives of Freeburg, copilot Joe Kimm and six passengers. All aboard were enjoying a beautiful springtime flight until a loud thump reverberated through the cabin, jolting everyone. Freeburg dipped his wings, looked out the window and immediately spotted the problem; his number one engine had broken free of the port wing and was wedged in the landing gear struts. As the Ford Tri-Motor passed over Wabasha, Minnesota, the captain and copilot discussed their options. Neither could be sure what would happen if the wayward motor fell from the Tri-Motor, but they certainly would be unable to land with it fouling the landing gear.[6]

Freeburg decided to shake the 500-pound engine from his plane. He guided the aircraft over the Mississippi River as Kimm reassured passengers. Once there, he banked left and then whipped the controls right. The pilot repeated the violent maneuver as frightened air travelers held on. "I flew around for eight minutes until I shook the motor loose," Freeburg later told a newspaper reporter. The engine fell to earth about 200 feet from a Wabasha farmer busy building a chicken coop.[7]

The falling engine damaged the landing gear and jammed a tire. Now Freeburg and his passengers faced a one-wheel landing. The pilot eased the Tri-Motor toward the ground, gingerly touching down first on the undamaged wheel, then on what remained of the undercarriage, and brought the plane to a halt. "Just one of those things that happen in ten million miles of flying…half the propeller snapped and flew away," an action that tore the motor from its mooring, Freeburg later explained.

Back in St. Paul, Northwest officials and Freeburg's wife listened to radio reports from the Tri-Motor. He assured those on the ground that everything would be all right. After the landing, the pilot and most of his passengers boarded a back-up aircraft flown in from the Twin Cities. They continued to Chicago.[8]

In 1932, an engine from a Tri-Motor such as this broke free of its mounting and fouled the plane's landing gear. Heroic efforts by pilot Mal Freeburg saved the plane and the passengers it carried.

Freeburg's report of the entire incident was as brief as it was modest. "Delayed on account of motor trouble. Changed ships at Wabasha." The pilot seemed about the only person unimpressed with his performance. President Franklin D. Roosevelt called Freeburg to Washington, D.C., and personally awarded him the Air Mail Flyers Medal of Honor. *Colliers* Magazine published an article about the feat.[9]

President Franklin D. Roosevelt personally presented Freeburg with this Air Mail Flyers Medal of Honor. The award is in the possession of his son James.
Courtesy of James Freeburg

Mal Freeburg with his son James

Ace of the Base

By 1933, Mal Freeburg ranked as Northwest's chief pilot. In that role, he and two of his pilots set about proving wrong those in the American aviation community who said the airline could not maintain an all-season northern transcontinental air route from the Twin Cities to Seattle. The Northwest group would have to fly over the formidable Rocky Mountains and the majestic Cascades to prove their point. Croil Hunter, an Ivy Leaguer and future Northwest president hired by the airline to publicize the event, decided to fly along. He also invited his friend Amelia Earhart, the world-famous American aviatrix and idol who just seven months earlier had become the first woman to fly solo across the Atlantic Ocean.[10]

On January 28, 1933, in the face of a swirling snowfall, pilot Hugh Rueschenberg guided a Northwest Ford Tri-Motor into the air for the first leg of the journey. Joe Kimm sat in the copilot's seat, with chief pilot Freeburg riding in reserve, along with Earhart, Croil and four others. The aircraft reached Helena, Montana, in three days but faced a treacherous final leg to Spokane. After a terrifying trip through blinding mountain snow squalls and escaping mistaken trips into two box canyons, the pilots found a route into Spokane. There, they landed in yet another snowstorm. The trip, lengthened by weather delays, took six days.[11]

Freeburg literally took a back seat to Rueschenberg and Kimm on this heralded trip, but the flight proved the ability and courage of the three pilots in making this dangerous, path-finding journey. Before the exploration team left Seattle to fly back to St. Paul, a representative of United Airlines warned Northwest chief Col. Lewis H. Britten, "If you Swedes from Minnesota don't keep out of these

Northwest Airways became Northwest Airlines in 1934. This mid-30s ad shows its service system and depicts two Lockheed Electras, the airplane that carried most of its passengers.

gave Woodhead the controls and went to remove seats immediately behind the cockpit. The pilot told passenger Celia Hanzlick, "Guess we'll have to make it without the wheels."[14]

Finally, Freeburg dumped some of his remaining fuel and began the landing. As the drama unfolded, a crowd gathered and looked on while fire and police units stood by. Spotlights picked up the aircraft as it neared the ground. Sensing his approach speed was too fast, Freeburg executed a quick climb and came around for another try. He kept the plane level as it scraped the ground and began a 700-foot slide, spewing sparks and debris. It was a perfect landing. Passengers cheered Freeburg and his faultless touchdown.

mountains, you're gonna break your goddam necks!"[12]

Mal Freeburg was back in the "hero" business the following year. The 28-year-old flying veteran took off from St. Paul heading to Minneapolis on the last leg of a night flight from Chicago when a control panel light began flashing. The plane's retractable landing gear had jammed. He flew back toward St. Paul and then circled for 90 minutes trying to shake the recalcitrant wheels down.[13]

Copilot John Woodhead told tales of Freeburg's previous exploits to calm the five worried passengers. He also moved them to the rear. Then Freeburg

TIME magazine lauded the skill displayed by "hero Freeburg" during the belly landing in St. Paul and reminded readers of his past heroics as a pilot.[15]

In 1938 Freeburg helped find a solution for pilot drowsiness while flying the mountain routes near Seattle. Dr. Charles Mayo, a co-founder of the famed Rochester, Minnesota, clinic that carried his name, diagnosed the problem as high altitude oxygen deficiency and assigned a team of his doctors to work on it. They perfected a lightweight mask through which pure oxygen and surrounding air, properly mixed inside a small rubber "lung," could be sent to pilots. A meter and valve controlled oxygen flow. The mask fit over the nose while leaving the mouth uncovered. This system, tested in Mayo Clinic pressure chambers, worked well up to 40,000 feet.[16]

Mal Freeburg joined in the July 17, 1938, experiment by Northwest that tested an oxygen-equipped aircraft. With Freeburg at the controls, the system worked perfectly at 20,000 feet. This advance meant pilots could fly at high altitudes with no loss of function. Combat aircraft were fitted with similar systems during World War II. Eventually airlines flew passengers several miles above the earth using pressurized cabins.

Freeburg continued to fly for Northwest but showed an interest in the politics of Richfield, where he was elected mayor in January 1942. Joking about his victory, Freeburg said, "I stand for bold, honest and progressive government by the people, for the people, etc. etc. etc." In December of that year Freeburg loaded 21 friends onto a plane and flew them over the Twin Cities during a Civil Defense blackout. He circled until the lights came back on. He resigned as mayor in July 1943 after buying a home in Bloomington.[17]

Mal Freeburg's career with Northwest ended in frustration. He took an airline office job with a promise of running it as he saw fit. When he found he did not have the autonomy he expected, the forthright Freeburg told airline executives he was through. "My father was an honest, outspoken man," recalled his son Jim, "and wouldn't compromise on the issue."[18]

Freeburg accepted a job with Transocean Air Lines and became

director of operations in Guam. Starting in 1946, TAL flew all over the world, and Guam was an important stop between the United States and Asia. The Minnesota pilot qualified to fly seaplanes but spent most of his time on the ground. Japan Airlines hired Freeburg as a consultant when they started operations in 1953. He lived in Tokyo for the next two years before returning to America, first moving to Hawaii and then California.[19]

At the outset of his own career as a Northwest pilot, Jim Freeburg got the chance to fly with his famous father. The younger Freeburg soon learned much more about his legendary parent from the countless stories related to him by other NWA flyers and crew. During his California years, illness, later diagnosed as multiple sclerosis, slowed the veteran pilot. He died in 1963.

Freeburg and young son James pose at Wold-Chamberlain airport. James would follow his father into the employ of Northwest as a pilot. The inset shows father and son teamed as pilot and copilot.

To the American flying community, Mal Freeburg was an outstanding pilot who, in an emergency, always seemed to know what to do. He was inducted into the Minnesota Aviation Hall of Fame in 1990.[20]

LOUISE WHITBECK FRASER STARTS OVER

"…survived by his widow and three small children."[1]
    Strikingly sad notes often close newspaper accounts of law officers killed in the line of duty. The quote above was printed following the 1928 Minnesota murder of a federal prohibition agent. Louise Fraser, the widow in the story, was a woman already tested and tempered by tragedy, and she still faced a painful challenge—finding help for a physically disabled daughter. In doing so, Fraser laid the foundation for future programs that created better lives for thousands.

Wesley Fraser's murder in January 1928 left his widow, Louise, with three children to care for, including eight-year-old daughter, Jean, severely disabled by a bout with spinal meningitis.

Wes Fraser looked forward to completing his final assignment as a Twin Cities-based federal agent fighting America's war against the manufacture or sale of alcoholic beverages. The 34-year-old family man and World War I veteran, about to be promoted to a new position, was riding along with two workmen assigned to remove bootlegging materials from a South St. Paul house. Fraser knew the building; he had led a recent raid on the premises. Now, on January 2, 1928, he was performing a routine follow-up. Fraser, who disliked carrying a pistol, was unarmed.[2]

The federal agent and the workers found no one home at the 5th and Poplar address. Fraser entered the house. Suddenly, three men drove up to the home. One, carrying a pistol, jumped from the car and ran toward the house yelling, "I told you to keep out of here!" He fired two shots through the window, hitting and mortally wounding Fraser. His enraged attacker, who owned the house and had rented it to the bootleggers, was still furious about the agent's earlier raid on his property.[3]

A newspaper account of the tragic incident named Wesley A. Fraser's three children—Mary Lou, nine; Jean, seven

PRICE THREE CENTS IN ST. PAUL.

DRY AGENT SHOT DEAD ON SOUTH ST. PAUL JOB; SLAYER GIVES SELF UP

"Mad at Prohibition Men," Says Gun Wielder, Owner of House Victim Raided Recently and Where He Was on Duty When Killed.

TWO WITNESSES OF MURDER ARE HELD

Wesley A. Fraser, 2116 Berkeley avenue, a Federal prohibition agent, was shot to death in South St. Paul Monday noon while removing confiscated coal from a house that he had raided for a moonshine distillery two weeks ago. He was unarmed.

Fraser was the first St. Paul Federal agent to be slain in line of duty.

One hour after the shooting at Fifth avenue south and Poplar street, Gulob Nickolich, 46 years old, 500 Fifth avenue south, South St. Paul, a butcher, surrendered to police and admitted having killed Fraser.

Nickolich gave no reason for the murder except that he was "mad at the Federal prohibition agents." He owns the house where the shooting occurred, but does not live there.

and Wesley, Jr., two—but did not mention his widow by name. Louise Whitbeck, who married Fraser in June 1917, had already experienced far more than her share of tragedy. Both of her parents had died from illness by the time she was three. Her first son, Bobby, fell out of the family car when he was three and was killed.[4] In 1920, her infant daughter, Jean, contracted spinal meningitis, with accompanying fevers of 106–107 degrees for 23 days. The little girl was later erroneously diagnosed as suffering from "mental retardation."[5]

Life's cruel lessons had steeled rather than shattered Louise Fraser. After her parents' deaths, she lived with an austere aunt who held the girl to very strict Victorian social standards. Once, while her aunt was away, Louise stormed up to the attic and yelled in frustration over her situation, "Damn, Damn, Damn!" Although the brief explosion of temper proved cathartic, from that time onward, she carefully maintained her self-control.[6]

After completing high school, Louise Whitbeck earned a normal school instructional certificate and became a classroom teacher. Young Miss Whitbeck displayed a knack for developing good relationships with difficult students, a talent that resulted in having more troubled pupils sent her way. She later recalled, "If there was a problem child, they always said, 'Give 'em to Whitbeck.'" Upon the arrival of one new student, her principal advised, "Give him a good spanking" to make him behave. "I thought it was terrible," Whitbeck said, "You just have to give them a little love."[7]

Four years after her husband's death, Louise moved the family to Minneapolis and into a house on 38th Avenue South. Daughter Jean, now 11, demonstrated wild behavior swings that prompted her mother to have the child tested at the University of Minnesota. There, Jean was found to have a profound hearing impairment—an explanation for her challenging conduct. While Jean awaited an opening in a program for hearing-impaired children, her mother began working with her, using music as an educational tool. Jean's positive response—she was able to hear high and low tones—was encouraging, and news of Fraser's innovative techniques spread. Parents with special needs children at home appealed for Louise's help in educating them. She agreed.[8]

Louise Fraser had looked for educational programs that might

Louise Fraser used music as an educational tool to help her hearing disabled child. Music education became an important part of her Home Study School, opened in 1935 to serve children with serious learning challenges.

help Jean and other children whose needs were not being addressed. She found none. Wesley, Jr., recalled his mother's frustration when she contacted government agencies that offered no help and no hope. "She was told by one woman, what she was doing was no better than teaching tricks to animals."[9]

In 1935, Fraser formally opened Home Study School, designed for children with major learning disabilities. The all-day school, in the family's new house at 5019 38th Avenue South, cost four dollars a week. University of Minnesota experts did not believe in Fraser's methods, and some even called her a fraud. But Fraser's music-therapy-based teaching style reached students, enabling them to improve their attention span, physical coordination and verbalization.[10]

An America struggling through the Great Depression in the mid-1930s faced a host of challenges. Educating children with learning disabilities did not rate among the major issues of the day. But specialized programs, although uncommon, did exist. In 1935, teenager Jean Fraser entered Agassiz School for the Deaf located in Minneapolis's former East Side High School. For four years, Jean worked with Roman Catholic nuns at Agassiz as she learned to lip-read and speak.

Jean mastered the streetcar transfer process, using three different cars to get to school. When her older sister, Mary Lou, began attending the University of Minnesota law school in 1939, she joined Jean on the trolley ride. Yet another

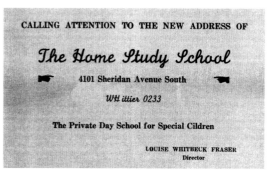

CALLING ATTENTION TO THE NEW ADDRESS OF

The Home Study School

4101 Sheridan Avenue South

WHittier 0233

The Private Day School for Special Cildren

LOUISE WHITBECK FRASER
Director

Fraser started her first school in a vacant home near 51st Street and Nicollet in south Minneapolis. She moved the program to 4101 Sheridan Avenue South in 1940–41.

tragedy struck the Fraser family when Mary Lou contracted a staph infection and died within three days. The loss of her sister staggered Jean, and she lapsed into depression. The staff at Agassiz suggested Jean, who had been helping them work with learning disabled students at the school, join her mother as an instructor at Home Study School. It was a move that worked well.

Louise Fraser's educational program continued its steady expansion through the late 1930s and 1940s, overcoming two major roadblocks—the pressing need for more space and resistance to having Home Study School in a residential neighborhood. Fraser found some storefront space in Uptown at Lake and Hennepin, and later at 43rd and Upton. By 1949 the school had 32 students enrolled, with others on a waiting list, and still more being turned away.[11]

A former Richfield machine shop at 63rd Street and Penn Avenue became the site for a new school. Parents had helped Fraser raise money for a building, yet it was ultimately the teacher who had to mortgage her house to pay for its purchase and refitting. The three-room Home Study School, complete with a modest playground, was ready for the fall 1949 term. In 1955 the school incorporated, and its directors collected money to remodel and expand the building.

The Fraser program did not seek publicity, but the school received national recognition in 1963 when Victoria, granddaughter of Senator Hubert H. Humphrey, Minnesota's most prominent politician and a future presidential candidate, was enrolled. Muriel Humphrey, the senator's wife, took an interest in her three-year-old granddaughter's new school and became an outspoken supporter.[12]

In 1965, Home Study School's board of directors renamed the structure Louise Whitbeck Fraser School. Two years later they opened a new building at 2400 West 64th Street in Richfield. The administration erected a major addition in 1971. At that point, the Fraser staff served 100 children and adults.

The Humphreys' prominence placed Fraser programs in the national spotlight, a fact that helped with fund-raising and expansion. Muriel Humphrey also brought notoriety to the school in June 1974 when she sold personal gifts from a Somali official and donated the money received to the Richfield school. Humphrey was unaware that, due to a 1966 law, such presents were to be turned over to the U.S. government. Considering Humphrey acted on behalf of Fraser programs, the minor flap quickly blew over.[13]

Louise Fraser, 1894–1976

When Louise Fraser died on January 27, 1976, the community lost an inspired educator and instructional innovator. She had created new approach to teaching children with special needs. She possessed a fundamental belief that all children deserved the opportunity to be educated.

Expanding from that modest beginning, ambitious 21st century Fraser programs reach hundreds of people each year: children with autism, Down syndrome, traumatic brain injury and emotional and behavioral disorders. Later programs included aid to families facing critical in-home care problems, mental health issues and evaluative screening for children, along with rehabilitation and education services. Fraser's innovative programs for adults with Down syndrome provide living spaces and support personnel that allow them to live more independent lives.

The exceptional Louise Whitbeck Fraser stands as a steadfast and courageous woman and that most rare of human beings: one whose vision and achievements helped thousands of lives change for the better.

Louise Whitbeck Fraser School opened in 1965 and was expanded in 1971.
It is located at 2400 W. 64th Street, Richfield

Safety in the Suburbs, Augsburg and its Move Toward Richfield

With the image of Minneapolis battered by corrupt politics at the beginning of the 20th century, leaders of the city's predominantly Norwegian-American Augsburg College contemplated the advantages of moving to the agricultural suburb of Richfield.

A portion of an 1898 Hennepin County map shows the area originally intended to become Augsburg Park in Richfield. The location is to the immediate east of Wood Lake.

Some lingering Old World problems shadowed Scandinavian immigrants newly arrived in Minnesota in the 1860s. Their long journey across the Atlantic and the eastern half of the United States gave them the feeling that they had reached a new world. But as they took a look around, they discovered former Northern European adversaries had also made the trip.

The training of students for service in American Lutheran churches provides an example of such old rivalries. Augustana Seminary in Paxton, Illinois, trained most of those young pastors by the 1860s. To Norwegian and Danish newcomers, Augustana, with its primarily Swedish orientation and cultural traditions, did not seem the place to educate their churchmen. The solution appeared obvious—divide the Scandinavian Lutherans into separate assemblies or "synods."[1]

In 1870, the Swedes created their own Augustana Synod while, at the same time, a new Norwegian-Danish Augustana Synod began operations. A splinter group of 14 pastors soon abandoned the latter group and formed the Norwegian-Danish Evangelical Lutheran Church in America. A consequence of the schism was the creation of two Minnesota private colleges: Augsburg in Minneapolis, serving the Evangelical Lutheran branch, and St. Olaf in Northfield, affiliated with the Norwegian-Danish Augustana Synod. Swedish Lutherans in Red Wing had already launched a college in 1862 that would eventually become Gustavus Adolphus in St. Peter.

For non-Lutherans, keeping track of the many denominations could be challenging. Even comparatively small Minnesota towns often held two Norwegian Lutheran churches, a Swedish Lutheran church, along with German Lutheran and, later, English Lutheran congregations. Services were conducted in the traditional language of the "Old Country." The switch to English in these churches was not easy. In 1901, when German Lutherans in Red Wing discussed using English, opponents within the church voiced strong dissent. Recalled one member, "…of course when others started talking about having English services, why man alive! God was German! He couldn't understand English! You know it was sacrilegious to them…and the Swedes and Norwegians were no different."[2]

Edward Murphy offered generous assistance to the Norwegian community in Minneapolis when, in 1872, he donated four undeveloped lots from his Murphy's Addition, not far from the west bank of the Mississippi. The campus sat on the prairie at the future intersection of 7th Street and 21st Avenue South. Of Augsburg's early years, student John H. Blegen remembered, "On the south side there was not a single house as far as the eye could see, except a decrepit uninhabited hut." Swampland along the Mississippi River and prairie further isolated the school from the center of Minneapolis, to Augsburg's west and north.[3]

Carl G.O. Hansen, in his history of Minneapolis, claimed the establishment of Augsburg Seminary in 1872 proved "a major factor in making Minneapolis a Norwegian center." During his years at the school (1889–90), Hansen reported a "vast majority of the 100 or so students were born in Norway."[4]

Shame of Minneapolis

Minneapolis, as the 20th century opened, suffered from an image problem. Investigative author Lincoln Steffens released *The Shame of the Cities*, a book about corruption in a number of America's urban centers. He devoted a long chapter to Minneapolis under the rule of its glad-handing mayor, Albert Alonzo "Doc" Ames, and his associates. Steffens described him as "the good fellow—a genial, generous reprobate." Doc Ames was the son of the highly esteemed Alfred E. Ames, the first Minneapolis physician on the west side of the Mississippi. Doc Ames had married Sarah Strout, daughter of Capt. Richard Strout, a founder of Richfield and Edina.[5]

After the 1901 election, the Ames administration ran amok. Steffens charged that Ames "laid plans to turn the city over to outlaws who were to work under police direction for the profit of the administration." Gambling parlors, houses of prostitution and illegal saloons, known as "blind pigs," thrived. The city used "liquor patrol limits"—supervised areas in which saloons were legal—to control alcohol sales. These limits ran

A. A. AMES,
SEVENTH MAYOR OF MINNEAPOLIS.

Albert Alonzo "Doc" Ames, mayor of Minneapolis in 1901, was at the center of a corruption scandal exposed by author Lincoln Steffens. Augsburg College later planned a move to suburban Richfield, in part to escape such influences upon its students.

along the riverfront and business section, reported Steffens, "with long arms reaching into the Scandinavian quarters, north and south."[6]

Fast-growing Minneapolis soon reached out to and then surrounded Augsburg campus and school, and the nearby neighborhood was no longer a Norwegian-American preserve. By 1910 the area south of the school, nearly empty 35 years earlier, flourished, and the Minneapolis city limits extended to 54th Street. Although Minneapolis reformers labored mightily to clean up the city's poor image, it was still easy to walk down Cedar Avenue and find a welcoming saloon. Augsburg student Carl Hansen reported that to those looking for a drink, the phrase "'å gå på Cedar' (go down Cedar) meant one thing: to tank up."[7]

Steffens also noted Minneapolis held a large class of wealthy and influential "Yankee" business leaders, citizens with roots in America's northeast who profited from the sweat of low-paid immigrant workers. They sent "Scandinavians to get the timber of the forests and raise the wheat" for Minneapolis mills, wrote Steffens. He wasn't alone in his criticism of Minnesota's dominant Yankee business class. Norwegian-American Thorstein Veblen, a contemporary of Steffens and a world-renowned, Minnesota-born economist and social critic, lashed out at the grasping Rice County Yankee

Knute B. Birkeland, president of Augsburg's Board of Trustees, discovered land in Richfield where he hoped to create Augsburg Park, a new site for the college. Birkeland's disappearance and the later discovery of his body created a Minneapolis scandal. This Minneapolis *Tribune* newspaper photo of Birkeland appeared at the time of his disappearance.

middlemen, storekeepers and bankers of his youth.[8]

Major changes came to Augsburg in the 1920s. After careful consideration and occasional heated debate, the school administration decided to admit females. That meant overcrowding of facilities on the small campus and a need for additional space. For those concerned about big city temptations within easy walking distance of Augsburg, it seemed time to move the school elsewhere. The board of trustees agreed to undertake a search for a suitable location.[9]

Knute B. Birkeland, president of Augsburg's board, had his eye on a building site in Richfield, a quiet agricultural community far from the enticements of Minneapolis. A former Lutheran minister turned real estate investor, Birkeland had become business manager of the Augsburg Park Association when it incorporated in 1922.[10]

The Augsburg Park group planned on creating a dual-purpose, 113-acre campus that provided ample room for the college facilities as well as lots where members of the Lutheran Free Church could build homes. The site had much going for it. The handsome tract bordered Wood Lake and stretched east to Nicollet Avenue, north to 69th Street and south to 72nd. Lyndale Highway (Avenue), the widened and paved main arterial road running south from Minneapolis, helpfully sliced through the proposed development, while trains and nearby streetcars provided access to the city when needed. The college announced the opening of Augsburg Park tracts on July 13, 1924.

Augsburg Park featured plenty of open space upon which to build. Sparsely settled and liquor-free Richfield, with its well-educated, church-going populace, completed the picture. An Augsburg church periodical reminded readers of another reason to move: "a more or less undesirable class of people of varied race and color" now populated the school's Minneapolis neighborhood.[11]

In early December 1925, shocking news swept through the Augsburg community. Knute Birkeland's body had been found in a vacant Minneapolis house. The 68-year-old Birkeland had disappeared a week before. His body was discovered fully clothed and placed in a bedroom. Officials believed the clergyman had been poisoned and were searching for a "bob-haired young woman" who rented the apartment four days prior to Birkeland's disappearance.[12]

Floyd B. Olson, Hennepin County Attorney and future Minnesota governor, told news reporters he believed Birkeland had *not* died a violent death and noted vaguely that he held evidence that "would defeat justice if made public."[13] Talk spread that the former churchman collapsed while involved in a sexual encounter. A formal inquest into the matter included three hours of closed-door testimony from an undisclosed number of unidentified women. They had secretly been taken to a jury through a back door.

Outraged members of Birkeland's family denounced Olson's theories,

This aerial view shows part of what would have become Augsburg Park's campus and home sites. Wood Lake is top left and Central School is the E-shaped building at center. The Augsburg plan failed, and the village of Richfield bought the land and built its senior high school there. Augsburg Park and library are also on the site.

claiming the former pastor had been kidnapped and murdered and the circumstances of those events covered up. His son, Howard Birkeland, embarked upon a long, two-pronged campaign: clear his father's name and expose what he believed was Olson's part in smearing Knute Birkeland.[14]

Olson biographer George H. Mayer wrote that Birkeland was a Norwegian Lutheran minister "with a reputation for peddling 'blue sky' stock" to members of the church community. Yet lot sales at Augsburg Park had moved slowly, and annual costs for interest, taxes and private loans worried investors. Following Birkeland's death, Augsburg Park Association found itself owing more than $18,000 to his estate because of his complex dealings as business manager.[15]

A year after Birkeland's death, the Norwegian-language newspaper *Folkebladet* printed correspondence from the Rockford, Illinois, Circuit of the Lutheran Free Church. It declared, "the alarming fact [is] that Augsburg Park Association finds itself with a debt of $67,120, which the people of the Free Church must pay off or lose the large sums of money they have already paid in."[16]

The advent of the Great Depression in 1929–30 only made matters worse for the Augsburg Park Association. Fred Paulson, who served as treasurer of the college, had also become an early settler in the Augsburg preserve. Paulson and a few other landholders held on as they watched the decline in value of their properties and Richfield land in general. Interest in Augsburg Park lots dried up. The Lutheran Free Church gave up on the idea of moving the college; meanwhile, Augsburg Park Association maneuvered to keep afloat.[17]

At the close of World War II, a real estate firm tried to "low-ball" the Augsburg board of trustees with a bid for Augsburg Park's remaining lots. A movement to once again consider

moving the campus to the Richfield site sprang to life. In the meantime, a dispute arose when the Lutheran Free Church and the college discovered the village of Richfield was directing storm surface waters into a pool on Augsburg property. The village offered to buy the land for $36,000, but nothing came of the attempt.[18]

Augsburg College, with the assistance of the Minnesota legislature and the power of eminent domain, purchased blighted property near its Minneapolis campus in 1945–46. This halted talk of a move to Richfield and led village leaders to offer to buy Augsburg Park for $60,000. The land changed hands on May 1, 1949.

New housing and construction of Richfield High School claimed the majority of the old college enclave. The community saw fit to use the remainder as a park and a site for a library. Appropriately, they both carry the name Augsburg.

Along with a new campus for Augsburg College, Knute Birkeland provided land Lutheran Free Church members could buy and upon which they would build homes. Lots were sold at Wood Lake Shores sales office.

THE COUNTRY CLUB DISTRICT

The able and ambitious home builder J.C. Nichols learned, after long study, why many early 20th-century housing subdivisions failed: Developers relaxed restrictions requiring high standards for homes and their owners. Nichols finally hit upon a surefire way to assure the success of his proposed upscale development: Create "perpetual restrictions" limiting what a buyer could do with a house and, with the help of homeowner associations, rigorously enforce those rules. Nichols's upscale Kansas City Country Club District became a great success, one to be imitated in Edina by his good friend Samuel Thorpe.[1]

Minnesota-born, Princeton-educated Samuel S. Thorpe, Jr., spent 35 years steering his real estate firm into a "position of leadership among the realtors of Minneapolis" and readying himself to meet the biggest challenge of his professional life. On June 8, 1924, he launched lot sales for an upscale housing subdivision the likes of which Minnesota had never seen—Thorpe Brothers' Country Club District in Edina.[2]

Thorpe openly admitted he was following a formula for success fashioned by developers of Kansas City's Country Club District, Cleveland's Shaker Heights and Baltimore's Roland Park. In these exclusive housing neighborhoods, developers purchased a suitable piece of undeveloped land and prepared it for houses by grading and paving streets and installing sidewalks, electrical service, water, gas and sanitary sewers *before* offering a single lot for sale. Then, these entrepreneurs established and maintained control of building operations by requiring customers to agree to a detailed set of restrictions designed to preserve both the quality of housing stock and the character of the community.[3]

Starting Out

Twin brothers, Samuel and James Thorpe, were born in Red Wing, Minnesota, on April 20, 1864, to Samuel and Caroline Thorpe, northeasterners of long-established families, his from New York, hers from Maine. Reverend Thorpe, a Methodist minister, had moved to Red

Samuel Thorpe's advertisements for his new Country Club District in Edina emphasized elegant country living for "discerning families." This 1924 image shows the area beginning to blossom.

The Crier

Published for the Residents of the
COUNTRY CLUB DISTRICT

VOL. VI NO. 5   VILLAGE OF EDINA, MINNESOTA   JULY 1935

Country Club, 11 Years Old, One of Nation's 4 Finest Subdivisions

Cleveland, K.C. And Baltimore Are Listed As Three Others

ONE of the four outstanding subdivisions in the country—that is the description applied to the Country Club District by men whose experience and observations over long periods of years make them qualified judges.

The other three subdivisions in that select group, located at Kansas City, Cleveland and Baltimore are older than the Country Club, and the experiences in the developing of these three contributed to the making of the Country Club. The best features of its predecessors, plus new ideas, went into the youngest of the four subdivisions of highest ranking.

That the Country Club is something more than just another subdivision is illustrated by the words of its founder, S. S. Thorpe, a man with a record of 51 years in business, who said he wanted it to be his valedictory, and now that it is well developed and 11 years old, he is satisfied that "if I did it all over again, I don't know that I could do anything different."

Saw Them All

During his 40 years in business, which included 10 years as an executive officer of the National Real Estate association, Mr. Thorpe traveled to all

FOUNDER S. S. THORPE

subdivisions, but until the Country Club idea was brought to reality, he said, he "never did a real good job." With few exceptions, the general practice was to obtain a piece of land, mark out streets and lots, and go ahead and sell the lots.

Except in its bare fundamentals, the development of the Country Club bore little resemblance to the customary method. Two years of preparation pre-

District Is The Valedictory Of Noted Founder Sam S. Thorpe

on the site of what is now the Country Club.

When the farm was obtained from the Brown heirs, including Earle Brown, careful planning and painstaking work got underway in preparation for the opening of the district to home builders.

More than $75,000 was spent in engineering fees. Such expenditures were necessary, Mr. Thorpe said, because the planning of a first class subdivision is "a nice trick."

Streets Are Curved

Take the matter of streets, for example. For appearance sake they must not be too straight. At the same time, for practicability and safety, they must not be too curved. Streets plotted in curves without careful foresight would be a constant menace to motorists and pedestrians because the view ahead would be cut off. Completion of the major plans was the signal for the moving in of men and machinery, and soon the transformation of a farm into a populated residential district was well underway. More than $700,000 was spent on grading streets, laying pavements, and placing sanitary and drainage sewers before the first lot was offered for sale.

Nothing was done until every assurance was given that the results would be the best possible. Numerous sam-

This July 1935 edition of *The Crier*, the Country Club's free monthly magazine, reports about the District's national reputation. Samuel Thorpe, on the cover, viewed this project as the challenge of his professional life.

Wing and a faculty position at Hamline University, founded there in 1854.[4]

Sam Jr., began selling real estate while still in college in St. Paul and, with his brother's help, soon built a firm worth $80,000. During the 1890s, Thorpe Brothers' first decade in Minneapolis, Samuel developed a business relationship with the shrewd New York investor John Emory Andrus. The New Yorker had picked up a sizeable chunk of real estate in the distant and undeveloped Minneapolis following an 1870s loan

default. Andrus saw great potential in Minnesota and soon partnered with T.B. Walker in timberland investments that made millions for both. It was just one of many shrewd investments by the New Yorker. The extraordinary John Andrus, according to his 1935 *TIME* magazine obituary, was among America's 10 richest people when he died. He also had a daughter, Margaret, with whom Sam Thorpe developed a romantic relationship.[5]

In October 1899 Samuel Thorpe traveled to Yonkers, New York, to marry Margaret, the third daughter of John and Julia Dyckman Andrus. Sam brought his brother James along to serve as best man. Yonkers, just north of New York City, was the site of the stately Andrus mansion (it made the cover of *Scientific American* in 1895) overlooking the Hudson River's palisades.[6]

The up-and-coming Thorpe didn't need much help from his father-in-law, but his family and business relationship with John Andrus didn't hurt. Thorpe Brothers directed construction of the impressive Andrus building (present-day Renaissance Square) at Fifth and Nicollet in Minneapolis and immediately made it their headquarters. Andrus occupied an office on the ninth floor. The Thorpes engineered construction of a number of Andrus's Minneapolis projects, among them, the Palace and Plymouth buildings, Dyckman Hotel and Century Theater.[7]

Although the name "Thorpe Brothers" remained with the firm, Samuel's twin brother, James, did not. He retired to Denver, Colorado, in 1904 in the interests of his wife's health.[8]

Creating Country Club

Thorpe Brothers purchased the farm of Henry and Susan Fairchild Brown and the site of Edina Mill in 1922 and soon began negotiating with the Edina village council to bring roads and sewers onto the Browndale site. The council harbored memories of the long and arduous struggles with the rebellious and citified citizens of the Morningside district, perhaps making them more agreeable to planned development. Whatever the reason, Samuel Thorpe got what he needed from the village.

In early May 1923, the Edina council, in three different meetings, sought permission from the Minnesota Board of Health to deal with "sewerage from the County Club District" The council authorized a 25-year charter on the Country Club's water and sewer operations and gave Thorpe that charter. More such enabling acts that year facilitated the developer's plans. He received permission to make a new platting of the Brown farm and added a portion of the former George and Sarah Baird property to the district.[9]

In all, Samuel Thorpe spent more than $700,000 improving the site. Along with water and sewage service, he paved streets with high-quality asphalt and installed concrete sidewalks and curbs and planted trees. The district mirrored, on a smaller scale, the Kansas City Country Club development of his close friend J.C. Nichols. Streets gently twisted through the neighborhood, with Minnehaha Creek and the old Edina Mill pond forming its western border. The

clubhouse itself and adjacent 18-hole golf course were soon in operation.[10]

There was a widespread belief that Sam Thorpe handled most or all of the design work on the Country Club project. However, in a 1995 study, Country Club resident Robert D. Sykes, an associate professor in the Department of Landscape Architecture at the University of Minnesota, suggested that the Minneapolis landscaping firm of Morell and Nichols was involved.[11]

On June 8, 1924, Thorpe Brothers released newspaper advertisements declaring Country Club lots were

Country Club District in the mid-1920s looking to the southeast

available for sale. During that opening week, the developers announced plans for constructing the district's first house, to be built on Browndale Avenue in the heart of the neighborhood. Thorpe also sold $40,000 worth of home sites. Some families moved into their houses by the end of November.[12]

Sales of County Club lots did not go as well as hoped, however, with only 25 homes built in its first year. Thorpe's son, Samuel III, attributed the problem to competition from "established Minneapolis neighborhoods." Indeed, the City of Lakes featured highly desirable housing districts surrounding Lake of the Isles, Lake Calhoun and Lake Harriet, all much closer to the business and entertainment sectors of the city. Although some might have worried about the effect of restrictive covenants, in the senior Thorpe's view, the requirements made of customers did not hamper lot sales but actually helped. He believed the rules could have been more stringent.[13]

Thorpe made the restrictions specific. Only single-family residences at least one and one-half stories high could be built or occupied, no "flats, duplexes, apartments...public garages, oil stations or any other buildings whatsoever except a detached dwelling house to be used exclusively as a residence for a single family...." No residence or any other structure could be built on "any lot until the plans, specifications, elevation,

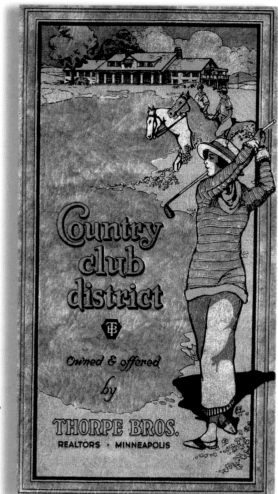

A fashionable young woman golfing, a couple horseback riding and the golf course clubhouse in the background combine on the cover of this promotional booklet to project Thorpe Brothers' image of the Country Club District.

location and grade thereof, with color scheme for said residence or structure, shall first have been presented to the vendor and approved in writing...." Sam Thorpe controlled all aspects of construction.

There was more. Outbuildings needed to correspond to the style and architecture of the residence, no above-ground tanks for fuel storage, no sign greater than 480 square inches, no shedding poplars, box elders or other objectionable shrubbery, no garbage, ashes, refuse or refuse receptacles placed or exposed to view, no horses, cows, goats, sheep or any domestic animals poultry or fowls of any kind, except dogs and cats (riding horses were allowed with Thorpe Brothers permission), no soft coal or fuel of any kind giving off black smoke...or obnoxious odors.

Restrictions on people moving to Country Club were also precise. "No lot shall ever be sold, conveyed, leased, or rented to any person other than that of the white or Caucasian race, nor shall any lot ever be used or occupied by any person other than of the white or Caucasian race, except for such as may be serving as domestics for the owner or tenant of said lot...."

Restriction by race raised few, if any, eyebrows. America faced a remarkable 1920s-era resurgence of the nativist Ku Klux Klan, particularly in the Midwest. The Klan had expanded its horizon of hatred to include the nation's newest immigrants, radicals, communists and more traditional targets—African Americans, Catholics and Jews. The segregationist traditions of the Jim Crow South also gained acceptance in the North, especially in big cities where a new generation of immigrants tended to congregate.[14]

County Club's promotional pamphlet spelled out the reasons for the restrictive covenants. "While it is not the intention of Thorpe Bros. to make the Country Club District a community of 'Snobs,' it is and will be…exclusive and select. A community where you can be proud to live, proud of your home, your grounds and your neighbor's home as well—a place where you can rear your children with the freedom of mind that comes with knowing they are more protected than would be possible in any 'hit or miss' city neighborhood."[15]

To stimulate disappointing sales, Samuel Thorpe hired local architects Jacob (Jack) Liebenberg and Seeman Kaplan, later known for their Minneapolis-area movie theaters including the Edina, to design model homes while drawing on historic styles as a guide. Five houses went up along Edina Boulevard and two on Moreland Avenue. Liebenberg-Kaplan set an impressive architectural example that influenced the style of future district homes. Lot sales picked up, and by 1930 County Club contained 269 houses and more than 1,000 residents.[16]

Map of Country Club from the March 1936 *The Crier*

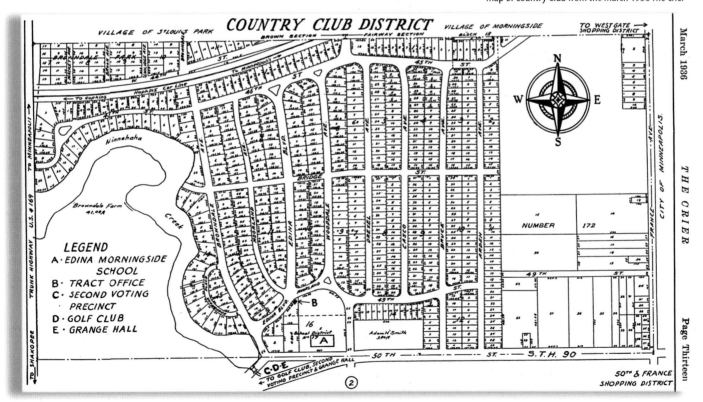

Country Club Influence

Members of Edina's village council took note of Thorpe Brothers' success in laying out Country Club and began doing some organizing of their own. In 1929 the council established a planning

Thorpe Brothers' advertisement comparing lot costs of "Desirable Minneapolis Residential Property"

commission, thus becoming the first community other than cities of the first class—Minneapolis, St. Paul and Duluth—to take such action. Within two years it had carefully crafted zoning ordinances to regulate future growth

and soon became the first suburb to hire professional planning experts. This foresight placed Edina in a strong position to face the post-Second World War growth boom.[17]

Edina adopted as a goal the Country Club concept of large lots—Thorpe Brothers required 65-foot frontages at a time when Minneapolis houses had lots with fronts of 25 to 50 feet—upon which single family homes would be built. The village amended zoning ordinances in 1948 to create lot standards that guaranteed a minimum size of 7,500 square feet with a frontage of no less than 65 feet. Larger, more expensive lots resulted in larger, more expensive homes. During the immediate post-World War II boom years, Edina did not develop at the stunning pace of Richfield or Bloomington—those suburbs held, in succession, the title of Minnesota's "fastest growing community"—but, in the tradition of Country Club, the village attracted wealthier home buyers.

A demographic study using the district's 1930 directory confirmed an expected community image—an upper-middle-class neighborhood of 591 adults, 344 minors and 97 servants. The analysis showed that of the approximately 150 men in Country Club for whom data was collected, "…26 worked in wholesale or retail merchandising, 25 in real estate or insurance, 26 in the professions, 14 in finance and 28 in various self-employed businesses."[18]

Sam Thorpe's vision for the Country Club District moved forward at a pace satisfying to its founder. In July 1935, 16 months before his death at age 72, Thorpe said of the development, "…if I had to do it all over again, I don't know that I could do anything different." Country Club was still growing, but by then, so was Edina. Other housing encroached upon the district, making less distinct the once clear boundaries of the area.[19]

It is fitting that the Country Club District enveloped the site of Edina Mills, the pastures through which Henry and Susan Brown's prize shorthorn cattle roamed, and George and Sarah Baird's beloved home—important and representative parts of the 19th century village. The inevitable advance of suburban development doomed the prosperous rural hamlet, while the Country Club District, the first incarnation of future subdivisions, provided a valuable template for the Edina we know today.

Country Club's no list: no above-ground tanks for fuel storage, no sign greater than 480 square inches, no shedding poplars, box elders or other objectionable shrubbery, no garbage, ashes, refuse or refuse receptacles placed or exposed to view, no horses, cows, goats, sheep or any domestic animals poultry or fowls of any kind, except dogs and cats (riding horses were allowed with Thorpe Brothers permission), no soft coal or fuel of any kind giving off black smoke…or obnoxious odors.

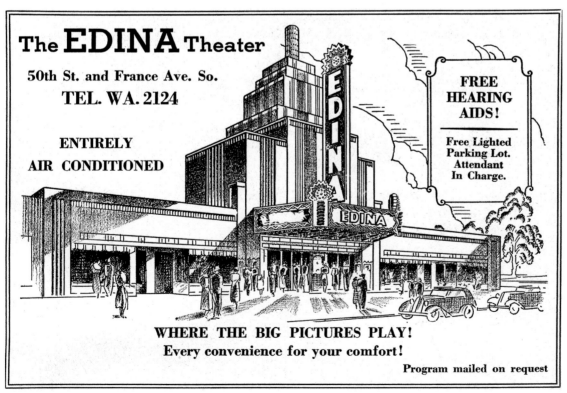

Local architects Jacob (Jack) Liebenberg and Seeman Kaplan designed model homes for the Country Club District. They became better known for their Minneapolis-area movie theaters including The Edina, shown here in the 1937 *Suburban Directory*.

–Four–
Boomlet to Boom

Signs of suburbanization south of Lake Street materialized early in the twentieth century and led to a building boomlet in the 1920s. Automobiles proliferated and brought once distant rural villages within range of Minneapolis. Housing developments overflowed the boundaries of that expanding metropolis, crossing into Richfield and forming a wall of homes on Edina's eastern border. Yet these changes mattered little when compared to a post-Second World War surge that transformed the once small rural hamlets of Richfield, Edina and Bloomington into large Minnesota cities.

"AUTOMOBILITY" AND HENNEPIN SOUTH

By November 1891 Tom Lowry, the creative force behind Twin Cities Rapid Transit Company, had finally made the streetcar business profitable. He had built an electrified system of trolleys that connected the "furthermost limits of Minneapolis to the outmost limits of St. Paul…." But new technologies threatened the old. By spring 1893 America's onrushing bicycle boom filled downtown streets with biking commuters competing with trolleys. And later that summer the Massachusetts Duryea brothers were toying with a gasoline-powered, wheeled machine that they drove at 10 miles per hour. What might their work portend?[1]

Martin Pahl, a 1920s Bloomington market gardener, has crammed his truck with fresh produce.

A less than perfect storm made up of farmers, bicyclists and devotees of gas-powered buggies called automobiles combined to make the nationwide Good Roads Movement of the 1890s a major force for change. Outside of urban centers, America's roads of that era were little more than unpaved trails prone to winter impassability, spring washouts and summer potholes. When the bicycle fad of the mid-1890s captured the public fancy, bike riders demanded proper roads for their use. For the same reason, auto enthusiasts clamored for reliable byways for their less-than-reliable vehicles. Farmers were no friends of bikers or autos—both unnerved their livestock—but they needed improved farm-to-market highways to speed fresh produce and dairy products to the city. Yet by 1900, the nation held less than 10 miles of concrete road.[2]

As the century turned, Americans looked on with satisfaction as the nation's infrastructure underwent dramatic improvement. Farmers thrilled to the arrival of RFD (Rural Free Delivery) that, according to the U.S. postmaster, brought the farm "within the daily reach of the intellectual and commercial activities of the world." Postal service across improved roads brought better access to "mail order" goods, described in alluring detail by Montgomery Ward and Sears

Roebuck catalogs. Though Americans owned fewer than 8,000 autos in 1900, that number swelled to 17 million by 1915. They drove on a rapidly improving network of roads.[3]

The Automobile Club of Minneapolis, from its headquarters in "Bloomington-on-the-Minnesota," launched a 1915 membership campaign titled, "Why Every Man Who Owns an Automobile Should Belong To The Automobile Club." A pamphlet explained that the club repaired and maintained several miles of road each year and also dealt with the frustrating lack of road signs. Unmarked roads greatly troubled drivers, a problem the auto group labored to correct by placing over 200 "malleable cast iron signposts." Members also could check maps and touring information held on file at club offices in the Radisson Hotel, the group's Minneapolis "city" headquarters.[4]

The Minneapolis auto club, an affiliate of both the Minnesota and U.S. automobile associations, joined the movement that was demanding a vast expansion of the nation's road network. Members liked nothing better than an after-work, 15-mile drive to their

This Cities Service Oil Company outlet at 66th and Lyndale was Richfield's first gas station.

Bloomington country club to relax. They also enjoyed longer rides on roads, some of which they built and maintained. The club reported Hennepin County commissioners had delivered "substantial aid" for their road projects. Nationally, auto club members, including those in Minneapolis, tended to be wealthier than the typical American. Yet, by 1914, there were more than a half-million owners of affordable Model T Fords sharing the road. Drivers joined elements of the

The Automobile Club of Minneapolis maintained a city headquarters in the Hotel Radisson, but members preferred a drive to their country club in "Bloomington-on-the-Minnesota" to relax.

Workers check forms on a freshly paved Bloomington section of Lyndale Avenue in 1918. Lyndale, also known as Lyndale Highway at that time, was the major route south for Minneapolis traffic.

Bloomington's first school buses, shown in 1918

each day; the highway was then made wider. In the meantime, the Minnesota Highway Department designated Lyndale, from Snelling-Shakopee Road to the end of paving in Lakeville, as State Highway 50.[6]

Some of those autos carried people in the market for a new home. The improved roads and technological advances in the car industry that made vehicles more dependable combined to bring housing developments within reach. Even Bloomington, to the far south, was experiencing subdivision platting by 1921.

Yale Realty Company began sales of lots on the 240-acre Waleswood subdivison, site of the Charles E. Wales estate near the Minnesota River. The fabulous home of Wales, a longtime leader in the Twin Cities coal trade, was also for sale. The mansion and other buildings included 80,000 square feet of space. Costs for one-acre lots started at $459, with $45 down and five dollars monthly. Developer Ara Berdan soon subdivided another 40 Bloomington acres, these were located east of Nicollet Avenue at 87th Street.[7]

Nonetheless, in 1923 and 1924 most south Minneapolis housing developers moved to the immediate southern sections of the city, working along Lyndale and Penn Avenues before

fledgling auto industry—oil companies, service station owners, parts suppliers, tire makers, road builders and land developers—in calling for better streets and highways.[5]

America could boast 25,000 miles of paved roads by 1925, which were viewed primarily as the automobile's domain. Lyndale Avenue, the auto gateway to southern Minneapolis, Richfield, Bloomington and points south, was among them. Work crews first paved this route, also known as Lyndale Highway, in 1918. Just seven years later, 22,000 autos and streetcars crowded that road

crossing the 54th Street border with Richfield. The Minneapolis *Journal* reported booming housing sales in the city's 13th Ward in spring 1923, with sales moving "beyond the southern boundary" into Richfield. The following year a *Journal* headline noted, "Blocks rectangle bounded by 54th Street on the north, 70th on the south, west to Penn Avenue and east to the Fort Snelling reservation. Subdivisions soon appeared. Growth rates then slowed dramatically, dampened from 1930 to the later 1940s by the Great Depression and Second

Peter and Amanda Christiansen pose in the front seat of their new automobile. Margaret Blaylock is one of the women in the back seat and Fritz Holm sits on the running board. The Christiansens lived in south Richfield.

of Homes Rushed in Villages Near City Limits." Six hundred acres were platted in Richfield for May marketing.[8]

Richfield real estate values rocketed upward, quintupling in a year's time. The *Journal* noted the escalation: "Acreage values in certain sections of Richfield jumped from $600, the top price in last year's (1923) transactions, to approximately $3,000." The newspaper pointed to the "concrete Lyndale avenue highway" as an important factor in the development. By 1924 Richfield was almost entirely platted. It formed a

World War. Endnote nine lists the 11 Richfield subdivisions placed on the market in 1924.[9]

Driven in large part by the new "automobility" of the 1920s, land developers migrated from the outlying districts of America's large urban centers toward the rural environs just beyond city borders. Thus, they created a foundation for a far more expansive suburbia and set the stage for an explosion of post-Second World War growth few could have envisioned.

MORNINGSIDE SECEDES FROM EDINA

While the farming community of Edina in the 20th century's first decade appeared to look much as it had during its formative years, change was under way. The large farms of the settlement period had been divided, often into produce gardening operations. Signs of suburbanization were appearing, particularly on the site of the old Grimes family homestead. Part of it had been platted into a new residential district known as Morningside.

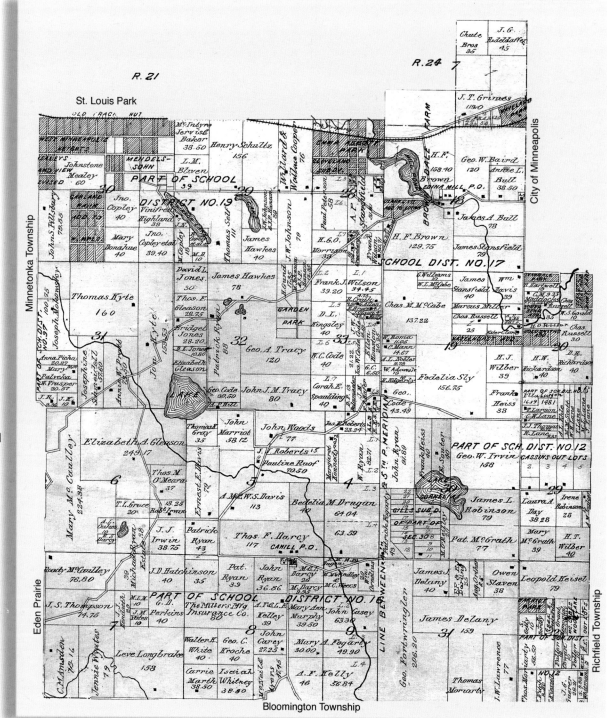

This 1898 plat map shows the McCrory "Motor Line" track to the north. In 1881 it reached Lake Minnetonka with stops in Edina. This link to Minneapolis was later abandoned, but not until a few housing subdivisions were built along it. In 1905 Twin City Rapid Transit Company's Lake Harriet line traced the old rail route, bringing about new housing built mostly on the Grimes farm. It was called Morningside.

By 1920 the progressive people of the increasingly "citified" Morningside section of Edina believed the village's reactionary rural majority was keeping them down. Morningside residents saw the farmer element in control of the council repeatedly reject their pleas for tax-supported community improvements.

In essence, Edina played Mr. Bumble to Morningside's Oliver Twist. "More?" sputtered Edina elders to those making spending requests, "There is no 'more'!"

Creating Morningside

The Morningside district owed its creation to the 1905 extension and electrification of the Twin City Rapid Transit Company's Lake Harriet line. The new tracks ran along present-day West 44th Street through Edina's northern districts. Heirs of prominent settlers Jonathan and Eliza Grimes had decided to plat the family farm for development, with 55 acres becoming part of the new Morningside district.[1]

The Minneapolis *Journal* reported on the project. "[The] new district, Morningside, is composed of sixty-nine lots, 100 by 200 feet each, to cost from $250 to $1000. The district lies between 42nd and 44th streets and will be crossed by three new avenues, Alden, Scott and France. Electric cars will stop at three stations adjacent to the [Grimes] property. Tenants living outside the city limits will have low taxes and at the same time only 5-cent carfare to town."[2]

The *Journal* article mistakenly credited Charles I. Fuller as developer. Part of the Grimes property had earlier been divided through the platting of Waveland Park, Kensington, Rutland and Lake Harriet Park. Three hundred acres still remained of the old farm, including

The Harriet News masthead caption:

A letter in the September 17, 1920, Harriet *News* served as a call to action for Morningside residents to break their political bonds with Edina.

Morningside's 55 acres at the property's east end. The Grimeses granted the railway company right-of-way through the new residential district.[3]

Originally the name "Morningside" referred only to the small 55-acre parcel, but it was soon attached to the entire southeast quarter of section seven. The first sale of Morningside land took place on July 25, 1905, when the Grimes family sold lots eight and nine to Charles Reynolds.[4]

To developers of the Morningside district, the community's future was assured. They would build a residential suburban retreat designed largely for commuters heading by streetcar to Minneapolis. Lots, nicely sized for an urban setting, would hold houses, not farms. The "new suburbanites," as the *Journal* was calling them, were expecting improved streets, curbs, sidewalks and other city conveniences.

Such expectations did not sit well with Edina's traditional and influential farmer leadership. They had little need for such costly improvements and were in a good position to thwart what they saw as "high-hat citified ideas." These Edina old-timers

The Harriet News

MINNEAPOLIS, MINN. FRIDAY, SEPTEMBER 17, 1920.

In the Morning Mail

To the Editor of the Lake Harriet News:

It is time that Morningside emerged from its chrysalis stage and became a recognized entity instead of being a revenue appendix of 8,500 acres of pasture, woodland and cornfield. During the past few months I have made a careful survey of various features of the community listed below in statistical and comparative columns. What is termed the Morningside territory embraces land to the south line of section seven, or including the residence portion south of the railway tracks to what is known as the Bail property, thence west to the intersection of the south line of section seven with the railway tracks and Wooddale avenue, where it joins the village of St. Louis Park. These are interesting figures relating to Morningside:

Population		502
No. of families		147
No. owning homes		147
Renters		0
Voters		352
Telephones		106
Children under school age		50
Children in grades		66
Pupils in high school		14

	Edina	Morningside
Valuation	$1,134,867	$142,733
Rate (Village)		
mills	13.20	13.20
Tax (Village)	14,980	1,884
Population (1920	1,833	502
Acres	8,688.11	240

Thus it will be seen that Morningside pays one-seventh of the taxes of Edina; contains nearly one-third the population, and comprises only one-thirty-sixth of the territory; or, to make a still further division, the entire residence portion is contained in 122 of the 240 acres, 71 times less than the area of the entire village. Is there any reason why an intelligent, wide-awake and up-to-date community should not administer its own affairs instead of being governed by "absent treatment"? We have young men in Morningside—attorneys, bankers, realtors, engineers, contractors and other business and professional men, who are admirably equipped to administer its affairs, whom we would meet face to face daily, and who would listen to our requests for service in a sympathetic and respectful attitude.

With the purpose of "starting something" a Morningside indoor family picnic will be held at the Odd Fellows' hall tomorrow evening, the 18th inst., under the auspices of the Morningside Civic League, to which every family, and the entire family, is invited. After acquiring a comfortable interior we will "talk it over" in a neighborly and friendly fashion. The very fact that nearly every family in Morningside owns its home should be a source of pride to the community and make us feel like one big harmonious family, willing and able to co-operate to perpetuate such an eminently desirable situation.

MORNINGSIDE RESIDENT.

spent most of the following two decades trying to keep a lid on Morningside projects.[5]

In 1904 the council put a brake on demands for new roads in the future Morningside area by passing a resolution regarding the opening and improving of streets. They declared, "*not less* than one half [of the cost] shall be assessed against the property benefited by such improvement..." [emphasis added].[6] Four years later the council agreed, under pressure from Morningside, to provide materials for road building if petitioners handled the job. In 1909, two Morningside men asked the council to buy six streetlights at $3.50 each and promised they would install them.[7]

The newly organized Morningside Improvement Association, represented by Dudley Parsons and B.T. Emerson, tried its luck with the council beginning in 1911. The community, meanwhile, worked to get Morningside people on the council. Nils N. Leerskov,

The route of the Twin City Rapid Transit Company, its tracks visible at center in the 1930s photo, ran along West 44th Street crossing through southern Morningside.

The 119 acres of the Jonathan and Eliza Grimes farm made up much of the Morningside community. The northern 80 acres of Browndale Farm, owned by Henry and Susan Brown, also extended into Morningside.

Plat Book of Hennepin County, 1898

a local builder, won election in 1912 and became the first neighborhood man to serve on Edina's governing board.[8]

The drumbeat of Morningside requests grew louder at Edina council meetings. In 1914, speakers from Morningside asked for an equal share of roadwork projects, more sidewalks and lighting. By 1916, they had added curbs and gutters to their wish list. Morningside citizens appeared at every council meeting in 1918, each time bringing new requests. Long meetings that often extended toward midnight and beyond made it difficult on Morningside attendees, most of whom needed to be up early, heading to work in Minneapolis.[9]

Morningside residents George Woodling and Leerskov, angered over a special assessment passed by the Edina council for work near 44th Street and Grimes Avenue, demanded reconsideration of the fees during an August 7, 1920, meeting. A number of other Morningside residents also faced assessments. The council listened to the men and then reaffirmed its decision.

R[asmus] L. Jensen spoke about Edina's "unfair tax distribution," and asserted Morningsiders needed to take "the yoke off our necks."[10]

Morningside's Declaration of Independence

On September 17, 1920, Harriet *News*, a Linden Hills-based newspaper, printed what amounted to a Morningside Declaration of Independence, protesting unfair taxes and mistreatment by a dominant Edina. This declaration, in the form of a Letter to the Editor, called upon citizens to break ties with its mother community in favor of self-government. The letter opened, "It is time that Morningside emerged from its chrysalis stage and become a recognized entity instead of being a revenue appendix of 8,500 acres of pasture, woodland and cornfield."[11]

Indignantly, the anonymous writer asked, "Is there any reason why an intelligent, wide-awake and up-to-date community should not administer its own affairs instead of being governed by 'absent treatment'? We have young men in Morningside...who are admirably equipped to administer its affairs, whom we would meet face to face daily and who would listen to our requests for service in a sympathetic and respectful attitude." The letter, somewhat Jeffersonian in tone and substance, if not style,

concluded by inviting Morningside residents to a community picnic the following evening.

The *News* covered that gathering. Speeches and welcomes kicked off the festive Saturday evening affair at the Odd Fellows Hall, 44th Street and France Avenue. Most of the 150 residents, who enjoyed picnic suppers during the meeting, supported a move to incorporate their community. Morningside Civic League president A.G. Long explained the incorporation process, followed by the crowd singing their new anthem, "Morningside My Morningside," sung to the tune of "Maryland My Maryland." After more speeches, including some strongly against secession, 25 property owners signed a petition requesting the Hennepin County Board call an election regarding incorporation of Morningside.[12]

Dudley Parsons, writing in the Harriet *News*, advocated for secession. His October 1 summary noted that Edina was a "large rural territory save only for the settlements made by people who have left the city but who work in the city and desire improvements. These settlements naturally are along the (street) car line." He pointed out that a community of farmers would not be expert in concerns of "city people," and listed sidewalk, curb, electric lights, parking, weed-

The Morningside children's band poses outside their school in the early 1940s.

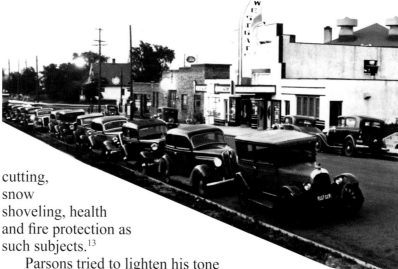

Westgate Theater on Sunnyside Avenue near 44th and France, pictured in 1935

cutting, snow shoveling, health and fire protection as such subjects.[13]

Parsons tried to lighten his tone at the finish, but failed. "It's a merry contest—this separation business—to be carried on with good heart and sweet spirit, not in acrimony...If the fates decree that Morningside shall still wait from eight until twelve o'clock...in the gloomy Grange hall before the bewhiskered tribunal that dispenses curb and gutter and other favors and then walk a mile and a half home to learn the next morning that Yancey or Rutledge or some other statesman had awakened in time to reconsider the question, so be it...."[14]

Some opposed secession or urged caution, including B.T. Emerson, Morningside resident and former Edina village council president. He believed Edina had treated the district fairly. He

feared unknown cost factors in separation and that Morningside was too small to be viable. Five leaders—Emerson, William Walker, Carl Brackey, Starr Whiton, S.S. Alwin—presented detailed budgetary information in the *News* and asked those on both sides of the issue to consider their figures.[15]

Excited Morningside community members met on October 26 to prepare a slate of officers for an upcoming election. Those elected were to attend the November meeting of the Edina village council and begin the process of dividing the assets of the two communities upon their formal separation. On October 30, R.L. Jensen was chosen to head the new Morningside

community as president. The fact that Jensen was then serving as Edina council president somewhat complicated matters.[16]

On November 5, 1920, the Morningside village board appeared before the Edina council with their formal request for division of assets. Edina's representatives decided to assess their own legal standing and consider the Morningside request. At this meeting, Jensen resigned as president of the Edina council, followed by Constable Robert Jackson and Justice of the Peace Alfred Bjorkland. Jackson and Bjorkland joined Jensen in the new Morningside government. By May 1921 the villages had completed their political divorce.[17]

The two communities clashed at times in the years that followed, particularly in the mid-1920s when both wanted a new school in the district they shared. A safecracking incident in which ballots on the school construction issue were feared stolen (they weren't) was a low point in the struggle. They resolved the dilemma in 1925 by putting up a schoolhouse in each village. Both communities shared the Edina-Morningside junior and senior high school.[18]

Remarriage

By the mid-1960s, the people of Morningside readied for another important vote. Mayor Jack Beegle openly questioned the village's ability to meet growing obligations and expectations and, along with his wife, Charlotte, led a drive to annex their community to Edina. A petition drive netted signatures of 164 Morningside residents, while the Edina city council and the Minnesota Municipal Commission consented to a remarriage of the two communities. All Morningside needed to do was get a majority of voters to agree.[19]

Feelings ran high in the village during the run-up to the vote. Morningside councilman C. Wayne Courtney made a passionate stand against annexation. Courtney had a high profile, thanks to television coverage of Minnesota state tournaments showing this feisty coach of Minneapolis Roosevelt High School's powerful basketball teams. A combative Courtney nearly came to blows with the Edina village manager, Warren Hyde, during the annexation debate, illustrating how this hot-button issue stirred discussions and arguments throughout Morningside.

On May 6, 1966, 85 percent of Morningside's 1,100 eligible voters went to the polls and by a two-to-one margin approved the annexation to Edina. Hard feelings lingered after the vote. Former mayor Beegle recalled people turning their heads when they saw him coming. Others harbored grudges over the decision.

But 13 years later Courtney admitted he had been wrong to oppose the reunification. "I thought we'd lose our identity, [our] representation, and that taxes would go up." Openly and somewhat sheepishly he said, "I was wrong on all three counts."[20]

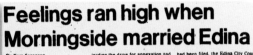

Feelings ran high when Morningside married Edina

By Tom Sorensen
Staff Writer

It was almost anti-climactic when Morningside residents voted on May 3, 1966, to determine whether to become part of Edina. By then the fun was over.

C. Wayne Courtney, of Morningside, and Warren Hyde, the Edina village manager, had already almost come to blows at a public hearing on the issue. Former mayor Jack Beegle had already had his share of late night phone calls wondering why he was leading the drive for annexation and who his ancestors really were. Roger Johnson, then the pastor at Edina-Morningside Congregational Church, had already expressed his feelings about annexation — from behind the pulpit.

The campaign had left a trail of sore hands and tired voices. Proponents and opponents of annexation knocked on doors, recited speeches, written letters to newspapers and argued over coffee, drinks and backyard fences. A petition with the signatures of 164 Morningside residents had been filed, the Edina City Council and Minnesota Municipal Commission had approved and the only remaining barrier along the road to annexation was a majority vote from the Morningside electorate.

So they voted.

There were 1,100 eligible voters in Morningside at the time and 85 percent showed up to cast their ballots. The issue that put Morningside on the map ultimately took them off it: 605 voted in favor of annexation, 302 against it and on Sept. 1, 1966, Morningside became part of Edina.

"It was fun," said Charlotte Beegle, 58, who led the annexation drive with her husband, Jack. "But I wouldn't want to do it again."

The Beegles had gone door to door pleading their case. Their case, essentially, was that the duties and obligations of city government had grown too big, too fast for a village of 2,000 people to keep up with. "We worked like sons-of-guns not to go," she said. "Until the last shot was fired we didn't want to go, but we had to."

Of course, there were 302 voters who disagreed. It was a dog-eat-dog, neighbor-versus-neighbor campaign that sharpened tempers and fractured relationships. After the results were in, it took time for some of those relationships to heal.

"I like everybody to like me," said Beegle, 60, the mayor in 1964 and 1965. "After the election, there were a few who turned their heads when they saw me coming. Poor losers, I guess. They felt so strongly they were right."

A.H. Halweg, Morningside's mayor at the time of annexation, said he wasn't sure he wanted to talk about it. Like the village's council at the time, Halweg was against it. "It happened 13 years ago," he said. "I've got no axes to grind."

Staff Photo Bruce Bisping

Morningside Mayor Jack Beegle and his wife, Charlotte, led a successful drive to annex their small community to Edina.

Rubbing Out Richfield

Soon after Morningside's secession from Edina in 1921, a determined band of north Richfield residents organized their own breakaway movement. They hoped to become part of Minneapolis. When Richfield's village council resisted their efforts, the northern secessionists countered with another idea: completely dissolve Richfield and make it all part of Minneapolis.

This Minneapolis *Journal* map from April 1924 illustrates how Minneapolis housing developments were pushing south.

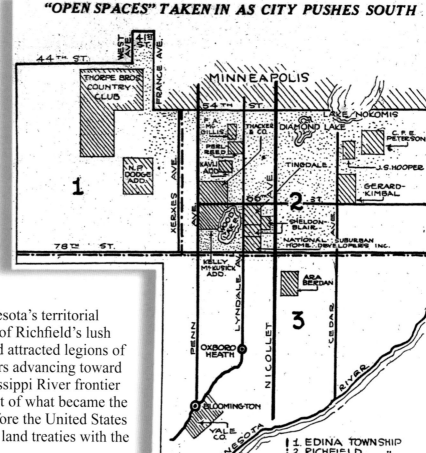

Since Minnesota's territorial days, the allure of Richfield's lush prairie lands had attracted legions of admirers. Settlers advancing toward the upper Mississippi River frontier snapped up most of what became the village even before the United States ratified its 1851 land treaties with the native Dakota.

Artist Frank Blackwell Mayer took a look at the future Richfield in 1851 and reported a scene that would make a farmer's mouth water: "The eye can pierce an unobstructed distance of several miles across this beautiful lawn, for such it seems to be, & one is constantly expecting to see neat farm houses appearing at every turn...its rolling & hilly surface being varied with open prairies and wooded hills, the trees appearing in clumps and masses of a few acres, looking like the orchards of the Eastern states...."[1]

Small wonder the first settlers of Richfield, almost all Eastern farmers, excitedly staked claims in the area. With water, wood and easily tillable land readily available, failure to succeed seemed remote. And succeed and prosper they did.

Nevertheless, by the early 20th century the rolling prairies, creeks and lakes of Richfield drew the attention of a new brand of entrepreneur—the land developer. Real estate speculators had done well in subdividing south Minneapolis and the city's Lake District area, nearly all of which was within original Richfield borders. Naturally, they hungered to develop similar lands available even farther into the sparsely settled south. Only the shock of America's crushing 1893 economic depression kept Richfield temporarily free of the developers' grasp.[2]

Minneapolis subdivisions advanced towards Richfield's northern border at 54th Street, and then crossed it by 1900. Buyers snapped up lots in the Minnehaha Falls section of north Richfield. The Mortimer Addition straddled the border at 54th and Lyndale, and Minnehaha Heights was wholly in Richfield east of Mother Lake at 60th Street.[3]

In spring 1911 a new building boomlet was started when the village council accepted four plats near its northern limits. Growth prompted a council member to make a motion to buy a Minneapolis map "to get an idea for platting Richfield property so that the streets correspond...."[4]

Developers kept up a steady pace, bringing a series of Richfield plats to the village council for approval. Lake Harriet Hyland, Brookside Park, Lake Harriet Terrace Addition, Minnehaha Highlands Park, Diamond Lake Hyland, Diamond Lake 2nd Addition and Wilson Park all received approval.[5]

Development slowed during the World War I years but returned with renewed vigor in the early 1920s. Buyers could look over lots near Grass Lake, Wood Lake and farther south near 70th Street. But most of Richfield still retained a rural character. Its Civic Association boasted in 1920 that the village had "One of the best known flocks of thorough-bred sheep in the country and the greatest herd of Holstein cattle, in this or any other country."[6]

An "airplane view" illustrates how Richfield's Fairwood Park Addition was in the "Profitable Path of Expansion" in May 1923. Developers typically avoided using the word "Richfield" in their advertising, focusing more on a property's proximity to Minneapolis.

The Bachman family, forced by what this May 1924 ad calls "the Onward Sweep of Progress," began selling large parcels of its Richfield produce gardening fields for housing development.

Breaking Away

But not everyone living in Richfield believed the community was a rural Eden. Those with homes near the Minneapolis border, like their neighbors in Edina's Morningside neighborhood, wanted big city amenities—modern schools, police, fire and water services among them. In spring 1923 the *Journal* reported Minneapolis was "southern bound" with housing sales in its 13th Ward booming. Further south, a "young city was springing up…between Fort Snelling and Penn Avenue," and these homes were being built "beyond Fifty-fourth street, the city's southern boundary."[7]

Two weeks after that growth report, the *Journal* informed readers of a major purchase in Richfield. The farm of Gilbert Graham, a prominent Richfield resident, had been sold to the development firm Tingdale Brothers for $200,000. Much of the future Richfield's economic heart—Lyndale to Nicollet between 66th and 69th streets—lay within the original confines of the Graham farm. It appeared to some that

Wood Lake, the "Last Lake in the Lake District," was a drawing card for developers of the Lyndale Shores addition in June 1924.

A CITY LOT $495

Just Outside of Minneapolis Limit—Low Taxes

$10.00 Down Will Hold a Lot **$2.30 A Week** Will Keep It

Opening Sale Starts Today

Salesmen on the addition all day and evening.

"LYNDALE SHORES ON WOOD LAKE"

The New Addition to the Lynnhurst District

Lyndale Ave. South at 67th St.
Only 108 Lots, but every lot a picture.

The Last Lake in the Lake District

Come and see the Most Beautiful Addition in direct line of our City's better growth—Large magnificently wooded lots overlooking Wood Lake on Lyndale Avenue South

50 to 60 foot Lots, $495 to $995 A Few Higher

Terms 10% down and 2% per month.

$10.00 paid today will hold a lot until you can arrange for the balance of the 10

5 to 10 per cent discount for excess down payments

This survey crew worked along the Bloomington section of the Lyndale Highway around 1920.

Minneapolis growth would swallow a large portion of northern Richfield.[8]

In May 1924 the leader of a new civic group calling itself the Richfield Improvement Association (RIA) announced it had gathered 300 signatures on a petition. Jacob Andresen, the RIA president, declared his group wished to annex to Minneapolis "the part of the village (Richfield) south of the city to 66th Street and from Xerxes Avenue to the Fort Snelling reservation."[9]

Andresen told newspaper reporters the area to be annexed had undergone "such a tremendous growth in the past few years," city facilities were now required. He explained that in 1919 three one-room schools were available to children in the area. The village now had three buildings and a total of 24 classrooms, yet they were not enough to handle all the students. He noted housing developments around Lake Nokomis, half of which was in Richfield, had added to the student influx.[10]

The Minneapolis *Tribune* picked up on the story and announced a large section of Richfield might soon become part of the city. Its reporter wrote, "With the possibility of Richfield, from the city limits to Sixty-Sixth street being annexed...new interest has developed in the property of the village." The publicity provided encouragement to RIA members. On April 16, 1924, the Association announced it would work to see all of Richfield merged with Minneapolis.[11]

Richfield voters addressed the annexation issue on May 29, 1924. The *Tribune* reported, "A heated campaign between advocates and opponents of the proposal caused practically every voter in the village to cast a ballot." Citizens rejected the idea by nearly a three-to-one margin. The RIA ticket running for village council also suffered defeat. Incumbent John B. Irvin, of the Richfield pioneering Irvin family, was re-elected president, while Robert Graham, clerk, and Walter Bachman also returned to office. Dr. L.J. Hann was the unsuccessful RIA candidate for president.[12]

But Richfield voters were swimming against the tide. During the week of the election, newspaper stories and ads appeared with a revealing story about a Richfield institution. The Bachman family, owners of a leading Twin Cities truck farming operation, announced the sale of most of its land. A new housing development, Bachman Estates, would take over their fields around Lyndale Avenue and 58th Street.[13]

A headline on an advertisement for Bachman Estates sounded a death knell for the rural life in northern Richfield:

"Forced Into Being By the Onward Sweep of Progress." The copy continued, "The main stream of overflow population is steadily Southward," and advised, "[I]f you ever expect to share in the

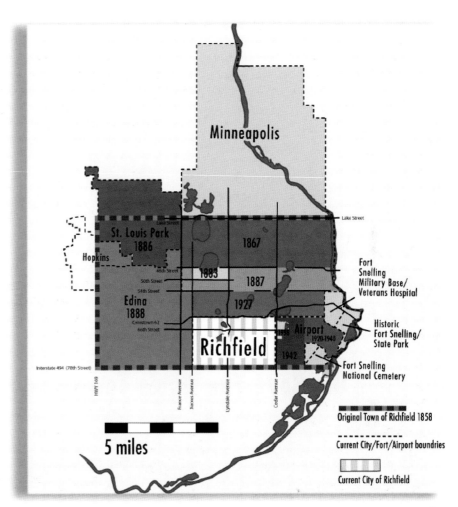

This map illustrates how Richfield was reduced from its original 1858 size of 63 square miles to today's seven.

Map by Joseph Hoover, research by David J. Butler

increasing values of Greater Minneapolis, we believe your opportunity has arrived HERE and NOW." If the developers were right and the population increase in the southern suburbs inevitable, what did that portend for Richfield, Edina and Bloomington? The highly respected Bachman family assessed growth trends and subdivided its Richfield holdings under pressure by the "onward sweep of progress." Who would be next to sell?[14]

The resilient Richfield Improvement Association, meanwhile, bounced back from its election defeat and returned to the village council on December 4, 1925, with another request to bring their neighborhood into Minneapolis. When that effort stalled, the RIA upped the ante and brought a new petition to the council just 10 weeks later. This one requested the *entire* village of Richfield be dissolved and annexed to Minneapolis. The association requested a special election on March 10, 1926, to decide the issue.[15]

A large majority of the 153 people signing the newest petition lived between 54th and 62nd streets. Many residents of New Ford Town, the impressive housing development that had opened in 1924 between 63rd and 66th streets, and 24th Avenue South and Cedar Avenue, also supported a consolidation with Minneapolis. Years later, Fred Bachman discussed the 1926 petitioners and mentioned the New Ford Town element. That subdivision was marketed

to workers at the new Ford auto assembly plant across the Mississippi in St. Paul's Highland Park neighborhood. Bachman said of the petitioners, "A lot of them moved away but we're still here. And we're in Minneapolis whether we want to be or not."[16]

The RIA did not get their requested March 10 referendum but did receive a sympathetic hearing from north Richfield members on the village council. Frank A. Drew, Jr., council president, lived at 5504 Emerson Avenue South, and recorder Raymond A. Gleason's address was 5600 Grand Avenue South, both in the heart of secessionist territory. Council members O.J. Samuelson and C.G. Erickson also resided in that district.[17]

A well-timed compromise proposal for annexation submitted by the RIA gathered support and promised an end to the long dispute. The secessionists now wanted to annex a portion of northern Richfield about one mile long and five and one-half miles wide; in all, about five square miles. The ceded district ranged between 54th and 62nd streets south, and from Xerxes Avenue South to the Fort Snelling reservation. Voters approved the move by a healthy margin, 1,658 to 675.[18]

Thus, Richfield lost its village hall, two schools and four elected leaders. The Hennepin County Auditor's Office took on the job of equitably dividing and apportioning the property and obligations of the two communities. In 1927, Richfield's northern boundary became 62nd Street, later Minnesota 62.[19]

That is where it remains.

Developers of New Ford Town, another 1924 Richfield subdivision, capitalized on the new Ford plant in nearby St. Paul. The small oval labeled "U.S. Postal Field" grew into Minneapolis-St. Paul International Airport that later engulfed the neighborhood.

Oh, Boy! The Whole Town's Coming!

YES, FOLKS, the big sale is on. We're here to sell every last one of our remaining New-Ford Town lots. Hundres have phoned us since we first announced this great close out sale. To them all—to everyone we say"Come out to the greatest feast of values in homesites that it has ever been your good fortune to attend." One glance at the map above tells the story of New-Ford Town's advantages as a homesite. Comesee for yourself. Comeshare in these values.

THE BOOM BEGINS

The post-World War II demographic phenomenon known as the baby boom changed America's growth patterns for decades to come. This population surge took a year to unfold as the nation hastened to get members of its wartime military back home. American armed forces had more than 16 million men in uniform as the war ended in 1945, the majority in their teens and twenties. As they returned, marriage and birth rates climbed at an astonishing rate.

World war and the mobilization of American manpower reduced the national birthrate, but "good-bye babies," conceived shortly before husbands left for military service, helped keep the annual number of births near three million. Following the war, birth numbers soared upward by a half-million in 1946, and the 1947 totals topped that record by 400,000. Demographers soon discarded their prewar population projections.[1]

Lack of housing for families emerged as the first of many challenges being generated by this population explosion. The Great Depression had slowed home construction for a decade, and the wartime absence of millions of American men and women caused an even greater reduction. By December 1945, four months after the war's conclusion, the Army was discharging soldiers at a rate of one million per *month*, while the Navy sent home a quarter-million monthly. Just over a year later, six million families had doubled up and were living with relatives or friends, while another half-million were housed in hurriedly put up temporary housing. Millions in the world's richest nation,

Quonset huts, prefabricated, lightweight buildings designed for wartime military use, were pressed into postwar service as temporary family homes. The Quonsets shown here in a 1946 photo were part of a Minneapolis neighborhood.

reported historian Harold Evans, lived in "garages, coal sheds, chicken coops, tool sheds, granaries, old trolley buses, Army Quonset huts."[2]

So where would returning veterans find suitable housing? Many would choose the rapidly growing suburbs that ringed large cities. The federal government authorized billions of dollars of FHA and VA financing to returning GIs, enabling veterans to afford a home of their own. In the war year of 1944 the country saw 114,000 houses started; the next year there were 937,000. At that point, the peacetime economy began taking hold, and construction materials

Housing districts such as this began covering Richfield's adaptable farm land following the Second World War. In 1950, the suburb's population had swelled to 17,502; four years later Richfield had 31,756 residents.

were more readily available. Housing starts reached 1,183,000 in 1948 and peaked in 1950 at 1,692,000. Large home building firms, capable of handling construction of massive tract developments, dominated the market. Ten percent of the nation's builders erected 70 percent of the housing. Between 1950 and 1970, America's suburban population doubled to 74 million, amounting to 83 percent of the nation's total growth.[3]

Americans understood a new

Bloomington Athletic Association (BAA) Little Leaguers and their coaches pose for a photo in August 1957. Note the "BAA" insignia on their caps.

Norling Collection, Bloomington Historical Society

The home building industry created jobs and helped get money flowing, while consumerism kept it moving. American farmers helped feed a world short on food as nations in Asia and Europe worked mightily to recover from six years of war. With employment and wage rates up, Americans could afford automobiles, refrigerators and labor saving devices (electric clothes dryers and dishwashers were popular) for the home. In 1947 the television age, a cultural and communications revolution, stirred the country. Americans bought more than 200,000 televisions each month in 1948 and 1949; three million owned sets by January 1, 1950.

Sewer construction became high priority in fast-growing suburbs like Bloomington and Richfield that had depended upon wells and septic systems. Needed upgrades began in the early 1950s.

Norling Collection, Bloomington Historical Society

house in the suburbs would likely cost about $5,000. In 1946, auto workers, among the higher paid factory employees, earned around $3,000 a year, about $600 more than those laboring in other manufacturing sectors. By 1950 the average weekly salary for all workers doubled the prewar rate, rising to $44.39. Women added to the family income. During the war, more than three million women took jobs who would not have done so otherwise. The number of women workers slowed when ex-soldiers returned home, but then grew larger, approaching 20 million by 1950.[4]

Television sales skyrocketed in the nation and the Twin Cities during the late 1940s. Lyndale Hardware sold TVs and also invited football fans without sets to watch games in the store.

Americans then bought seven million TVs in 1950 *alone*.[5]

Despite its problems in retooling the nation for peace, America after the Second World War clearly dominated the world through its economic and military prowess. After a visit to the United States, British historian Robert Payne wrote in 1949, America "...sits bestride the world like a Colossus; no other power at any time in the world's history has possessed so varied or so great an influence on other nations." Payne reported the U.S. controlled more than half the world's wealth and more than half of its productivity. "[T]he rest of the world," he asserted, "lies in the shadow of American industry...."[6]

South Suburbs Emerge

To the south of Minneapolis the postwar housing tidal wave first washed over Richfield and Edina then headed for Bloomington. Richfield served as a Minnesota model that reflected new American growth patterns. From its prewar 1940 population of 3,378, the village more than quintupled during the following decade to 17,502. Four years later it held 31,756 people, nearly 10 times the prewar number. Edina's population increased, growing from 5,855 residents in 1940 to 9,744 in 1950. Bloomington, from the 1940 starting point, came close to tripling its population by 1950, from 3,647 to 9,942.[7]

Creating an infrastructure to keep pace with these impressive growth rates caused a headache for America's new suburbia. The urgency for new schools (lots of them), and expensive water and sewer service typically ranked high on the "needs" list.

Edina, with impetus from its Country Club District, began the postwar era with a head start on Richfield and Bloomington. Thorpe Brothers installed Country Club sewer and water links with Minneapolis even before the district's mid-1920s construction. The village added artesian wells for drinking water in 1936 and began expansion of sewage treatment service two years later. Edina finished the work in 1946.[8]

Richfield's water and sewer wars became legend in the community, resulting in thorny political challenges. The village's reliance on a well and septic system for each home turned

Construction at Bloomington's Lincoln High School in September 1956 with newly constructed homes across the street

Norling Collection, Bloomington Historical Society

into a potentially dangerous health dilemma.

Minnesota's polio epidemic of 1949 hit Richfield the hardest of any community, with three deaths and 38 surviving victims. Some, including village health officer, Dr. John J. Heisler, expressed concern about the "sanitation situation." Construction of a sanitary sewer system commenced in 1953. Bloomington's sewage issues mirrored Richfield's and were finally solved after the Minnesota Health Department found 80 percent of the village's private wells contaminated. The community then quickly dealt with the situation.[9]

New Englanders brought their tradition of free public schools with them to Minnesota and south Hennepin County. One hundred years later the people of Richfield, Bloomington and Edina struggled to preserve that heritage by building schools fast enough for their baby boomers. Edina still relied upon Cahill and Edina-Morningside schools, both badly overcrowded after the war. Richfield's East and Woodlake buildings were overflowing with children before and during World War II. The village consolidated those two buildings in November 1945 but was soon inundated by a wave of boomers. Rather than build high schools, both Edina and Richfield paid tuition to send older students to Minneapolis secondary schools.[10]

Bloomington first modernized its school system in 1918, merging its rural programs into Bloomington Consolidated District 142. The new building, at 10025 Penn Avenue South, housed grades one through 12, with busing provided for those needing it. Edina High School opened in 1949, and Richfield High, after protracted effort, began operations five years later. Until that time, Richfield (population 31,756) was believed to have

This September 5, 1956, photo of the Nicollet Avenue and Old Shakopee Road area shows housing divisions on the march in a growing Bloomington.

been the largest community in America without its own high school.[11]

Students in Bloomington managed to squeeze into District 142's lone school building until the postwar boomers reached first grade. The village pressed the old two-room Kimball School into emergency service and then operated grades one and two using split shifts until 1950 when Cedarcrest Elementary began operations. Across the nation other districts replaced one-room schools, but there were still nearly 60,000 remaining by 1950.[12]

Dazzling growth statistics helped tell the story of America's expansion from 1946 to 1950, and most citizens could bear witness to their truth. But the postwar boom was far from finished. Who, in 1950 Bloomington, for example, would have believed their community would build on average more than one public school a year for the next two *decades*?[3]

LET MARV ANDERSON BUILD IT FOR YOU

Marvin H. Anderson earned high standing in the ranks of America's Greatest Generation. Born in Milaca, Minnesota, in March 1918, Anderson learned the carpenter trade before service as a combat infantryman in the Second World War. After military service, he became one of the Twin Cities' most prominent housing contractors. Marvin H. Anderson Construction Company and its competitors built houses by the thousands in the Twin Cities suburbs, including many in Bloomington where he lived.

Marvin H. Anderson is pictured at the height of his suburban Twin Cities home building career. The Bloomington resident's construction firm erected more than 3,000 houses in that city alone.

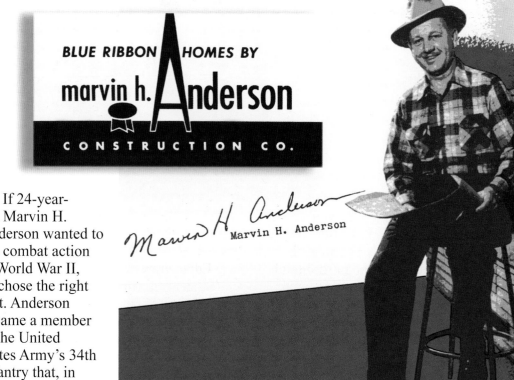

If 24-year-old Marvin H. Anderson wanted to see combat action in World War II, he chose the right unit. Anderson became a member of the United States Army's 34th Infantry that, in 1942, was the first American division shipped overseas. Anderson and the 34th took part in landings in North Africa where U.S. and German soldiers, for the first time in the war, met in combat. The Minnesotan was later wounded and awarded the Bronze Star for heroism during the protracted battle at Cassino in Italy, a struggle renowned for its length and ferocity.[1]

Following the war, millions of American veterans, Marv Anderson included, returned home to restart their lives. Anderson soon turned to home construction, working in the burgeoning Twin Cities' suburbs where veterans were among his first and best customers. They snapped up Anderson's affordable ramblers thanks, in large part, to the federal GI Bill of Rights and its mortgage assistance provisions. Anderson became active in veteran and labor affairs and successfully ran for the state legislature in 1946. He remained in office through 1957. During that time period, he helped create the Bloomington Chamber of Commerce and served as its president for five years.[2]

The postwar construction surge affected Richfield, Edina and Bloomington at different times and in

Keeping up with road construction needs was a continuing battle for fast-growing suburbs. This is Bloomington's unpaved 83rd Street and Portland Avenue in January 1961.
Norling Collection

different ways. Contractors, including Anderson, needed to adjust to building opportunities in these and other suburbs. Minneapolis expansion had pushed Richfield at a steady pace toward total development well before the Second World War. In the years following that conflict, builders such as Gust Fallden and Arvid E. Carlson & Son typically chose small one or two-block areas upon which to build. Richfield subdivisions averaged 9.66 acres, or about two city blocks. Of 176 early postwar plats, 107 were five acres or less.[3]

Edina grew in the years after the war, but not at the frenetic pace seen in Richfield and later in Bloomington. Its hilly landscape dotted by lakes made for attractive home sites, though it was not amenable to large tract-style

This 1956 photograph of Grover's Station at 78th and Portland shows a small outpost on the Richfield–Bloomington border, in the path of future Interstate 494.

The kitchen and dining area of a suburban house was small, but in advertising jargon, "efficient."

distance from the heart of Minneapolis's business district, Bloomington's postwar expansion started later and took longer to complete. Once under way, however, the growth spurt was remarkable. By the late 1950s, bulldozers were leveling the Bloomington plain with relentless precision, and houses arose, blocks at a time, in their wake. In 1953 the city held 12,600 people. Ten years later the population was 60,000 and rising.[5]

Marv Anderson and his wife, Luella, moved into Bloomington after the war and raised two children

development. The community's reputation as an upper-middle class suburb, first established by the Country Club District in the 1920s, persisted. At that time, Edina became the first Minnesota village to take control of development through use of lot restrictions and zoning ordinances. Builders there constructed higher-priced housing on larger, more costly lots during the postwar years and continued to find willing buyers.[4]

Bloomington's development followed the pattern cut by inner-ring suburbs like Richfield. Because of its greater

An advertisement for Marv Anderson's Blue Ribbon Homes

there. He jumped into the expanding Bloomington housing market in the 1950s and became its leading builder. He eventually put up 3,247 houses, outpacing second-placed Orrin Thompson's number by more than 1,000.[6] He advertised heavily, using a catchy jingle as a musical signature for promos boosting his "Picture Book Home" concept. Like them or not, the words and music burned into the mind of Twin Cities radio listeners:

Let Marv Anderson build it for you,

A Picture Book home that's stylish and new,

We'll build you a home, a real paradise,

A Picture Book home at a practical price,

So, let Marv Anderson build it for you!

Over the years Marv Anderson's home-building strategies evolved. In 1952 he started construction of his Bloomington Picture Book Homes, a grouping of small three-bedroom ramblers near 81st Street and Portland Avenue. Two years later Marv Anderson Homes introduced the four-bedroom, bath-and-a-half, "family-size" rambler that sold for $16,795. In 1956 he shifted gears and included in his inventory "split-level" houses that clearly separated living and sleeping floors and ranged in price from $16,000 to $24,000. These homes marked a step up in size and features.[7]

Anderson continued building through the 1970s before selling the business to his cousin, Marlin Grant, who later sold the firm to Pulte Homes. Marvin Anderson died in February 1998. He is remembered as a leader in Twin Cities' suburban home construction. Indeed, thousands of Twin City suburbanites had eagerly let Marv Anderson and his house-constructing colleagues "build it" for them.

R-105 .... **4 ROOMS & GARAGE**

THE use of frame siding combined with brick and wrought iron trellis on the large open front porch gives the exterior of this home unusual interest. Note the practical arrangement of the dining area adjacent to the kitchen. All rooms are readily accessible from a central hallway. Both bedrooms are large enough for twin beds.

· **data** ·

Living area, plan 1—1120 sq. ft., plan 2—1178 sq. ft., Garage area, plan 1—245 sq. ft., plan 2—260 sq. ft., Porch area, plan 1 or 2—142 sq. ft.; Cubage, plan 1—25,095 cu. ft., plan 2—19,248 cu. ft.

PLAN 1
WITH BASEMENT

PLAN 2—WITHOUT BASEMENT

Pictured is a standard floor plan for the three-bedroom rambler, a postwar favorite of home buyers. This blueprint labels the front hallway a "rec hall."

THE MURDER OF FRED BABCOCK

For the many rural villages and towns ringing America's great metropolises after World War II, the change from a peaceful farming community to a fast-paced, heavily populated American suburb could be startling. Along with the typical changes brought on by suburbanization—new sewers, new paved roads, new schools and acres of new housing—were unwanted aspects of urban life. In the summer of 1949, crime came to Richfield in a particularly ugly and tragic manner—the murder of a police officer trying to halt a burglary in progress.

The phone call reached Richfield police around one a.m. Saturday morning.

Eugene Reynolds, 7620 Garfield, had returned home from a baseball game and through his bathroom window saw some men behaving suspiciously behind the National Tea grocery store, located off West 76th Street. He also noticed an unusual light coming from a car parked between his and neighbor Walter Milford's vehicles. Reynolds phoned police about what he had seen.[1]

Richfield officers Fred Babcock and Leroy Poulter, on patrol in a squad car, received the report and headed to the scene. Babcock, at the wheel, slowed the car as they neared the store. Poulter stepped out and headed toward the building while his partner drove on to Garfield and pulled up in front of the Reynolds house.

Poulter neared the back of the grocery when he heard the screen door slam on the far side of the store. The

Law enforcement agencies of six states combined in the search for Babcock's murderers. The chase would end in Kansas.

officer stumbled momentarily, and as he regained his balance he heard Babcock's voice. His partner had stopped alongside the Reynolds car, shined a spotlight on a suspicious vehicle, and ordered its occupants out.

Suddenly, a man carrying a rifle ran from behind the Reynolds house toward the spotlighted car. The rifle-toting man fired once at Babcock and then ducked behind the left front fender of the Milford car and got off a second shot. The shooter steadied his rifle on the auto and pulled the trigger twice more. Babcock, who had not returned fire, fell to the street, bleeding heavily. Poulter and neighbors who witnessed the event attempted to assist the mortally wounded officer, but Fred Alton Babcock died within minutes of the shooting. The former Marine, 26, had been filling in on the Friday night shift for another officer.

Police uncovered the entire burglary plot within hours of the crime. Four St. Paul men, three with extensive criminal records, had teamed up to commit the break in. As Babcock drove up, Gustav Johnson, Jr., 29, was attempting to pry open the grocery store door. Johnson heard shouts and gunfire and raced back to the group's get-away car, only to see it and his accomplices disappear without him. Several hours after the shooting, Minneapolis police, summoned to assist with the case, caught Johnson in Bloomington near Lyndale and 90th Street.[2]

Leading the criminal gang were brothers Arthur and Carl Bistrom. Arthur, 37, had spent six years in St. Cloud Reformatory (1930–36) for grand larceny. He served part of a five-to-ten-year sentence in a 1937 St. Paul robbery, with an additional Minneapolis term that kept him locked up until 1946. Carl, 27, served terms in St. Cloud and Stillwater prisons for auto theft and third-degree robbery. He was paroled in 1948. As a

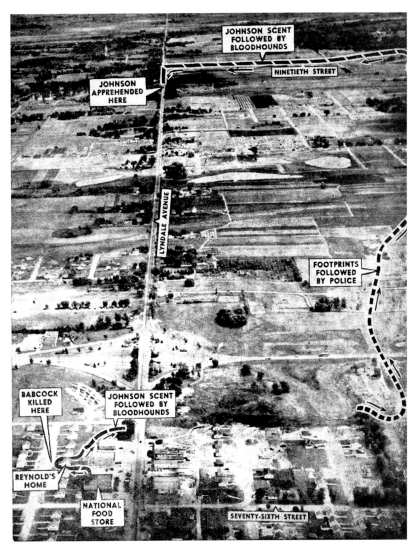

This newspaper photograph traces the first chapter in the tragic June 1949 murder of Richfield police officer Fred Babcock. Three of the men involved in the burglary and shooting at the National Tea store escaped, while police tracked down and arrested a fourth suspect near the crime scene.

youth, Gustav Johnson had been sent to the St. Paul Boys Farm program and the Red Wing Training School, in both cases for burglary, and later was given seven years in Stillwater for assault and robbery. Allan C. Hartman, a 20-year-old with no criminal record, rounded out the quartet.[3]

The Bistroms and Hartman fled in Hartman's Oldsmobile convertible, heading for North Dakota. Richfield, meanwhile, mourned the loss of Fred Babcock. The former Marine master sergeant, a decorated combat veteran, had spent 38 months in the Pacific theater during the war. He and his wife, Lorraine, lived at 1407 East 66th Street with their two children. Richfield's Junior Chamber of Commerce began coordinating community-wide, fund-raising events for the Babcock family, taking in nearly $9,000 in its first week.[4]

On Sunday morning, Mandan, North Dakota, police officer Ralph Senn stopped Hartman's car, unaware of its dangerous occupants. Police in Bismarck had spotted the auto and its wanted occupants, but word hadn't yet reached Senn. The Bistroms surprised and captured the officer. They threw him in the back of his squad car and drove south in the police vehicle. Senn asked his captors what they intended to do with him. Arthur Bistrom growled, "We'll dump you when we're good and ready."[5]

Carl Bistrom did most of the talking as the men drank coffee and nervously watched for unwanted visitors. Mrs. Buhrman later told a reporter, "They said no one would come up that lane alive."

A growing army of state and federal lawmen, aided by local police throughout the region, now knew the general whereabouts of the St. Paul gang and moved in. They watched the bridges crossing the Missouri River, while Iowa officials shut down its western border using heavy police patrols. Somehow, the fugitives managed to avoid authorities as they traversed South Dakota back roads.

The Bistroms and Hartman crossed into Nebraska where they released Senn, unharmed, at three a.m. Monday morning. Within minutes they stopped 16-year-old William Walz and sped off with his 1947 Plymouth and the teen as well. An hour later they left Walz and his vehicle for a blue Ford with Nebraska license plates. During the seven hours that followed, they pulled off a string of three Nebraska carjackings, taking and later releasing H.O. Langmeier outside Randolph, then kidnapping and soon freeing Mr. and Mrs. A.R. Andrews near Wisner. At 11:15 a.m. the trio seized Ray Falke at Norfolk.

Just before noon the gang barged into a farmhouse occupied by the tenant, Evelyn Buhrman, 23, and her three children. They held the family and Ray Falke at gunpoint on the West Point, Nebraska-area farm. Carl Bistrom did most of the talking as the men drank coffee and nervously watched for unwanted visitors. Mrs. Buhrman later told a reporter, "They said no one would come up that lane alive."[6]

But when the farm's owner, Fred Hatteman, drove into the yard, Carl Bistrom simply took him prisoner and ordered him inside. As they waited for dark, the trio discussed their options. Then, at eight, Carl Bistrom and Allan Hartman left. Art Bistrom stayed behind, saying, "We'll just sit here and listen to another news broadcast. Then you can call the sheriff."[7]

Bistrom waited two hours before handing his pistol to Evelyn Buhrman, allowing the other men "a good chance to get clear." Local police took him to the Wisner, Nebraska, jail. There, he talked freely to the authorities and claimed his brother had been the one who actually shot Officer Babcock.[8]

At Seward, Nebraska, 50 miles to the south, policemen James Skinner and William Kuds spotted a parked car with door ajar in an alley. "We thought kids might be in it," said Skinner. As they investigated, a man with a pistol confronted them. Another person, with a gun in each hand, appeared. The strangers took the officers' guns and ammunition, along with $1.50 cash, disabled the police car and drove off.

The Seward policemen noticed another man with the two fugitives. This was Bill Beaty, Jr., a hitchhiker who Bistrom and Hartman had pickup up earlier. Officer Skinner believed Beaty was a hostage, yet he did not appear to have any intent to escape.

Now, Carl Bistrom, Hartman and Beaty disappeared, driving through a heavy thunderstorm as authorities hustled to corral them somewhere near the Nebraska-Kansas state line. At four a.m. Tuesday morning their car crashed at a washed-out bridge in northeast Kansas. The bloodied Hartman left Bistrom and Beaty unconscious in the car and walked to the farmhouse of C.H. Smith for help. Smith went to the accident scene and recognized the car as the one the missing fugitives had reportedly been driving. He saw two men inside, neither one conscious. The farmer hurried off to phone in a report.

Smith then quickly rounded up a handful of neighbors who, armed with shotguns, returned to the scene. When the sheriff arrived at 8 a.m., the two men were still in the car and not moving. Authorities

took them, along with Hartman, to a Marysville, Kansas, hospital for treatment. Bistrom and Beaty suffered serious injuries, including fractured skulls, and by noon had yet to regain consciousness. Police formally arrested the suspects in the Marysville hospital later that day.

On the day of the capture, while the assailants of Officer Babcock languished in hospital beds or jail, Richfield gathered to bury its fallen police officer. All businesses closed for the funeral services, after which a procession of vehicles more than a mile long wound its way to Fort Snelling cemetery. They were met by a crowd of thousands of Richfield citizens and other mourners.[9]

An honor guard of fellow Marines laid Fred Babcock to rest.

Commies! The 1950s "Red Scare" in South Hennepin

It all seemed so terribly confusing in 1950.

Less than five years after thoroughly defeating the evil axis of Fascism during the Second World War, it appeared the United States was under threat again. The Soviet Union, the enemy this time, had been one of America's wartime friends. The increasing power of the Soviet Union, a confederation of states dominated by Russia, grew powerful and became master of Eastern Europe. And if that wasn't enough, Communist forces in China, another American wartime ally, subjugated that country and aligned with the Soviets.

The United States and its western allies had little time to relax following their resounding Second World War victory. Communist nations, led by an expansive Soviet Union, soon challenged America, ending "The Easy Life" for Americans, according to this July 17, 1950, Minneapolis *Star* cartoon.

In the aftermath of World War II, Communist nations appeared more than a match for the democracies of the United States and Western Europe. The Soviet Union, the world's largest country in size (taking up one-sixth of the Earth's surface) also pulled six Eastern European nations into the Communist orbit. On October 1, 1949, China's new pro-Soviet leadership proved equally intimidating, taking control of the world's most populous nation and creating the People's Republic of China, soon to be commonly known in the West as "Red China."[1]

THE END OF AN INTERLUDE

Powerful Soviet weaponry also concerned America and its allies. In August 1949 the Soviet Union detonated an atomic bomb, becoming the first Communist country to possess the super weapon. Worried Americans learned secret agents working for the Soviets had stolen atomic bomb secrets, and the search for spies, Communists, turncoats and double agents was on.

Then in June 1950, Communist forces in North Korea charged into democratic-leaning South Korea, threatening to overwhelm that nation. United States military forces led a United Nations-launched rescue effort to Korea, and

America was back in a shooting war. With the Soviets and Red Chinese supporting their communist brethren, it appeared the Korean conflict would be a long one. Twin City newspapers were already reporting the names of local dead and wounded in this Asian conflict.[2]

Atomic Bomb Threat to Bloomington and Richfield

The United States scrambled to reorganize its civil defense system to meet the new threats. The Soviet Union possessed atomic weapons and was busily building aircraft that could reach American targets. An alarmed U.S. defense establishment needed to get a public still recovering from World War II ready for a possibly bigger challenge.

Richfield and Bloomington civil defense organizations hustled to get started. Wold-Chamberlain Airfield, situated on the border of the two communities, was a likely target for Russian attack, and citizens needed to prepare for war. Editor Oscar B. Strand's September 14, 1950, Richfield *News* warned, "If the Russians attack either by atomic bomb or the so-called block busters, Richfield must be ready to care for the homeless, wounded—and dead." The newspaper carried a front page "Dollars for Defense" coupon, a collection being taken for civil defense. Wrote Strand, "each village" must care for itself.[3]

The following week Herbert E. Kossow of Bloomington, along with Richfield's Rollie Schweiger, both local civil defense chairmen, called a joint meeting regarding the threat. Reported the Bloomington *News*, the forum was "to prepare people against possible atomic and other bomb warfare by Russia…."[4]

Editor Strand, who ran both the Bloomington *News* and Richfield *News*, warned that the upcoming November general election would be "directly connected with the threatened atomic bomb which every mother and father fears for their children and themselves." He reminded readers, "The bomb, America knows, is in Russian hands," and Chinese Communists, together with Communist Russia, might widen the Korean War.[5]

The frustrated editor asserted angrily, "It is a well known fact that Russia could drop a one-way 'suicide' bomb near Bloomington at any time and Civilian Defense chiefs have tried almost vainly to get people to realize this fact." Strand reported Bloomington civil defense leader Kossow had learned "50% or more lives can be saved if we are prepared against atomic or other bomb attacks…."[6]

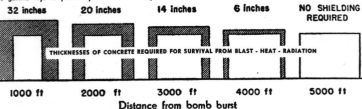

Worrisome pamphlets explaining to citizens how to prepare for a possible enemy attack circulated around the nation, including this page from a Bloomington publication, *The Atom Bomb and Your Survival.* It tells people how to build a bomb shelter in their own homes. Nearly 7,000 were constructed in Minnesota.

BLOOMINGTON CIVILIAN DEFENSE CORPS
IMPORTANT INSTRUCTIONS
Hang up for future reference; it may SAVE YOUR LIFE!

Mr. and Mrs. .... whose address is ...., and whose phone number is ...., have accepted the responsibilities and duties of Block Warden in your block which is listed in the records of the Bloomington Civilian Defense Corps as Area No. _12_, Block No. _5_.

Block wardens have many duties and perform them without pay. Please cooperate with them to the fullest extent, at all times.

Air raid alarms, as well as other warnings of anticipated disaster, will be given as follows: Fire department siren will sound continuously and your Block Warden or an appointed substitute, will drive past your house several times, sounding his or her auto horn.

When you are thus warned, take the following precautions immediately:

6 Survival Secrets for Atomic Attack

Always Put First Things First and

1. Try To Get Shielded
If you have time, get down in a basement or subway. Should you unexpectedly be caught out-of-doors, seek shelter alongside a building, or jump in any handy ditch or gutter.

2. Drop Flat on Ground or Floor
To keep from being tossed about and to lessen the chances of being struck by falling and flying objects, flatten out at the base of a wall, or at the bottom of a bank.

3. Bury Your Face in Your Arms
When you drop flat, hide your eyes in the crook of your elbow. That will protect your face from flash burns, prevent temporary blindness and keep flying objects out of your eyes.

Never Lose Your Head and

4. Don't Rush Outside Right After a Bombing
After an air burst, wait a few minutes then go help to fight fires. After other kinds of bursts wait at least 1 hour to give lingering radiation some chance to die down.

5. Don't Take Chances with Food or Water in Open Containers
To prevent radioactive poisoning or disease, select your food and water with care. When there is reason to believe they may be contaminated, stick to canned and bottled things if possible.

6. Don't Start Rumors
In the confusion that follows a bombing, a single rumor might touch off a panic that could cost you your life.

Five Keys To Household Safety

1. Strive for "Fireproof Housekeeping"
Don't let trash pile up, and keep waste paper in covered containers. When an alert sounds, do all you can to eliminate sparks by shutting off the oil burner and covering all open flames.

2. Know Your Own Home
Know which is the safest part of your cellar, learn how to turn off your oil burner and what to do about utilities.

3. Have Emergency Equipment and Supplies Handy
Always have a good flashlight, a radio, first-aid equipment and a supply of canned goods in the house.

4. Close All Windows and Doors and Draw The Blinds
If you have time when an alert sounds, close the house up tight in order to keep out fire sparks and radio-active dusts and to lessen the chances of being cut by flying glass. Keep the house closed until all danger is past.

5. Use The Telephone Only for True Emergencies
Do not use the phone unless absolutely necessary. Leave the lines open for real emergency traffic.

This card provided as a Community Service by your friendly
RICHFIELD STATE BANK
6608 Lyndale Ave. So.   PL 6867

On November 16 the Richfield *News* grabbed the attention of readers with a startling front page story, "A Letter to Joe About Your Home!" dated July 10, 1970—20 years in the *future*. The fictional missive described what had happened to unfortunate Richfield during an aerial attack on Wold-Chamberlain Field. Some bombs missed the airfield and devastated the village.[7]

The letter from the future told of a lack of preparedness in the community. Local civil defense officials could not overcome "the smug security" of a populace holding a "collective opinion" that they were in no danger. But then the bombs started falling.

The front page message described a truly frightful scene: Richfield in the wake of an attack by enemy bombers. Anarchy reigned. "Wild, undisciplined mobs" ran wild, giving way to "primitive emotions." Infected by " blind animal rage," the citizens attacked and murdered the few police officers and fire fighters responding to the disaster. Bombs and mobs destroyed municipal records, thus Richfield had to be governed "as a protectorate of its wiser neighbors."[8]

If this lurid story of chaos and death hadn't shaken Richfield enough, the *News* then gave residents a blow below the belt. In the fictional emergency, the state legislature ceded to Edina what was left of a bombed-out Richfield. Readers of the *News* knew the communities shared a common border and history, and a natural rivalry between the two was sometimes in evidence. Having Edina take over a shattered Richfield would be an ignominious end for the village.

The creative device of writing from the future allowed Strand to adopt an "I told you so" tone. The letter scolded those who said they were too busy to help or refused to organize a defense program. Richfield citizens needed to act. Each family was expected to send a dollar to

ADDED ATTRACTION

YOU'RE A LIAR!

YOU'RE A SPY!

COLD WAR DIPLOMACY

MINNEAPOLIS STAR

Uncle Sam tries to deal with "Cold War Diplomacy" while American politicians keep him off balance arguing about Communist spies.

Minneapolis *Star*, May 9, 1950.

The increasingly strident messages of warning were getting a reaction. The *News* advertised a speech to Richfield's Mothers Clubs, ominously labeled as "The Bomb, How will it Affect Us." University of Minnesota radiology expert Dr. Asher A. White actually titled his talk "Radiological Safety in an Atomic Bomb Attack." Richfield women's groups had a long and continuing record of community activism that often included leadership in current affairs and politics. That they sought expert advice on a new threat facing their community was not surprising.[10]

assist in creating a civil defense program, as well as volunteer their services to the organization.

On November 16 Bloomington *News* continued its campaign to arouse citizens to the danger of modern war. Col. E.B. Miller, Minnesota director of civil defense, assisted with a rousing speech in the community. The colonel was "indignant and alarmed at the lack of interest in civilian defense not only in Bloomington but all over the area." Miller asserted, "It is likely that Minneapolis will get bombed some winter night and their water supply knocked out."[9]

Herbert Kossow, meanwhile, chided residents of Bloomington who, to his mind, continued to ignore the danger. In a letter to the *News* editor, he renewed the charge that some in the community were not helping civil defense officials. And now, he added a new claim: some citizens were "actually hindering it (civil defense preparations) and, by talking against it, ridiculing the program…." He reminded everyone what was at stake, writing, "[It's] a known fact that Wold-Chamberlain Airport is high up on our enemies list for early attention in case of war."[11]

As director of Bloomington's newly formed Civilian Defense Corps, Kossow organized a comprehensive survey of the town. He wanted to know how many people were living in each home as well as the number of cars, telephones and radios they possessed. He was also beginning to recreate the World War II-era system of air raid wardens.[12]

As the new year opened, Bloomington's Oxboro Theater announced it would show a two-minute film, "You Can Beat the A Bomb!" In Richfield, Rollie Schweiger told of local preparations "in case our enemy should strike." The community had civil defense control centers at Lincoln Park and Central Park schools. National and state civil defense leaders, meanwhile, were marshaling resources to defend against a possible attack.[13]

Readying for the Onslaught

Minnesota's Office of Civil Defense warned that a military strike against America would mean World War III had started, and "nothing short of TOTAL WAR would result." State and federal governments would mobilize. The office reported the Air Force designation of Minneapolis, Duluth, Brainerd and Rochester as state air raid warning centers. Officials created plans to evacuate civilians from stricken communities, started developing a system of public air raid shelters equipped with food and water, and organized a national public warning system that would use television and

By DAVID LAWRENCE
Why Are 1,000 Commies Centered on Capital?

Throughout the early 1950s, Americans worried that Communist spies had infiltrated United States governmental agencies. Sensational trials, particularly those dealing with the theft of atom bomb secrets, kept the nation on edge.

radio to advise the populace. Meanwhile, school children practiced air raid drills.[14]

Citizens received instructions on how to build a bomb shelter attached to their own home or adjacent to it. The plans included information on thickness of a concrete wall needed to withstand the shock, heat and radiation from an atomic blast. One Twin Cities bomb shelter plan noted encouragingly, "some crude, semi-buried shelters only 900 feet from ground zero" had withstood the American A-bomb dropped on Nagasaki, Japan, during World War II. Minnesotans built 6,841 basement or backyard bomb shelters.[15]

America and the Soviets continued to perfect super-weapons, and by 1952 the United States had developed a hydrogen bomb, vastly more powerful than an atomic device. The first hydrogen bomb, detonated on a Pacific island, created a four-mile-wide fireball that rose five miles into the sky while creating a 175-foot-deep trench in the ocean floor. The Russians set off their own H-bomb nine months later. No wonder civil defense specifications for civilian identification bracelets called for metal "with an extremely high melting point"— specifically, 2600° Fahrenheit.[16]

Edina Takes Cover

By 1955 Edina had taken measures to protect residents from enemy attack, stocking eight shelters with food, water, medical and sanitation supplies enough to last 11,000 persons two weeks. The community promised an additional eight areas would be provisioned and available for another 26,000 people.[17]

Fallout shelters in Edina and elsewhere soon featured federal government-provided emergency materials. Boxes of food—crackers, biscuits, bulgur wafers and hard candy—enough to supply each person 10,000 calories for two weeks, took up much of the shelter space. Fiberboard drums served as the first water containers but were later replaced by 22-inch-high steel barrels lined with plastic and holding 17.5 gallons of water. When emptied, they become toilets. Fiberboard sanitation kits, once their contents were removed, also converted into toilets. Medical kits and instruments to measure radiation completed the shelter inventory. In July 1964 Edina's Southdale

Mall received four semitrailer loads of approved supplies for its lower-level shelter.[18]

A drawing of a devastated and dying metropolis shrouded by a large mushroom cloud produced a suitably terrifying cover for *The Atom Bomb and Your Survival*, the 1951 Twin Cities civil defense booklet published by Bloomington-based WDGY radio.

Bloomington-based WDGY radio produced this 1951 atomic bomb survival guide.

The manual's cover made a strong case that Twin Citians needed to prepare for nuclear attack. Such printed images of these massive bomb explosions, coupled with television and movie theater newsreel coverage of the real thing, led many to believe that such a super-bomb showdown would make long-term survival of humankind doubtful.[19]

The survival manual carried sobering letters from a chorus of local leaders. Minneapolis Mayor Eric Hoyer wrote, "By use of the global bomber in modern warfare, the city of Minneapolis is vulnerable to an attack by a foreign enemy." Edward Delaney, mayor of St. Paul, reported, in case of attack, "it will be practically impossible to eliminate all the enemy bombers before they deal their deadly and destructive missiles." U.S. Senator Hubert Humphrey offered, "Russia has the atomic bomb. We know this, and we know that Russia has the means to deliver it."[20]

Treachery from foreign agents added to the worries of Americans now bewildered by a new Red Scare—the sensational trial of a Soviet-run spy cabal that stole atomic bomb secrets while operating within the United States. On March 29, 1951, a jury found four members of the spy ring guilty. Two defendants received prison terms, while Julius and Ethel Rosenberg, a husband and wife team, were executed. Defections of double-agents, spy trials, congressional investigations, and FBI reports, all leavened by heavy media coverage—

> *"The Russians set off their own H-bomb nine months later. No wonder civil defense specifications for [American] civilian identification bracelets called for metal "with an extremely high melting point"—specifically, 2600° Fahrenheit."*

particularly television and motion picture newsreels—made Americans suspicious of anything Communist-related. "Better dead than Red" became an American mantra.[21]

America's Red Scare and the fears of atomic warfare that accompanied it during the 1950s morphed into a new kind of conflict called the Cold War—a period of sullen mistrust and suspicion in which political battles at times sparked smaller but deadly regional wars. The Cuban Missile Crisis of 1962 came breathtakingly close to triggering a catastrophic nuclear exchange between the Soviet Union and the U.S. That near-disaster led to an agreement between the United States and Soviets to install safeguards that controlled use of their nuclear arsenals. For both sides, the Cold War years consumed thousands of lives and billions in treasure. This long stressful struggle ended with the 1991 collapse of the Soviet Union.

Cold War scholar John Earl Haynes described the gnawing fear under which the people of Richfield, Bloomington, Edina and the nation lived, particularly in the early 1950s, as they grappled with and then came to understand the threat of nuclear warfare. Wrote Haynes, "[Americans faced] the constant psychological pressure of maintaining a strategic nuclear capacity which, if ever used in the context of nuclear war with the Soviet Union, would have also destroyed most of the United States and ended modern civilization."[22]

PICTURING BLOOMINGTON AND RICHFIELD:
THE NORLING AND ADELMANN COLLECTIONS

To the great good fortune of those interested in south Hennepin County history, Irwin Norling and Robert Adelmann shared an abiding interest in photography. They used photos to document the stories of Bloomington and Richfield, the towns in which they lived. Both men took and also collected photographs that, together, covered some 80 years of community events ranging from the commonplace to the unusual. Upon the deaths of Norling and Adelmann, their families donated the men's photo archives, appropriately enough, to those dedicated to the preservation of local history. Today the public can access the Adelmann and Norling collections at the Bloomington and Richfield history centers. In 2008 Minnesota and Bloomington Historical Societies cooperated in publishing Suburban World: The Norling Photographs. *The photos that follow come from the collections of both Adelmann and Norling.*

Bloomington's fire department responded to this February 1956 fire. Community services were improving after the decision to organize as a village in 1953, following 95 years as a township.
Norling Collection

Irwin Norling photographed this February 1960 fatal head-on collision on the old Lyndale Bridge. He worked with the Bloomington Police Department as a volunteer photographer.
Norling Collection

Fisher's Oil Station and Eat Shop on the south side of 78th Street between Lyndale and Nicollet is pictured in 1932. Cleo Salden is to the left and Grover Ehrhardt, right. Fisher's sold White Mule gasoline, fuel with a "kick."
Adelmann Collection

Rudy Adelmann, Louis Peske and Joe Alt cut ice at Diamond Lake in this 1915 photo.
Adelmann Collection

A potato picking crew takes a break on the Elmer Haeg farm on the southwest corner of 24th Avenue and 66th Street in the 1940s.
Adelmann Collection

Ed Fyten stands between two Greyhound buses at the 78th Street and Lyndale bus stop in November 1930.
Adelmann Collection

A row of 1960 Studebaker Larks are lined up at the Osterberg dealership in Bloomington.
Norling Collection

The Bloomfield community on the Bloomington-Richfield border was little more than a post office, church and trading point, yet those living in the area developed real loyalty to it. Pete Scholz, with his foot on the axle, stands next to a truck from Bloomfield's Scholz General Merchandise store. His brother-in-law Merle Blaylock is to the right.
Adelmann Collection

George Degan and George Christian try to get their wind-powered ice boat underway.
Adelmann Collection

Local television personality Clellan Card hosted a popular afternoon TV show for children titled "Axel and His Dog." He also made appearances at community events such as this one in Bloomington.
Norling Collection

Children pose next to a placid Grass Lake in 1912.
Adelmann Collection

Esther A. Bowles's Happiness Troupe rides in a Ford convertible during a June 12, 1954, Bloomington parade.
Norling Collection

Apprehensive Bloomington children prepare for their shots.
Norling Collection

Wards Southtown, Bloomington's newly-opened shopping mall at Interstate-494 and Penn Avenue South, is pictured in November 1960.
Norling Collection

The William T. Collins circus drew a large crowd to the Richfield-Bloomington border at Interstate-494 and Chicago Avenue during a 1987 visit.
Adelmann Collection

-Five-
Suburban
Satisfaction

In the years following the Second World War's end, America's suburbs struggled to keep pace with the phenomenal growth of their communities. Providing the basics—schools, water and sewage treatment, streets, police and fire protection— seemed a never-ending struggle. Yet cities like Richfield, Edina and Bloomington were maturing by the mid-1960s. They now had what was needed and then some—excellent housing stock, modern shopping and business centers, new school facilities, maturing parks, updated roads and sewer systems, and low crime rates. It was a good time to be a suburbanite.

SHOPPING TOWN, USA

Victor Gruen, architect of Southdale Shopping Center, America's first indoor retail mall, asserted in 1960 that, when properly designed, such facilities assume "the characteristics of urban organisms serving a multitude of human needs…thus justifying the designations: Shopping Towns."[1] Using Gruen's definition, Edina and Bloomington became the national leaders in establishing trendsetting retail centers.

During the early post-Second World War era and throughout the 1950s, the Twin Cities and their suburbs held a distinction of compelling interest to developers: The metropolitan area had one of America's lowest population density rates.[2] That meant plenty of developable land remained within easy reach of builders and their bulldozers.

The downtown districts of both Minneapolis and St. Paul still dominated the retail shopping scene in 1950, but some suburban entrepreneurs had hopes of stealing at least a few of their customers. With the population in communities such as Richfield, Edina and Bloomington growing rapidly, developers readied to serve a legion of potential consumers by building shopping centers. Certainly the need for suburban retailers existed. By 1955, residential construction still "…accounted for 80 percent of the value of all building permits in the principal developing suburbs of the Twin Cities."[3]

Builders erected auto-oriented shopping centers at busy and visible street intersections, but, unlike downtown districts, parking was free. Richfield's HUB center at 66th Street and Nicollet Avenue opened on February 25, 1954, serving as an example of the new wave in suburban retailing. The HUB advertised itself as "The Center of the Wheel of Richfield–Bloomington Progress," and enticed car owners with the pledge, "…it takes less time to drive to 'The HUB' than it takes to find parking in other parts of town."[4] Developers of such outlets did well, but, according to one detailed study of the trend, "underestimated the requirements of the private automobile and the size of the retail market." It pointed to the HUB as an example of centers that were too small and poorly sited at "chronically congested" intersections. Noted one observer in 1956, many shopping centers "…already are suffering from downtown's biggest headache—inadequate parking in peak hours."[5]

The HUB proved a hit with shoppers, becoming a leader in "customer preference" among the 20 Minneapolis suburban shopping centers that had been developed between 1955 and 1959. The Richfield complex featured a J.C. Penney store, three women's clothiers, Walgreen's Drug Store, hardware, appliance, and jewelry stores among its 24 retailers. Shoppers listed the HUB, along with Knollwood Plaza and Miracle Mile in St. Louis

Richfield's HUB Shopping Center opened in 1954 and by the end of the decade had attracted strong support from suburban shoppers.

HUB SHOPPING CENTER OPEN EVENINGS

66th & NICOLLET
OPEN EVERY EVENING

Park, as their top three favorites. But by October 1956 a new kind of shopping complex stood ready to steal the hearts of suburban shoppers.[6]

Edina Bombshell

"A $10 million bombshell with far-reaching social and economic implications for Edina exploded Tuesday in the form of a proposed shopping-residential center." The headline in the June 19, 1952, Edina Morningside *Courier* called attention to a plan to build a 500-acre, $15-million development (early cost figures varied) known as Southdale. An 84-acre indoor shopping center lay at the heart of this proposed retail complex. Donald C. Dayton, head of the well-known Twin Cities Dayton's department store chain, personally brought his formidable proposal to the public. Unlike his competitors who had chosen busy neighborhoods for their shopping plazas, Dayton would build in a sparsely settled corner of Edina.[7]

Dayton's architect, Austrian-born Victor Gruen, was charged with breathing life into the revolutionary Minneapolis south suburban project. He would build a "shopping town," a full-fledged community with a traffic-free shopping and residential district, recreation and entertainment areas, parks, lakes, office space, and sites for a hospital, schools and churches. Housing districts were planned for three general locations—north of West 66th Street (189 lots), south of West 66th and west of France Avenue (191 lots), and east of Southdale (87 lots)—with construction slated for completion in May 1955.[8]

Donald Dayton dealt his shopping center designer a strong hand. Gruen held three aces: ideal year-round shopping conditions in his indoor, three-level enclosed building, acres of free, well-lit on-site parking, and easy road connections for his auto-driving customer

base. The architect had heard about terrible Minnesota winters, "But here (Southdale)," he said, "flowers will grow, birds will sing and it's going to be spring."[9]

In an unguarded moment, the quotable Gruen put forward another, less grand, reason for building a shopping center at West 66th and France. "Families move to the sprawling suburbs where the women are bored to death and there is no social life because they are too far removed from the center of things." Gruen saw "bored" women both as potential shoppers and partakers of other shopping center opportunities—art fairs, concerts, community events and more.[10] He viewed local residents as, "involuntary suburbanites (who) don't like to drive miles into the cities."[11]

Dayton understood the business opportunities waiting in the targeted Edina-Richfield border area. He chose the site "because the section is growing rapidly and because much of the Dayton Company's downtown trade comes from that area."[12] Dayton was correct about the area's growth. Richfield's population stood at 17,502 in 1950, a total that would nearly double four years later. Edina held 9,744 residents in

An announcement of The HUB's February 25, 1954 grand opening

1950, a number that grew in five years to 17,000. In another telling development, total 1954 sales at America's suburban shopping centers surpassed those of downtown retailers for the first time. This occurred as construction of Southdale commenced.[13]

Although scheduled for a largely undeveloped section of east Edina, Dayton said of this new shopping town, "We are planning to create a community. We are not being put into an already existing community." Edinans forgave Dayton's overreach—the sparsely settled Southdale site was located in Edina near the Richfield border, still within the village boundaries—but they had questions about his plans.[14]

Edina, with the creation in the 1920s of the Morningside neighborhood and the Country Club District, committed to becoming a community of single-family

homes. The Edina village council modernized its municipal government in the late 1920s, passing ordinances that protected its housing developments from unwanted businesses that could be "dangerous, hurtful, unwholesome, offensive and unhealty [sic] to the neighborhood."[15]

When Donald Dayton showed up with his plans for commercial development in 1952, some Edinans greeted him with skepticism. Dayton's design promised increased village tax revenues while challenging the single-family housing concept, a tradition residents still favored. The Southwest Edina Better Government Association later worried, "Will it be necessary to condemn hundreds of brand new homes in Edina for the proposed Southdale highways?"[16]

The powerful vision of Southdale, shared and promulgated by Donald Dayton and Victor Gruen, gradually brought community members on board. "Southdale is not the usual strip-of-stores plan.... We'd like to have residential, park, road and recreational development," said Dayton. Gruen viewed the enclosed shopping center as a "crystallizing force for this sprawling suburban area," and expansively declared, "[Southdale] is the town square that has been lost since the coming of the automobile." They planned on creating a unique alternative to downtown Minneapolis.[17]

Along with the seemingly unlimited

The HUB targeted both the Richfield and Bloomington markets when it opened. Residents responded to the "one stop" shopping center concept.

promise of modernity touted by its developers came a reminder of Edina's past. Samuel Thorpe, Jr., son of the prominent developer of the Country Club District in the 1920s and a member of the village planning commission, handled local land acquisition for Dayton. He resigned his commision role when the plans for Southdale were announced.[18]

A National Story

Following a special preview for those living near the new Edina shopping complex, Southdale staged its official Grand Opening on Monday, October 8, 1956. Marty Rud, the mall's publicity director, marveled at the national interest in the project. "We had coverage that you could not have even hoped for," Rud recalled. All major publications, including the New York *Times*, *TIME*, and *Life* magazine, sent representatives. Minnesota newspaper reporters joined the crowd.[19]

Southdale is "the last word in modernity," wrote James Holton, real estate editor for the New York *World-Telegram*. Holton said the retail center left him "a bit breathless." *FORTUNE* described the center's look as "strikingly handsome and colorful." Syndicated columnist Sylvia Porter called the shopping center "the newest symbol of [a] revolution in retailing" that had taken place after World War II. America, she noted, now (1956) had "between sixteen and eighteen hundred shopping centers...against next to zero only 10 years ago."[20]

"Families move to the sprawling suburbs where the women are bored to death and there is no social life because they are too far removed from the center of things... involuntary suburbanites [who] don't like to drive miles into the cities."

Victor Gruen, architect of the Southdale complex

Observers had yet to come up with an acceptable name for this new kind of shopping complex—Gruen informally called it a "satellite downtown" in 1954. Eventually the Southdale complex in Edina, and its enclosed, climate-controlled imitators, would be known as shopping malls.[21]

TIME reported in its feature "Pleasure-Domes with Parking" that Southdale and other mammoth suburban shopping areas were "designed to siphon shoppers from an entire region." The weekly news magazine declared free parking lots, never more than a few hundred feet from entrances, were attractive to women shoppers. "With an eye out for women drivers," noted a chauvinistic *TIME* magazine writer, some centers allotted nine-foot parking slots, wider than the standard eight feet. Southdale made its parking spaces nine-and-one-half feet wide, angled at 45 degrees, advertising it for the "convenience of all."[22]

Upon its opening, 60 stores filled the mall, anchored by long-time retail rivals Dayton's and Donaldson's department stores. In a counter-intuitive move, Donald Dayton decided to enlist his retailing adversary as a tenant, believing their traditionally strong competition would result in more customers for both. Donaldson's management agreed to the deal a year before the mall's opening. Dayton's was still Southdale's largest retailer with 195,000 square feet and 164 departments, while Donaldson's covered 140,000 square feet. The mall's organizational plan called for fashion and specialty shops on its top two floors, hard goods on the lower level, and service shops plus a kiddie land entertainment center at the basement level. Tenants filled 58 other retail outlets or offices in the indoor mall. There were only two vacancies.[23]

Southdale's opening weekend proved a monumental success. "A tidal wave of shopper-spectators (188,000) and a battalion of experts from every field of trade and industry opened the giant Southdale shopping center in Edina…," reported the St. Louis Park *Dispatch*. "They came away mumbling in incredulous amazement at the nation's newest and most unique experiment in suburban shopping…."[24]

Marty Rud hustled to elevate the excitement and interest level in the shopping mecca. Within two months he had the Twin Cities talking about Southdale's Cruise Show, an exciting concept for a Minnesota January. The program included five stages used by 120 "beautiful models in their skimpy resort outfits," recalled Rud. "We continued to do spring and fall shows," he added. Visitors flocked in from all over the Upper Midwest.[25]

Rud recalled Bob Barker bringing his popular national television game show *Truth or Consequences* to Southdale for an entire week. The center later hosted

three-ring circuses with the Hammond-Morton Shrine Circus, art shows, a Hawaiian Show, yearly Easter animal farms for children, a *Sports Illustrated* special featuring national sports stars and three symphony balls. Southdale created, with assistance of Great Britain's Vice-Counsel Gene Harrison, British Trade Shows so popular that mall officials followed up with similar programs for all Western European countries. Dag Hammarskjold, Secretary-General of the United Nations, attended one such event.

The "Southdale effect" appeared in a survey of Minneapolis and suburban women in 1957, a year after the mall opened. A study of shopping trends showed 62 percent of the suburbanites visited the new mall during the year compared to 38 percent of city shoppers. Two years later the same survey showed 72 percent of suburban women had gone to Southdale in the year preceding the survey, while 49 percent of the Minneapolis group had. Asked which

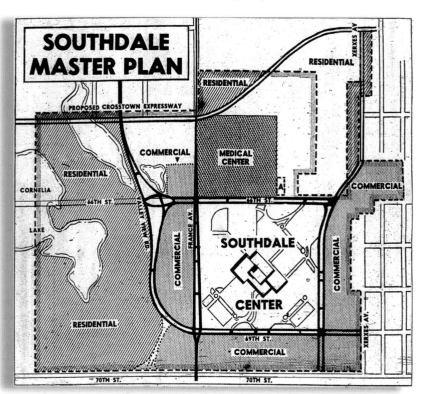

A preliminary plan for the proposed Southdale complex in Edina

shopping center they frequented most often, 30 percent of the Minneapolis women surveyed answered Southdale, with The HUB their second choice at 9 percent.[26]

Southdale's popularity and profitability led Dayton's to expand the "Dales" franchise, building Brookdale (1962), Rosedale (1969) and Ridgedale (1974). Indoor malls based on the Southdale template flourished throughout the nation but were showing signs of major shifts in tenants. At opening, 95 percent of Southdale's retailers were based locally. Chain stores found a home in the malls, steadily driving out local entrepreneurs who were unable to compete. Department stores such as Dayton's and Donaldson's had been regional powers, but larger national chains began absorbing their smaller rivals.[27]

Major cities, including Minneapolis, fought malls for market share. They closed downtown shopping streets to traffic and created pedestrian malls. Smaller rivals found they could benefit from the traffic created by their larger competitors. Developers erected modest strip shopping centers at the periphery of the indoor malls to pick off a share of the customers.

Critics Find Fault

Developers jumped on the indoor mall bandwagon, and as their retail centers multiplied, critics began taking shots. Familiarity, it appeared, bred contempt. A 1966 indictment, perhaps over-enthusiastically, called them "graceless buildings [that] are little more than merchandise barns," part of a larger "squalor-of-affluence spreading across the U.S. like a Technicolored fungus mold."[28] Even Victor Gruen, the architect of Southdale, became frustrated with his failure to fill what he originally saw as a suburban "vacuum created by the absence of social, cultural and civic crystallization points…." Gruen had claimed, in 1954, that he wanted to recreate "an old architectural form—the square or plaza. There people may relax—not just shop."[29] The architect later abandoned suburbia and became a city planner, revamping American urban downtowns.

Gruen eventually returned to his native Austria where he disowned his most famous creation, the American shopping mall. In 1978 he gave a speech, *The Sad Story of Shopping Centres*, detailing how his vision had been corrupted by American big business that adopted "only those ideas that proved profitable." He made that claim despite the fact he had openly promised profitability for Southdale. The bitter architect concluded with the declaration, "I refuse to pay alimony for those bastard developments."[30]

Here's How You'll Locate Car at Southdale

Free and ample parking for Southdale customers was part of the mall's allure. A system of well–labeled parking areas helped patrons remember where they left their cars.

A Megamall Challenge

While some still saw the Southdale-style enclosed mall as the perfection of American retail architecture, others were preparing to challenge Gruen's shopping towns. In 1981, developers of the West Edmonton Mall in Alberta, Canada, introduced their "megamall," a super-sized indoor shopping and entertainment center that boasted 800 stores, a hotel, amusement park, water park, zoo and 438-foot-long lake all under one roof. In the number of retailers alone, it was roughly Southdale times ten.

Pleased with their Edmonton triumph, the Ghermezian brothers—a quartet of Iranian-born Canadian real estate investors—looked to build another megamall, this time in the United States. They targeted Bloomington, Minnesota, and the former site of Metropolitan Stadium as home for their Mall of America. Despite Bloomington's concerted efforts to save the Met, the 1982 creation of a Metrodome sports venue in downtown Minneapolis made the old stadium obsolete. The Ghermezians and their Triple Five Corporation moved forward with the new megamall, later ceding project leadership to Melvin Simon

Southdale, the nation's first enclosed shopping mall, promised shoppers protection from Minnesota weather. This winter scene shows parking lots crowded with cars.

& Associates. Appropriately, they labeled their novel concept in American retail architecture the Mall of America (MOA). Its location in Bloomington was just 10 minutes away by car from the pioneering Southdale complex.[31]

Victor Gruen had viewed Southdale as a complete and civilizing "shopping town" for the new American suburb. Builders of the Mall of America hoped to convince visitors that they were entering a new kind of community that combined shopping and fantasy. The megamall was themed in its architectural design, with a diversity of stores and entertainments. Shopping in the MOA would be, in management's terms,

like "exploring different neighborhoods in an exciting new city." Four large retail outlets, Nordstrom, Sears, Bloomingdale's and Macy's, were linked by "distinct shopping streets"—North Garden, "a summertime shopping experience," West Market, "an international marketplace," South Avenue, "cosmopolitan," and East Broadway, a "contemporary, high energy avenue." The shops surrounded seven-acre Camp Snoopy, an entertainment park and its 26 rides.[32]

Along with its promise of a new kind of shopping experience for its customers, designers of the Mall of America provided a sprawling seven-acre indoor entertainment park.

Regarding plans for the new complex, the New York *Times* asserted, "the difference between the Mall of America and an ordinary shopping mall is the difference between a space station and a bus station"[33] Nader Ghermezian beamed, "You will love us, we will love you, and everybody will love it."[34] These were challenging words for Southdale and its sister malls that had won the hearts of many Minnesota shoppers. The old retail centers were now more similar to the *Times'* description of an "ordinary" mall than the MOA.

Twin Cities regional shopping centers fought to keep pace with their new challenger. In advance of the Mall of America opening, Southdale and Rosedale embarked on major makeovers, downtown Minneapolis launched a two-year "Do the Town" marketing campaign, and Rosedale Center in Roseville opened 22 new stores. Edina's Galleria expanded its footprint by 180,000 square feet, and

the city's traditional retail crossroads at 50th and France underwent an $11-million renovation.[35]

The MOA complex opened on August 11, 1992. The giant mall drew enormous crowds of the curious jockeying for position as they made their way around the grounds. A Minneapolis *Star Tribune* poll indicated about half the state's adults visited the mall within eight months of its opening. The important early news to the mall's retailers was good. MOA's assessments indicated customers were staying longer and spending more when compared to shopping trips by patrons of smaller malls.[36]

Mall of America's flashy start electrified the Minnesota shopping scene. Was an updated version of Gruen's Shopping Town a new apotheosis in American consumerism? In late summer 1992, this was a question about the future that no one could possibly answer.

THE MET: LURING BIG LEAGUE BASEBALL TO BLOOMINGTON

Americans never had it so good. As the only economic superpower in a war-ravaged world, the United States supplied two-thirds of all manufactured goods consumed by other nations. The country's work force saw income nearly triple by 1955, and a new middle class emerged that included 60 percent of America's families.[1]

How then, in this unparalleled period of growth and good times, could major league baseball, the nation's premier sports organization, be in a slump that would have embarrassed the game's weakest batsmen? More importantly, what could baseball do to halt the decline?

Unless you lived in America's northeast or the industrial corridor skirting its Great Lakes, viewing a major league baseball game in 1950 was a challenge. Big league ball quite naturally flourished in the nation's largest population centers with their guaranteed fan bases, but was out of reach for many. The majors had 16 teams operating in 10 large cities. New York City alone had three clubs—the Giants, Dodgers and Yankees—and four other towns had two each—Chicago (White Sox and Cubs), Philadelphia (Athletics and Phillies), St. Louis (Cardinals and Browns), and Boston (Red Sox and Braves).

Followers of baseball in America's North Central, Southern, and Far West regions tended to maintain a dual team allegiance.

They cheered their favorite major league ball clubs at a distance, while turning out in person to support a vast network of minor league competition. The minors were major elements in 1950s American

The Minneapolis Millers served as the Triple A minor league farm club of the New York Giants. When efforts began in the early 1950s to bring major league baseball to the Twin Cities, it seemed a given that the Giants would be the team moving to Minnesota.

Minneapolis *Tribune*, June 22, 1955

MINNEAPOLIS CHAMBER OF COMMERCE

1750 HENNEPIN AT GROVELAND TERRACE
NORTH AMERICAN LIFE AND CASUALTY BUILDING
MINNEAPOLIS 3, MINNESOTA

baseball, from the top rated AAA leagues and down through AA, A, B, C and D levels. "Town team baseball" had also flourished across the nation since the 19th century, with nearly every village and town boasting clubs. African American players, banned by racial codes from advancing to the major leagues, formed the Negro leagues.

Some Triple A baseball clubs developed a devoted fan base and reputations for producing great baseball. In the Twin Cities, fans could see the 1950 editions of the American Association's Minneapolis Millers and St. Paul Saints battle the league's Louisville Colonels, Milwaukee Brewers, Kansas City Blues, Toledo Mud Hens, Columbus Red Birds, Indianapolis Indians and, of course, each other.

While Americans continued to demonstrate their love of the national pastime, major league team baseball owners nervously pored over attendance figures and balance sheets. They saw disturbing signs. Big league baseball crowds were diminishing. Despite the booming economy and growing wealth of the populace, attendance at games peaked in 1948 at 21 million. The 1949 numbers showed a modest drop to 20.2 million, but by the end of the 1950 season, the figure had plunged to 17.5 million. The major leagues were becoming New York oriented. That city hosted the

1949 and 1950 World Series, the first two in a string of 10 straight New York championship playoffs.[2]

Aging ballparks, some in deteriorating older sections of cities, were shoehorned onto small sites with little parking, a major issue for an increasingly auto-dependent society. In the dynamic postwar American culture, baseball was going out of style. The game, in the words of one observer, was a vestige of another time, "…one that held ever less appeal for a nation moving to new split-level homes in the suburbs. The game was old and America was not interested in old."[3]

Bring on the Braves

While nervous owners fidgeted, baseball-minded entrepreneurs in cities across America were scheming to bring major league ball to their towns. The nation's largest metropolitan areas without baseball included Los Angeles, San Francisco,

> *"In the dynamic postwar American culture, baseball was going out of style. The game, in the words of one observer, was a vestige of another time, '…one that held ever less appeal for a nation moving to new split-level homes in the suburbs. The game was old and America was not interested in old.'"*

Earthmovers carved the outline of the future Metropolitan Stadium as construction began in summer 1955.

other communities wide-eyed with wonder, and no one was watching more closely than leaders in Minneapolis and St. Paul.

The Boston Braves managed to make it to the 1948 World Series singing the famous refrain "Spahn and Sain and Pray for Rain"— Warren Spahn and Johnny Sain were the team's one-two pitching punch—but in 1952 the club

Baltimore, Minneapolis-St. Paul and Buffalo. In Minneapolis, Jerry Moore, president of the Chamber of Commerce, urged Charlie Johnson, the influential sports editor of the *Star* and *Tribune*, to make inquiries regarding franchises to the commissioner of baseball. Johnson was assuming a role he would play for nearly a decade: impresario of a movement to bring major league sports to Minneapolis—barring that, to the Twin Cities.[4]

Other communities were also interested in big league ball, and Milwaukee was on the march. In 1951 that city broke ground for County Stadium, a ballpark for its Triple A Brewers. The Brewers never got to use it. The struggling St. Louis Browns and Boston Braves eyed the new venue as a possible home and began maneuvering to move to Wisconsin. The National League gave the Boston club—it already possessed a working relationship with the minor league Brewers—the go-ahead. The Braves immediate and remarkable success in Milwaukee left

neared collapse. Braves attendance in 1948, a profitable 1.5 million, slumped to 281,000 during the 1952 campaign. Less than a month before the 1953 season opened, Braves owner Lou Perini announced the Milwaukee move. In the first year at their new home, the Braves drew 1.8 million fans. The following season more than two million attended. They doubled the average attendance of the seven other National League clubs. Baseball-mad Milwaukee stamped mail "Home of the Braves," police calls dried up during radio broadcasts of games (none were televised), while department stores tuned radios to Braves coverage to keep customers happy.[5]

In early 1953, Minneapolis and St. Paul teamed up to create a major league baseball committee. Bill Boyer, Lyman Wakefield and Kenneth Dayton represented Minneapolis, and Fred Sperling, Walter Seeger and Don McNeeley made up the St. Paul contingent. The committee expanded in June 1953, adding more influential citizens to their lineup. Among the group's first moves was an August lobbying effort to convince St. Louis Browns owner Bill Veeck to move his club to the Twin Cities. The Minnesotans took their case to a New York meeting of American League club owners the following month, but the league approved a Browns move to Baltimore.[6]

Milwaukee emphatically proved that a new venue captured the interest of major league club owners—and the Twin Cities most certainly needed a new ballpark. Nicollet Park at 36th and Nicollet was home to the Minneapolis Millers and was "pretty well done for," in the words of Tommy Thompson, Minneapolis city engineer from 1948– 1967. A Navy man and a civil engineer, Thompson later served as city manager,

1967–1978. Nicollet field, built in 1896, was cramped and needed major repair. Similarly, St. Paul's Lexington Park could not meet major league requirements. A new big league stadium was needed, but in which city would it be built?[7]

The Twin Cities major league baseball committee soon fractured over a predictable fault line—their inability to agree upon a site for the new ballpark. St. Paul preferred a location in its industrialized Midway area, while the Minneapolis group took a hard look at a St. Louis Park location just west of the downtown district. The Mill City faction then shifted its interest to a site near the Minneapolis-St. Paul International Airport, conveniently located at the intersection of the Twin Cities' fastest growing suburbs, Bloomington and Richfield. The Minneapolis Minutemen, a group of 16 ten-person sales teams, got to work raising $4.5 million to build a Bloomington ballpark at 8000 Cedar Avenue.[8]

St. Paul, meanwhile, had already moved into the ballpark-building lead. Voters passed a $2 million stadium referendum in November 1953. Walter Seeger, a member of the St. Paul half of the Twin Cities baseball committee, guided the effort. The Seeger family, of the Arcade Street refrigerator factory that bore their name, was a leader in supporting St. Paul institutions. The city planned to build on its Midway site.[9]

Minneapolis Moves

Minneapolis moved forward as well. Jerry Moore used a letter from a Milwaukee *Journal* executive to preface his July 1954 Minneapolis baseball committee prospectus regarding a major league baseball facility for the Twin Cities. Said the newspaperman, "Big League Baseball put Milwaukee on the map and brought it into national prominence more quickly and more completely than anything else in the community's history. That includes our reputation for beer."[10]

The exploratory committee working to secure major league baseball discovered a unifying theme during their talks with team owners. Moore wrote, "...a number of major league franchise holders were eyeing with intense interest the Twin Cities area," but then cautioned, "…major league owners would not (commit to move) until adequate major league stadium facilities were available."

Minneapolis committee members, in the midst of their stadium fund drive, passed on a July 1954 opportunity to buy the Philadelphia Athletics franchise. Creditors of Connie Mack, the legendary owner of the Athletics, met secretly with newspaperman Charlie Johnson, a member of the baseball committee. They would sell Mack's team for $3.2 million, with half needed for a down payment.

A skeletal Metropolitan Stadium is shown on April 10, 1956. The Bloomington ballpark debuted just 15 days later when the Minneapolis Millers hosted Wichita.

When Minneapolis declined, the A's headed for Kansas City in 1955 to play in the city's refitted Blues Stadium that now held seating for more than 30,000.

Those making the Twin Cities' case for major league baseball centered upon the need for a new stadium. Big league franchises that had already moved reinforced their point. After losing out to the Braves in Milwaukee, the St. Louis Browns headed to Baltimore in 1954 when the city added a second deck to its four-year-old Memorial Stadium. The A's shifted to Kansas City in 1955 to play in an expanded ballpark.

A bidding war for major league teams was under way—terrific news for club owners still worried about waning fan support. The 1948 high point that produced 21 million fans at the ballparks seemed ages ago in light of the 1954 attendance figure of 15.9 million. It was a loss of nearly 25 percent. Walter O'Malley and Horace Stoneham, owners of two of baseball's most storied franchises, the Brooklyn Dodgers and New York Giants, were among those thinking about greener pastures.

O'Malley's Triple A farm club happened to be the St. Paul Saints, and the Giants' Triple A affiliate was Minneapolis. When plans to replace the Giants' Polo Grounds ballpark fell through, Stoneham looked to Minneapolis as a new home. O'Malley preferred to stay where he was, having been led to believe he would soon have a new stadium for his Dodgers. He was blindsided by a furtive veto from the imperious Robert Moses, the "emperor" of New York, who had the power stop any city project he didn't like. The Dodgers boss began to consider leaving town.[11]

Stoneham later recalled, "I was unhappy playing in the Polo Grounds. The ballpark was old, and it was darn near impossible to finance one in that area. I had intended to go to Minneapolis. We had a ball club there so I had rights to the area...Also Minneapolis was well within transportation range of the league (National). Aviation at this time had been accepted by everyone."[12]

Newsday writer Stan Isaacs confirmed Stoneham's recollection. When plans for a new stadium in New York City fell through, the reporter remembered the owner's decision to leave. "His first choice was Nordic Minneapolis," wrote Isaacs, "the lilliest of lily-white suburbs."[13]

Horace Stoneham did more than just talk about Minneapolis. In the spring of 1951 he had purchased the 40-acre St. Louis Park site that later came under consideration for the proposed major league baseball stadium. By January 1954, with the Braves profitably ensconced in Milwaukee and the Browns and Athletics packing their bags, Stoneham nearly jumped on the bandwagon that could bring him to Minneapolis. During a lengthy planning session in his hotel suite, Stoneham told George Brophy, the Millers general manager, he would bring his New York Giants to Minneapolis.[14]

Building a Ballpark

Minnesota's state legislature moved into the major league ballpark debates in March 1955 by approving a Metropolitan Sports Area Commission, controlled by Minneapolis, Bloomington and Richfield. It was charged with handling issues regarding the new stadium. A Minneapolis *Star* editorial claimed forming the commission showed "Minnesotans mean business."[15] In May, the Minute Men completed their bond sale providing funds to purchase 164 acres of Bloomington land from 28 property owners in the area bordering 78th Street (the Beltline) and 81st Street, along with Cedar Avenue and 24th Street. The cost was $487,899.[16]

Recalled Minneapolis city engineer, Tommy Thompson, "Richfield, Edina and Bloomington were developing fast, both in numbers and a certain amount of sophistication. The idea of a ballpark appealed to a lot of the citizenry and, of course, location was a big question." Thompson mentioned discussing the

Met Stadium's grandstand, with which Minnesota baseball fans would become very familiar, begins to take shape in spring 1956. It was believed a major league baseball club would be making its home here in short order.

land sale with one Bloomington landowner while in the popular Smokey's Barbecue, located at present-day Cedar Avenue and Interstate-494.[17]

This September 6, 1956, view looks south over Richfield's southernmost housing district to Met Stadium and beyond.
Norling Collection

Thompson, echoing the feelings of many Minneapolitans, stated, "I felt, when we were getting the Met Stadium deal done, that perhaps major league ball out there [in Bloomington] was a bit of a fantasy." Yet city residents had great affection for their longtime minor league club, and getting a new ballpark for them was a plus. "[T]aking care of the Millers was considered a heckuva good idea by just about all involved," observed Thompson. "You have to remember that they were really popular at the time and they had some great players, too."[18]

The Sports Commission had to include both Bloomington and Richfield, even though most of the money for the park would be supplied by Minneapolis. Bloomington had natural prerogatives as the new stadium's hosting community, but Richfield supplied a more basic need. The water supply in Bloomington could not handle the ballpark's needs, and Richfield, after years of rancorous debate, had begun modernizing its water and sewage system in 1953. The commission thus included Richfield representation.[19]

Last-minute disputes over land cost were settled, and ground breaking took place on June 20, 1955, with 500 people in attendance. Minneapolis Miller team manager Rosy Ryan declared, "...major league baseball is closer than you think." The *Tribune* reporter on hand did not lead with the construction angle, instead he opened, "Amid increasing talk about the possible transfer of the New York Giants to Minneapolis, the first shovels of earth were turned Monday for the Bloomington stadium."[20]

Talk about a possible New York Giants move took place over lunch at the Nicollet Hotel. Stoneham sent his head grounds-keeper to Bloomington to help lay out the new field, and word was passed that "All stadium plans are being submitted to Horace Stoneham...for approval."[21]

The three-tiered Metropolitan Stadium neared completion in spring 1956. Its reinforced steel and concrete

Metropolitan Stadium was constructed with possible expansion of its seating areas in mind. Seats along the left field line were among the first added, as this late 1950s photo shows.

Stadium facts...

Foul line distances (right and left)	316'-3"
Center field distance	405'-0"
Height of Centerfield fence	8 feet
Height of Tubular Steel Light Towers (14)	138 feet
Height of Light Towers on Stadium (2)	154 feet
Structural Steel (450 tons steel deck)	1,650 tons
Reinforcing Steel	540 tons
Concrete	8,400 cu. Yds.
Brick	1,300,000
Pipe Rails	4 Miles
Outside aluminum fence (10' high)	1.650 ft. long
Number of Turnstiles	32
Number of Concessions	16
Number of Public Washrooms	12
Number of Lockers in Home Team Locker Room	50
Number of Lockers in Visiting Team Locker Room	44
Length of Dugout	51 feet
Height of Center Field Flagpole	100 feet
Height of Uppermost seat above playing field	83 feet
Overall height of Stadium	93 feet
Length of Stadium measured along back wall	567 feet
Number of Ramp Towers (16' wide ramps)	2
Number of Doors	220
Elevation playing field below stadium entrance	16 feet
Parking Lot Capacity	15,000 cars

superstructure soared over the Bloomington prairie with stadium light towers reaching 154 feet. The grandstand ranged from home plate and along the first and third baselines. More seats were placed along the left field foul line, with bleachers built behind both the right and left field fences. The Met held 18,300 people but could be expanded upon the arrival of a major league team.

The Minneapolis Millers played American Association rival Wichita, Kansas, before 18,366 spectators on April 25, 1956, and inaugurated the new Bloomington ballpark. The field carried the name Metropolitan Stadium. If any fans were dreaming about major league action, George Brophy brought them back to earth. He complained that the Millers lost three dozen baseballs hit into the capacious seating areas, noting balls "cost three dollars each."[23]

On June 26 Commissioner of Major League Baseball, Ford Frick, viewed a game at the new venue and proclaimed to a meeting of its bond holders, Metropolitan Stadium "…is a tribute to Minneapolis [that] proves you are truly big league."[24] Horace Stoneham, also on hand for the occasion, received prolonged applause. A reporter had earlier quoted the Giants owner before the April 25 opener as saying, "This is a real major league park, and you'll have major league ball here in the near future."[25]

That team wouldn't arrive for another five years, and when major league baseball reached Minnesota, it wouldn't be with Stoneham's Giants. In spring 1957, an aggressive contingent of Californians attempted to lure the two available New York clubs to the Golden State. San Francisco would go after Stoneham, and Los Angeles would pursue Dodgers owner, Walter O'Malley. As spring training closed, Stoneham told the Brooklyn boss he still planned on moving to Minneapolis. O'Malley, now in the Los Angeles camp, suggested the Giants owner consider San Francisco. The National League wouldn't allow the Dodgers to move unless Stoneham shifted west as well. In the end both clubs, to the great disgust of their longtime fans, took the California option.[26]

"Horace Stoneham was darn well coming; he had as much as said so!" noted Tommy Thompson. "But then he fell out of bed on the project when he was lured out to California by Walter O'Malley. I've always felt there might have been more involved…than just O'Malley, like the league had a say."[27]

The New York Giants baseball team left the Polo Grounds for the last time on September 29, 1957. As the players headed for their center field clubhouse, fans chanted, "We want Stoneham! We want Stoneham! We want Stoneham with a rope around his neck!"[28]

In distant Minnesota, a jilted bunch of major league baseball fans no doubt would have been happy to join in the refrain.

Major League baseball officially arrived in Bloomington's Metropolitan Stadium on April 21, 1961. The Minnesota Twins hosted the Washington Senators.

On Being Goliath

According to Biblical lore, soldiers who faced the nine-foot-tall Goliath, and those who heard of his showdown with the teenaged David, longed to see the Philistine warrior lose. The phrase "David and Goliath battle" is among the most tired of sports writing clichés. When traditional powers meet supposedly weaker unknowns, the public inevitably cheers for the underdog. What about the modern day giants, the New York Yankee-like perennial favorites confronted by legions of jeering sports fans? In the 1960s and 70s, outstanding Richfield and Edina high school sports teams often found themselves in Goliath-like roles.

Richfield High School's 1960 varsity basketball team

"A" SQUAD

BACK ROW: Bystedt, Barton, Werness, Gjerde, Lary. FRONT ROW: Johnson, Lutz, Alevizos, Davis (Capt.), Szepanski, Sadek, McLenighan.

Lanky six-foot-six Bill Davis, captain of Richfield's Spartans basketball team, jogged up the steps to the elevated Williams Arena court, followed by his teammates. As they ran onto the floor, a raucous unwelcoming chorus echoed through the building. "We got booed by 19,000 people," recalled Davis years later.[1]

The Spartans were about to play a critical role in one of the legendary sports events in Minnesota history: The 1960 ascent of tiny Edgerton Minnesota's Flying Dutchmen to basketball immortality in the state. Edgerton, a community of about 1,000, had come to the Minnesota State Basketball Tournament as fan favorites and prepared to collide with big city foes. Richfield, a still-growing suburban boomtown of 40,000, was represented by a squad rated number one in the state and selected by veteran coaches as the team to beat. The two schools met in the championship tournament's second round.[2]

Informal interviews for a front page news story, titled "Tournament Fans Like 'Little One,'" produced predictable comments. Asked whom she was cheering for, a 16-old from

Rochester said, "Oh I can't remember the name but you know—the little one." A Hibbing man smiled, saying he was "For Edgerton, of course. They're the darlings of the tournament." A St. Paul woman cheered on "the little farmers," adding, "I'd like to see the small town win," while a Worthington observer reported being "wild for Edgerton."[3]

This unscientific sample appeared quite accurate to Richfield players as they trotted onto the Williams arena floor in March 1960. Jeers from the crowd subsided, only to return, with gusto, to greet each Spartan as he was introduced during pre-game ceremonies. Said Bill Davis, "[W]e were the big school and everybody was pulling for little Edgerton. It was the small school. And the only ones cheering for us were our students...up in the balcony." The suburban squad was about to find out what it meant to be a basketball Goliath facing a very good small town club, undefeated at 24-0. Richfield would have to subdue the Flying Dutchmen and the packed house of screaming spectators who supported them.[4]

Considering fan interest, the annual high school basketball tournament ranked among the state's premier sporting events. In 1960, Minnesota had yet to field a single major league sports team. Davis pointed out, "There was the University of Minnesota and then there was Minnesota state high school basketball. The state tournament in hockey was just getting off the ground."[5]

"And this was a big deal. This was a big deal," said the Richfield captain, repeating his point nearly 50 years later. "It was on television. The newspapers were full of it. That's all we talked about."

The game itself was a see-saw affair of intense, exciting basketball that, at the end of the fourth quarter, was tied at 56-56. Players on both squads responded well to the pressure of overtime. But Edgerton made seven of eight free throws in the extra period to fend off clutch shooting by Richfield's Mac Lutz and Bob Sadek, and won 63–60.[6]

Richfield players and coaches put forth an excellent effort during the game and made an equally impressive showing following it. There may have been room for griping about the officiating from the Spartans, who made nine more field goals than Edgerton but watched the Dutchmen net 35 free throws. Richfield players and coaches offered no complaints about their harsh treatment from the Williams Arena crowd. A bitterly disappointed but generous Bill Davis paid tribute to the winners in a post-game interview with *Tribune* columnist Sid Hartman. "They deserved to win the championship. You'd figure a team from such a small town would crack under the pressure. Not this team."[7]

Other Richfield players, including Denny Johnson, Mac Lutz and Roger Alevizos, talked with reporters and praised the Dutchmen. Richfield head coach, Gene Farrell, was in the Edgerton locker room just 10 minutes after the game, congratulating the team, saying, "You played a wonderful game." Edgerton, again bolstered by crowd support, went on to beat Austin and win the 1960 state championship.[8]

A Richfield *News* editorial lauded the hometown team for its efforts—a performance that meant more to the suburb than the players might have known. "For years now, one of Richfield's few deficiencies has been a lack of community spirit. Perhaps this is an inevitable liability in a suburb. But a winning basketball team...can do more to stimulate civic pride than all the parades, dances, speeches and political campaigns of a hundred years of history." The newspaper later applauded team members for their "wholesome aggressiveness."[9]

Yet sports writer Jerry Hoffman spoke for many in Richfield who witnessed the shabby treatment dealt to the Spartan basketball tournament team by the Williams Arena crowd. Hoffman wrote just one sentence of complaint. "It is the first time that I have ever witnessed any crowd boo, roundly, a team that was being introduced." Considering their gentlemanly behavior during and after games, these teenagers deserved better.

In 2009 Bill Davis still remembered the crowd reaction when the Richfield

Richfield and St. Louis Park players struggle for position during a Lake Conference game.

basketball team ran onto the Williams Arena floor to meet Edgerton. People were everywhere, some sat in the aisles. "It was stunning as we first took the court, the roar of 19,000 people. And the jeers, yes. I think the team was taken a little by surprise, but we handled it well. During warm-ups the rhythm of getting ready was established and our focus was on the game, not the crowd. As the game moved along we could hear our fans cheering us, as well. They weren't completely drowned out."[10]

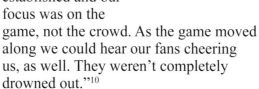

Bill Davis accepts team medals and trophies for Richfield's third place finish at the 1960 Minnesota State Basketball Tournament.

Davis continued, "It was a great ball game, and they (Edgerton) were really a solid team. They beat a good Austin team in the final and they were talented. It doesn't do much good to complain about the officiating in our game…. Both teams had key players foul out (including Davis, in overtime), and there's no question it was a hard fought battle….I'm proud of how we handled ourselves."

Members of that Richfield team are still asked about the Edgerton game today. Davis laughs, "If everyone who said they were at that game was actually there, it would have had to have been played in the Grand Canyon."

Other Richfield prep teams excelled during the 1960s, years when only one team in each sport could win a state championship. Spartan hockey teams reached the state tournament in 1962 and 1964, and its outstanding '64 football team was rated Minnesota's top squad.[11]

Members of Richfield's 1960 hockey team work out on the high school's outdoor ice rink.

But Richfield's powerhouse baseball clubs from that era drew the most attention statewide. The Spartans captured four state tourneys in an 11–year period and sent so many players to the University of Minnesota that coach Dick Siebert, a college baseball Hall of Fame member, called Richfield his "farm club." Three particularly dominant clubs earned special mention. Five members of the 1960 team, which Richfield coach Gene Olive pointed to as among his most outstanding, later played for Siebert's

a loss in 1968 broke that string. Edina entered the 1968 tournament looking for its third consecutive championship. With veteran senior center Bob Zender as its top player, it was the team to beat. It was also the club most high school basketball fans wanted to see knocked off.[13]

An undefeated Hayfield squad gave Edina a stern test during the basketball tournament's first game when they cut the Hornets once-healthy lead to 44–38. The Williams Arena audience screamed their approval of that development and begged

1964 National Championship team. The 1965 baseball Spartans recorded a perfect 25-0 season record, while the 1967 team overwhelmed the opposition by not surrendering a single run during the state tournament.[12]

Edina Takes the Heat

Edina's basketball Hornets assumed the unwanted role of Goliath as they dominated Minnesota State Tournament rivals in the late 1960s. The school won championships in 1966 and 1967 and rolled up 69 straight victories before

for more. Wrote one reporter about Edina's plight, "A lesser team might've folded under the pressure of a crowd hollering for its scalp, but the Hornets kept their cool." Hayfield finally wilted.[14]

Reporter Jim Kaplan explained what he termed "a psychological climate…not always pleasant" for Edina players. He continued, "Taking out their sociological frustrations on these sons of America's fourth wealthiest (per capita) community and their athletic frustrations on the onetime winners of a record 69 straight, fans outside of Edina's friendly

Richfield's 1960 baseball squad sent five players to Coach Dick Siebert's University of Minnesota team. They helped the Gophers win the 1964 NCAA National Championship. Siebert was soon calling Richfield his "farm team."

Bob Zender swats away a shot from a Bemidji player during a 1967 state basketball tournament game. Zender played on three Hornets state championship teams and later starred at Kansas State.

gymnasium often have been harsh."[15]

Edina heard fewer jeers during their second round 91-61 defeat of Duluth Central. Hornet coach Duane Baglien preferred to avoid discussion of what one reporter termed "the perennial raspberry his players get." The Hornets overwhelmed Central and quieted the crowd. "They didn't say much," reported Edina guard Mike Burley. "They just sat and watched." Edina players, used to the jeering, claim not to have been bothered in previous games either. "It gave us more incentive," said Burley. "The harder they cheered, the harder we tried." Observed Hornet team member Tom Miller after the Duluth game, "It's kind of subdued in here. That's good."[16]

With growing experience in the role of the heavily favored ball club, Edina basketball players accepted a fact they could not change: The Hornets would usually play the role of the bad guys in the minds of others.

Bob Zender, the 6-foot-8 center on Edina's three consecutive state championship squads, fondly remembers those seasons. "The late '60's Edina teams were very special. I consider it a once-in-a-lifetime coming together of some incredible athletes who were able to completely put aside ego and concentrate on the goals of the team. The guys who I played with were some very talented individuals who focused on winning games and had little regard for statistics. We usually had three or four players in double-figures, within a few points of each other." [17]

"When you have different leading scorers on a regular basis, that speaks to what I believe was the subjugation of ego on our squad. Great players, a smart team that could run fairly sophisticated offensive sets under coach Baglein, and a lack of selfishness were the key to our run."

Zender retains vivid memories of the loss that ended Edina's state-record-winning streak. It occurred on

Charlie Kelly, an Edina defenseman, checks an opponent into the boards during a 1970–71 season game. Kelly played on the Hornets state championship team that year.

the court of another Goliath of the 1960s—Richfield. "That's probably the game I remember best," Zender says with a laugh. "That was the loudest high school gym I ever played in, maybe the loudest anywhere, and they got the best of us that night. We had several tough battles during our winning streak, but that was the first time anyone had knocked us off in a long time."

Jon Nicholson was a ball-controlling guard and co-captain for Richfield that cold February night in 1968, and echoes Zender's recollection. Richfield used the energy in the packed Spartans' gymnasium to blast out to a 45-25 halftime lead, but Edina hadn't won 69 consecutive ballgames by surrendering. The Hornets clawed back to within eight, 57-49, entering the fourth quarter. They were still battling in the final seconds before Richfield's Doug Kingsriter, later a Gopher and Minnesota Vikings star, hit a streaking Nicholson for a breakaway lay-up to secure an 81-75 victory. "It was a tremendous high-school basketball game," says Nicholson, who had 17 points to back leading scorer Jim Thompson's 29.

The headline in the Richfield *Sun* read: "Proud Kids Go Down Fighting," but Edina was ready when the inevitable rematch was played for state tournament rights. "They (Edina) came back to win the rubber game against us at Williams Arena in the District final. There were 14,000 there for a District game— 14,000!" recalled Nicholson. "We felt we were among the best in the state, but the road was through Edina, and they proved they were champions."

Says Zender; "The Richfield game is very memorable, but the three state titles have to tell you the big story about our team." While Nicholson went on to play some college ball and become a successful Twin Cities businessman, Bob Zender became an All-Big Eight

basketball player at Kansas State and a business success. He speaks with great feeling about his Edina teammates of the late 1960s: Tom Cabalka, Bill Fiedler, Jay Bennett, Kurt Schellhas, Jeff Wright, Mike Burley, Jay Kiedrowski and all of the other Edina players who contributed to one of the most remarkable dynasties in Minnesota high school basketball history.

"We did get used to the experience of being the favored ball club," says Zender. "But we had to earn it, and we did, with a special group of guys and a great coach."

Kurt Schellhas maneuvers for position. He was a member of two of Edina's state champion basketball teams and one of four Hornet All-Lake Conference players in 1971.

Edina Hockey

Edina High School's hockey club took up where its basketball team left off. The 1969 Hornets didn't start out as favorites to win the state tournament— Greenway of Coleraine held that honor—but they captured a championship anyway. South St. Paul upset Coleraine in the first round but got trounced 7-1 by Edina in the semi-finals. That victory put the Hornets into the title round against tiny Warroad, setting up a big city/small town showdown. It resulted in a game still talked about today in state hockey circles.[18]

A talented Warroad club led by Henry Boucha stayed with the speedy Hornets, even after losing their star to a hard second period check. Spectators, who had been supporting the underdog Warriors throughout the contest, were further riled by Boucha's injury. The hard-fought, nerve-racking contest ended in a 4-4 tie, but Edina pulled out the overtime win for its first hockey state championship. There would be more.

Minneapolis *Tribune* hockey writer John Gilbert took a look at Edina's state champs and, with an understanding of the community's youth hockey system, pronounced it "one of the most productive…in the country." The headline on his column, "Edina, with First Hockey Title, has Personnel for No. 2," was accurate as far as it went.[19]

The Hornets returned to the tournament the following year and defeated Warroad once again, this time in double overtime. Edina then overcame St. Paul Johnson and its record-setting goalie Doug Long 2-1, also in overtime, before losing to Minneapolis Southwest 1-0, yet again in overtime. Despite their defeat in the final game, the tournament helped establish Edina as a "team to beat" in Minnesota high school hockey.[20]

That reputation grew in 1971 when Edina won another championship, but only after controversial plays in both the semifinal and final games. In the semifinals, the Hornets held a 2-1 lead over St. Paul Johnson when officials awarded Edina a disputed third goal. Tempers flared on the Johnson side of the ice, but the goal stood. Edina led late in the championship game 1-0 on a goal by winger Rick Wineberg when Roseau, their opponent, believed they tied the game. Officials didn't agree, and Edina held on to win.

The 1969–1971 tournaments established Edina as a premier prep program but also started a tradition of anti-Hornet sentiment that continued. To fans from outside the community, Edina hockey clubs displayed a winning combination of talent and good coaching with a penchant for great play at state tournament time. In 1974, sports columnist Sid Hartman wrote that Edina established "a record of dominance that might not be matched by any Twin City school in the future." During the six-year period beginning with 1969, noted Hartman, the Hornets "…either won the championship, finished second or won the Consolation championship."[21]

Over the years the Hornets dashed the ambitions of a number of great high school hockey teams, along with the hopes of Minnesota communities that supported them. Edina built a record to envy and a strong tradition of excellence along the way. Nearly four decades after those dominating days of the early 1970s, many followers of state high school hockey still hope to see a talented Hornet team knocked off come state tournament time.

In this team photo of Edina's 1971 state hockey tournament champions, Coach Willard Ikola is in the top row, far right.

ALL-AMERICA CITIES: RICHFIELD AND BLOOMINGTON MAKE THE GRADE

Both Richfield and Bloomington suffered serious growing pains during the years following the Second World War. Overwhelmed village governments struggled to deal with basic issues including inadequate water and sewage service, the need for road building and maintenance and the lack of schools. These neighboring communities earned All-America City status following major infrastructure improvements.

Some young Bloomington athletes show the community's 1960 All-America City banner in front of the town hall.

Along with sharing a border and history, postwar Bloomington and Richfield had an important yet disagreeable dilemma in common: what to do about a water and sewage problem that was growing steadily worse. Both communities lacked such public facilities, leaving homeowners to rely upon their own wells and septic systems. Richfield, and then Bloomington, faced serious health issues when skyrocketing population growth overtaxed the existing water safety procedures.

As early as 1946, Richfield's League of Women Voters pointed out that the city had 3,000 houses on lots of less than 10,000 square feet, all with septic tanks, and most with wells about 50 feet deep. League efforts produced a public vote to improve water and sewer service that earned strong support, but not the five-eighths majority needed to make the changes.[1]

Minnesota's 1949 polio outbreak hit Richfield the hardest of any community in the state, killing three and leaving 38 other surviving victims. The emergency raised concerns about Richfield's water supply. A Minnesota health department survey tested several wells and found "a little contamination." But Frank L. Woodward, the department's director, didn't like how the city's 4,500 wells were situated—nearly all in basements. Dr. John J. Heisler, Richfield health officer, stated, "the whole (sanitation) situation is bad."[2]

The Richfield City Council divided into what the community's manager, LeRoy Harlow, saw as a newcomer versus old-timer confrontation. Newer residents tended to support more costly improvement measures including sanitary sewers, while longtime citizens preferred to leave things as they were. Those new to Richfield also discovered favoritism

The National Municipal League

and LOOK Salute the

ALL-AMERICA CITIES

in the local tax system; assessed taxes on identical homes varied widely.[3]

One resident put the situation this way, "We had a Model T village government. The police station was closed most of the night, and in 1948, we had a single polling place for 4,000 voters." The reform-minded Richfield Tax Payers League organized, and voters put their members in control of local government. Federal officials settled the lengthy debate over sanitary sewers when they stopped issuing government-sponsored home loans to builders in Richfield until new housing could get access to a city water and sanitary sewer system. Sewer construction began in 1953 and concluded in 1956.[4]

The community faced another problem. With his hiring in 1944, Harry E. Rumpel, the forward–looking future superintendent of Richfield public schools, called for construction of a high school in the community. "Can anyone imagine a village of nearly 10,000 residents without a high school?" Apparently they could, because in 1950 the city had 17,502 citizens and was among America's largest communities *without* one.[5]

Leona Rumpel, left, of Richfield's Minnesota Valley Woman's Club, accepts a national award for the mid-1950s creation of a community Safety Council. Women's groups in Richfield traditionally held a leadership role in civic improvement projects.

Richfield finally solved that problem in 1954 with the opening of a new senior high school. The great majority of those students living in the city but attending Minneapolis high schools moved into the new building. Within a few years Richfield High was among Minnesota's largest.

In February 1955, the National Municipal League selected Richfield as a 1954 All-America City. The country learned of the honor in a *Look* magazine article. The publication reported, "Strange things happen when a tiny village increases its population tenfold almost overnight. Richfield, with no sewer system, had thousands of cesspools scattered throughout town." The community received praise for rectifying the situation.[6]

Look pointed out another major Richfield improvement, taking care of a tax fairness issue: "[T]ax bills on 12 identical houses varied as much as $175." The inequities were corrected and community activists credited with bringing change.

Bloomington Goes Big League

Bloomington and Richfield held historically close ties dating back to Minnesota's territorial days. The Bloomfield community that overlapped the borders of each village in the late 19th century was centered upon the German Catholic community's house of worship, today known as Church of the Assumption. The small crossroads' post office served residents on both sides of the towns' boundaries, as did Bloomfield School (District 88), a building located in Bloomington but open to Richfield children in the village's southeast as well.[7]

Mutual interests kept the two neighboring towns in contact during the years that followed. Entrepreneurs in these suburbs attempted to approach both communities simultaneously as when in 1954 Richfield's HUB advertised itself as "The Center of the Wheel of Richfield–Bloomington Progress," and when Northwestern National Bank opened a "Bloomington-Richfield" branch on 78th and Penn. The Chambers of Commerce of each city worked together, and even later two leading financial institutions, Richfield City Credit Union and Employees Federal Credit Union of Bloomington, merged to create the logically named Richfield Bloomington Credit Union. During the frightening early years of the cold war, the two neighbors toiled together to establish a civil defense plan of action dealing with atomic warfare.[8]

Bloomington felt the heavy impact of postwar population growth later than Richfield. Its population tripled to 9,647 between 1940 and 1950 but was well below Richfield's total of 17,502. Nevertheless, Bloomington's growth problems mirrored those of its neighbor. Nagging issues with homeowner reliance on septic systems and private wells became critical when the state department of health reported in July 1960 that 50 percent of Bloomington's wells held traces of sewage contamination. Over time, cesspool effluent had leached into the water. A central sewage and water system would cost about $20 million.[9]

A startled populace took immediate action. A sewer and water advisory committee was formed, pushed forward by the Chamber of Commerce and the League of Women Voters. A brigade

Bloomington made extensive expansions in industrial and commercial development during the late 1950s and early 1960s. This photo shows Ward's Southtown Shopping Center at Penn Avenue and Interstate-494.

of more than 1,000 volunteers brought petitions before Bloomington residents. Community members had been very supportive of public schools, passing every bond issue from 1949 onward. They also organized the Bloomington Athletic Association (BAA), a civic theater and a band. Now, they needed to take care of the dangerous sewage situation.

Bloomington was in the midst of its campaign to become an All-America City when the water contamination

Richfield's new senior high school is nearly ready for students. When it opened in 1954, the school enhanced the city's image.

The addition of Metropolitan Stadium and professional sports had a major effect upon the development of Bloomington. This photo shows the Met filled with spectators for a Vikings football game.

issue broke. It appeared to be a deal-breaker. A local team headed by Mayor Gordon Miklethun traveled to Phoenix, Arizona, to meet with a jury tasked to rule upon the community's All-America bid. George Farr, a member of the Bloomington Planning Commission, spoke to jury members addressing the sewage problem directly. He reported that the city had moved forward on a sewer and water project that was already producing pure water.[10]

Farr made a strong case for Bloomington. To bolster his argument he provided reports of the city's success in passing school bond issues, expanding parks and recreation and the adoption of a city charter. The fact that the city council had passed a policy statement in April 1958 calling for "encouragement and cooperation toward industrial and commercial development," was another major selling point. That decision spurred even more growth in the city.[11]

Bloomington's presentation featured some other news that impressed the judging panel. A new city charter had just been approved, along with an urban redevelopment proposal. The city proudly pointed to the Bloomington Athletic Association, community band and civic theater. The fact that Bloomington had just become a "major league city" as the home of the Minnesota Twins and Minnesota Vikings strengthened its already impressive resumé.

Duly impressed by Bloomington's arguments, the judging panel praised the "civic victories and living environment of Bloomington," and the "dedicated participation of thousands of citizens" that brought it about. They declared the community a 1960 All-America City.

EDINA AND THE "CAKE EATER SYNDROME"

In a nation teeming with post-Second World War suburbs, comparatively few earned any special distinction. Edina stood with this minority. Its reputation as "one of the wealthiest communities of its size in the country" eventually became known across the nation.[1] Later, some fellow Minnesotans attached a more unflattering label, "cake eaters," to Edinans, an appellation sometimes adopted by the national media. The pejorative comes from Marie Antoinette who, when consort of the king of France, became the first cake eater when she supposedly said of starving Frenchmen crying for bread, "Let them eat cake." A historical look at Edina and this "Cake Eater Syndrome" is in order.

Edina's history of economic prosperity dates at least to the 1880s and its formal organization as a Minnesota community. By that time, residents such as George and Sarah Baird, James and Mary Bull, Henry and Susan Brown, and Jonathan and Eliza Grimes had accumulated considerable wealth and lived comfortably in the rural community. Their fellow citizens also fared well, typically running farms on land of increasing value. Community leaders, including the Bairds, Bulls, Browns and Grimeses, did not, however, take on "airs." History tells us they were regarded as hard workers and important contributors to the new village.[2]

In the 1920s Samuel Thorpe, developer of Edina's Country Club District, was determined to have potential customers understand that he was building an upscale, restricted community. Thorpe's advertisements stated clearly the District would be "exclusive and select" while, at the same time, asserting Country Club would not be a "community of snobs." Nevertheless, the promoter required homeowners sign a formal agreement allowing Sam Thorpe to control everything

COUNTRY CLUB DISTRICT - *Thorpe Bros.*

While it is not the intention of Thorpe Bros. to make the Country Club District a community of "Snobs," it is and will be, by the very nature of its typography, restrictions, etc., "exclusive and select." A community where you can be proud to live, proud of your home, your grounds, and your neighbor's home as well—a place where you can rear your children with the freedom of mind that comes with knowing they are more protected than would be possible in any "hit or miss" city neighborhood.

"The Homesite Perfect"

When Samuel Thorpe opened his Country Club District in 1924, he used advertisements depicting the Edina neighborhood to be "exclusive and select" without being snobby. He achieved mixed results.

about the building arrangements, from the color of one's house to the color of one's skin.[3]

Thorpe's recipe for a successful housing development, roomy high-end homes constructed on spacious, more costly lots, naturally limited Country Club access to those with means. The cover of a promotional brochure for the District depicted powerful symbols of 1920s era wealth—a stylish, young female golfer with a couple riding horseback behind her and a golf clubhouse in the distance—illustrated the clientele expected to buy into the Country Club life. Thorpe's customers might or might not be snobs, but they would be wealthy. To America's agricultural and industrial workers of the 1920s, the good life depicted in Country Club's advertising was reserved for rich people, a lifestyle for which regular folks had neither the time nor the money.[4]

Those of wealth were not likely to identify with the working class. In the early 1930s, residents of Country Club chafed at being attached to Edina with its distinct but fading reputation as a rural precinct still run by farmers. A well-organized and funded effort by Country Club Association members, strongly supported by Sam Thorpe himself, moved the District toward secession from Edina. A formal proposal for separation in October 1931 included a budget for the new village along with several possible names for it—Edgebrook, Dry Gulch and Edina Mills. The movement focused on political autonomy, taxes and utilities, but conflicts about social class did not become part of the public discussion. Secession did not occur.[5]

The Crier, a free monthly magazine delivered to homes in the District, began publishing in March 1930 and became the unofficial voice of the Country Club District. It chronicled the lives

Golf Course from 18th Hole

The District's many amenities—including golf clubhouse, paved streets, sidewalks and sewer system—made it known as a refuge for the wealthy. By the 1930s, the neighborhood monthly magazine, *The Crier,* rated the Country Club among America's "four finest subdivisions."

The Club House

of Association members, their travels, parties, society news, sports events and the like. The magazine provided fodder for those who claimed the exclusive neighborhood was for haughty "high hats."

Country Club District in the late 1920s

A September article discussed the Minneapolis *Journal's* upcoming series on Country Club's "community of magnificent homes" and the opportunity to "educate the public in the matter of good taste in furnishing and decorating homes…." Readers would learn that, "Children who grow up in good surroundings, with pretty furnishings and comfortable living conditions are trained to like such things and will demand them all through life."[6]

In November 1931 *The Crier* printed a plea from Rufus Rand, chairman of the District's Community Fund, to assist those in need as the national economic depression deepened. He appealed to "every member of the family including the children and employees" to contribute money for the poor. Said Rand, "Many employees in our homes such as maids and chauffeurs are well paid this year in comparison to other workers and can well afford to give several times as liberally as they have in the past."[7]

Labeling Edina

Country Club growth slowed during the first years of the Great Depression, but building picked up in the mid-1930s as well as in nearby neighborhoods including South Harriet Park, White Oaks, Colonial Grove and Brucewood. This construction blurred the once clear boundaries of the District. Country Club Association would later join with Greater Edina Association to form Edina Civic Association. The newer subdivisions followed the Country Club model and fit in well with the residences of the District. According to architectural historians David Gebhard and Tom Martinson, such Edina housing, "…established a strong sense of place which is not often found in American cities."[8]

By now, however, the entire community had been labeled as wealthy. Calvin F. Schmid, in his 1937 study of the Twin Cities, noted, "Edina is a better-class residential district with no industries." The sociologist rated neighboring Morningside as a "typical residential suburb for upper middle class people."[9]

Edina's reputation as a "better-class" locale grew largely within the residents' circle of family, friends, and business associates during the run-up to World War II. Like most south suburban communities, Edina was comparatively unknown in Minnesota. The postwar boom would bring attention to area villages and, in Edina's case, cemented its reputation as a place of prosperity.[10]

Some residents came to understand that Edina's reputation as a refuge of the rich had the unwanted connotation of pretentiousness. Martha Mattson Johnson recalled moving to Seattle in the 1960s where she met some Minneapolis-trained nurses. They teased their visitor from Edina about being rich and called her a "cake eater." When Johnson later lived in Ann Arbor, Michigan, she found that nurses there referred to her as Edina an snob.

"From that point on I felt it was safer socially to not announce I was from Edina," recalled Johnson. "I said I came from Minneapolis."[11]

Edina's desire to maintain its status as a community of single family homes, to the exclusion of commercial enterprise, came under threat in the early 1950s. Home owners would bear the cost of future growth since Edina lacked a strong business and industrial sector and the tax dollars it could supply. Donald C. Dayton,

> *"[The] chairman of the [1931] District's Community Fund…appealed to 'every member of the family including the children and employees to contribute money for the poor.… 'Many employees in our homes such as maids and chauffeurs are well paid this year in comparison to other workers and can well afford to give several times as liberally as they have in the past.'"*

president of the successful Minneapolis-based department store chain, Dayton's, provided an attractive tax-producing answer when he proposed building a revolutionary new shopping complex in Edina. Dayton waged a vigorous campaign with Edinans and won approval for Southdale, America's first enclosed shopping center.[12]

Donald Dayton planned for more than just a fancy mall. He produced the commercial place to be, a destination for consumers that offered free parking, dozens of shops, two large anchor department stores (Dayton's and Donaldson's) and a guarantee of perfect year-round,

Plan Supervision and Other Wise Restrictions to Protect Property Owners

indoor weather. When it opened in 1956, customers flooded through Southdale's spacious open courts and into its stores.[13]

As Edina historian Paul Hesterman noted, "In some ways, Southdale was to Edina's commercial development what the Country Club District was to its residential development." The District set the "standard and tone" for the community's residential neighborhoods; the magnetic indoor mall proved that well-planned retail spaces could draw customers to the suburbs. Southdale became known for its fashionable shops and fashionable shoppers, a reputation later bolstered by the addition of the nearby Galleria complex.

Cake Eaters of Sport

In the 1950s and through the early 1960s, University of Minnesota football and the state's public high school tournaments dominated the sports scene. Fans were ecstatic when Gopher footballers won their fifth national championship in 1960.[14] The winner of the annual basketball tourney also earned high, albeit brief, statewide status each winter, while the state prep hockey champions gained more attention each year. Major league baseball and football, new to the area, were yet to dominate local sports news.

By 1966, Minnesota's professional clubs, baseball's Twins and football's Vikings, had moved into the sports spotlight. High school basketball and

The ambitious 1952 design for the Southdale complex included plans for a hospital. In the foreground is today's Fairview Southdale Hospital.

hockey tournaments, however, remained very popular. Only one team would emerge victorious as state champion in those sports. Edina's 1966 basketball Hornets, led by all-state juniors Jay Kiedrowski, Kurt Schellhas and Jeff Wright, along with sophomore Bob Zender, reigned supreme. It was not surprising that these veterans returned to help win the title in 1967, despite the fact most basketball fans were cheering hard to see them upset. Outside of Edina, few followers of Minnesota basketball were happy that the Zender-led 1968 club made it three straight for the Hornets. Between 1965 and 1968, Edina won 69 straight basketball games, still a state record today.[15]

Prior to the 1968 tournament, an Edina High graduate and student at the University of Minnesota-Duluth attended a Duluth Central High School basketball game with friends. Central

During the 1970s Edina produced two national beauty queens, Barbara Peterson, Miss USA 1972, and Dorothy Benham, Miss America 1977, and claimed to be the "No. 1 City of Beauty and Charm."

Edina students also adopted the cake eater "cheer" while winning this state tournament game.

"…all right with me. If we don't win the tournament we can buy it." Another student predicted that following the title match, "We'll be eating cake Saturday night." The student cheering section buzzed, " Beee-you-tiful you Wasps."[17]

The Saturday night championship resulted in another runaway, with Moorhead the victim this time. Reporters found Edina junior starter, Tom Cabalka, celebrating the victory, shoveling a post-game cake into his mouth by the double-handful. "We're good cake eaters, yes," declared Cabalka.[18]

If Minnesota high school sports fans didn't care much for Edina basketball, some came to resent its successful hockey teams. During the 1970s, Edina teams appeared in eight state tourneys and won four of them. In the following decade they made it to state seven times and took three titles. Edina held two high schools from 1973 to 1981—East in the original building and West in a new structure. The district merged the programs in 1982, sending all Edina High students to the West campus. Hornets coach, Willard Ikola (1958-1991), became a Minnesota legend during this era as his Edina teams recorded 616 wins against 149 losses and 38 ties.[19]

It is little wonder that such a record of excellence triggered envy and frustration

was expected to challenge Edina for the state championship. She reported, "One day I found a note in my mailbox, and all it said was "Cake-eater." An account in the Minneapolis *Tribune* noted that after stopping the Hornets' record-breaking winning streak, Richfield fans had taunted the Edina team as "Cake Eaters" because "of the town's supposed wealth."[16]

Edina students laughed off the insults as they awaited the 1968 tournament championship game. A 17-year-old boy said the cake eater comments were in rival teams and sports fans as well. "You'd go to a state tournament, and 15,000 people would all be rooting for the other team, no matter who it was," claimed a former Edina resident.[20] Minneapolis *Tribune* columnist Jim Klobuchar, who made frequent references to the community over the years—"the homes and palaces of Edina," "an enclave of prim prosperity," "Camelot of the suburbs," "a student body representing upscale suburbia"—captured the feelings of hockey fans at the 1988 Edina-Warroad state tourney semi-final. "It was a game for the lovers of fables and fairy tales, Munchkins (Warroad) against plumed knights (Edina), the homesteaders against the squires." The final score, in two overtimes: Plumed Knights 2, Munchkins 1.[21]

Klobuchar, like good writers everywhere, understood the need to use language their readers could quickly grasp. When his column needed some allusion to wealth and privilege, he often worked Edina into the story. Most in the Twin Cities, and much of Minnesota, understood the phrase "Camelot of the suburbs" just had to refer to Edina.

Similarly, Minneapolis *Tribune* cartoonist Richard Guindon enjoyed skewering the Edina image with 1970s-era observations. One sketch showed a mother having a serious talk with her suit-and-tie-wearing five-year-old son. She says earnestly, "Daddy and I weren't born in Edina, dear, we achieved Edina."[22]

The oversimplified images of Edina that prevailed in the region had an effect upon those living in the community. A 1971 poll of Edina residents conducted by Dr. Ronald Anderson, a University of Minnesota sociologist, showed 46 percent of Edinans used the words "rich, wealthy, snobbish" in describing the "public image" of their community;" 40 percent admitted they sometimes disguised the fact they lived in Edina. Sixty-seven percent of those polled, aged 18 to 24, claimed to mislead others about where they lived, but only 23 percent of those over 55 did.[23]

One woman polled said, "They think we're all a bunch of wealthy snobs." Other residents recalled hearing outsiders use phrases such as "cake eaters, mortgage row, rich bedroom society, and golden ghetto" to describe Edina and its people. Edinans' perceptions of their image aligned with the popular view, although most did not agree with it. The majority of poll respondents believed prevailing attitudes about the city were inaccurate. That group was satisfied with, or at least indifferent to, Edina's public image.

Eight years later a youth representative to the Edina Human Relations Committee asserted the children of Edina, those of "wealth, success, spiritual and material advantage," have "unique" self-concept problems. The spokesperson said, "Kids...are success-oriented and very competitive" and concerned with living up to "expectations of success-oriented and competitive parents." The statements seemed to square with Edina's public image. The committee and city council agreed to study the issue.[24]

EDINA the team you **LOVE** *(to hate)*

Edina High School students deflected the "cake eater" jeers they heard at athletic events, in this case with a button.

The National Council of Churches selected Edina to be part of a 1979 U.S. survey regarding quality of life issues. They chose the Minnesota suburb under an assumption, made at the national level, that "Edina would represent high income families…."[25] The survey's results showed a "feeling of excessive pressure" on residents, a result that aligned with the town's own Human Rights Commission study. That analysis noted, "People inside and outside this community accept the stereotype of the typical Edina resident as an intelligent, competitive, affluent, upwardly-mobile overachiever."[26]

The Icing on the Cake

Concerns about Edina's image did create, during the 1970s, an era of well-intended introspection and self-study within the community. The fact that its citizens were 99 percent white, with a poverty rate three times lower than Hennepin County's average, raised concerns of racial and economic segregation.[27] Overall, reviews found Edina had Minnesota's highest median income by a wide margin, excellent high school test scores and graduation rates, strong real estate values, efficient local government and ample municipal services. By most empirical standards, Edina had proven to be an excellent place to live. And, perhaps more importantly, residents no longer believed, if they ever had, that there was anything wrong with that fact.

As a new century dawned, Minnesotans appeared to understand that the once-accepted caricature of Edina had been overblown to the point of farce.

Reporters found Edina junior starter Tom Cabalka celebrating the victory, shoveling a post-game cake into his mouth by the double-handful. "We're good cake eaters, yes," declared Cabalka.

"Edina envy" seemed to be on the wane as other affluent Twin Cities communities and housing districts emerged.

So what of the "Cake Eater Syndrome?" Edinans began to laugh off the familiar taunts, or even embrace the label. Edina hockey boosters wore buttons with the words, "Edina, the team you love to hate." The words "cake eaters" still echoed through gymnasiums and across hockey rinks, particularly when Edina teams were contenders at tournament time. But after so many years, the cake was getting stale.

Edina's reputation, nevertheless, lives on in Minnesota and the nation. Few in the know were surprised in March 2009 when *Sports Illustrated*, the leading American sports journal of this era, casually referred to a loss by Edina's high school hockey team during the Minnesota state tournament. Noted *SI*, "The citizens of Edina, an affluent Twin Cities suburb, have been scornfully dubbed Cake Eaters for at least 50 years."[28]

Sports Illustrated claimed Edina's defeat in the state hockey tournament "…probably tickled the rest of the state." And despite assertions that Minnesotans no longer see Edina in stereotype, *SI* was safe in assuming that some still delighted in the vanquishing of the varsity Hornets.

Eddie Webster's	**FAMOUS "POOR BOY" SANDWICHES**	
"POOR BOY" No. 1	Generous slices of Broiled Sirloin Steak on a fresh loaf of French Bread, Onions, Lettuce and Tomatoes	2.25
"POOR BOY" No. 2	Broiled Ground Beef on a crisp Individual French Loaf, Onions, Lettuce and Tomatoes	1.95
"POOR BOY" No. 3	A Broiled King-Size Alaska Crabmeat Sandwich on a French Loaf, Tomatoes and Relish Tray Pickles	2.45
"POOR BOY" No. 4	Hot Ruben Sandwich, Thin Slices of Corned Beef and Turkey Over Marinated Sauerkraut With Swiss Cheese on a Fresh Pumpernickel Loaf, Kosher Dill Pickles	2.25

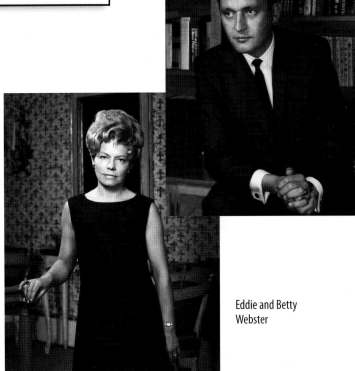

president, announced the Senators would be moving to the Upper Midwest.[13]

Bloomington became a major league city, twice over. Metropolitan Stadium went from a little-used minor league ball park in 1960 to the home of two professional sports franchises, the Minnesota Twins and the Minnesota Vikings.

The Bloomington Strip

Eddie and Betty Webster planned to open their new Bloomington restaurant in October 1965 at 78th and Cedar, the backyard of Metropolitan Stadium. By a happy coincidence the Minnesota Twins would win the American League pennant that year and host the first game of the World Series just as the classy eatery opened its doors. Betty Webster recalled, "The Series was a huge event…and we had a big sign proclaiming "Open for the World Series" out front…We knew that our sign was getting some local news coverage, and then we heard that pictures of the sign were going around the country. Our

Eddie and Betty Webster

Eddie and Betty Webster opened their new Bloomington restaurant during the 1965 World Series. It quickly became the anchor of the city's emerging hospitality industry.

opening became something of a national news story."[14]

"We were the first on the Strip, or, should I say, what would eventually be called the Bloomington Strip," stated Betty Webster. Her husband had learned cooking in the army and reportedly had once prepared food for Gen. Dwight Eisenhower. After returning to civilian life, the couple operated restaurants in Pipestone and Rochester. They saw opportunity in the growing Minneapolis suburb and picked a perfect location for their new place.

On October 6, 1965, nearly 48,000 spectators crowded into the Met to watch the Twins beat the Los Angeles Dodgers 8-2. The Twins won 5-2 the next day before 48,700. After both games, Eddie Webster's hosted throngs of happy Minnesota fans. Following games six and seven of the Series, local fans chose Webster's to commiserate over losses by the home team. The 1965 World Series gave Webster's its start and, in turn, the new restaurant served as a foundation for what became known as the Bloomington Strip. It would hold that place until Eddie Webster's untimely death in a 1980 snowmobile accident.

"Eddie's was the first of its kind in the area and the best place around, period, for a long time," said Bill Brown,

Bill "Boom-Boom" Brown

The Thunderbird Motel was an eastern anchor of the Interstate-494 strip, with Camelot Restaurant in Edina among its leading establishments to the west.

the popular Minnesota Vikings running back and member of the team's Ring of Honor. "You could go to Charlie's downtown, or stay home in Bloomington at a classy place. That was a big change. The people (at Eddie Webster's) were great and a big part of the new landscape in Bloomington, not just for me during my football career, but for everyone who was a sports fan of any kind. Baseball with the Twins had a big following and so did the North Stars when they arrived at the Met Center. Eddie's was the place to go, and really started the tradition of the 'Bloomington Strip.' Sometimes you might see athletes from a few different teams out on the dance floor, including the opposition! It was a lively time, let me tell you."[15]

The history of Bloomington's hospitality industry should include the pioneering role of the Thunderbird Motel. In 1963 the motel obtained the community's first liquor license. Like its suburban neighbors, Richfield and Edina, Bloomington had originally been a "dry" town with no liquor sales. Edina, however, issued a single off-sale liquor license to local businessmen Charles Hay and Arnold Stenson in 1934 and cautiously became "wet." Richfield voters approved the opening of municipal

liquor stores that produced profit enough to support popular community initiatives. Edina adopted the municipal liquor model in 1951.[16]

When Bloomington voters chose city status following a 1960 election, its new charter specified that the community remain dry. A charter amendment legalizing liquor sales passed in 1962, and Rodney S. Wallace, owner of the Thunderbird, received the city's first liquor license a year later. Without this option, the community's young hospitality industry would have suffered.

Eddie Webster's, meanwhile, developed a reputation for drawing professional athletes and leading entertainers. "Eddie's was about having fun and, of course, we were so close to Met Stadium that a lot of athletes would stop by," said Betty Webster. She mentioned Minnesota Twins from the 1960s as frequent guests, including Harmon Killebrew, Tony Oliva, Bob Allison and Billy Martin, who coached and managed the Twins. Ron Yary, Jim Marshall, Bill Brown, Scott Studwell

Viking all-pro defensive end Jim Marshall is pictured as the grand marshal of an Eddie Webster charity golf tournament.

and Paul Krause were among the Vikings who enjoyed Eddie's. Betty Webster recalled that singer-actor Frank Sinatra "was around a few times," as was comedian George Burns. Actor Paul Newman visited "with regularity" on his way to Brainerd and race car driving. Hubert Humphrey, United States Vice President and former Minnesota senator, stopped by "fairly regularly" on his way home from Washington."[17]

Tom Webster, son of the founders and an active manager of the establishment, recalls the evening New York Yankees slugger Reggie Jackson showed up at the door after a game at Met Stadium. When told by the doorman, Victor Barr, that there was a five-dollar cover charge, Reggie had a question for the young employee. "Do you know who I am?" Victor, who was aware that Jackson had recently signed a large contract, responded without hesitation; "Yeah, you're Reggie Jackson and if anybody can afford a five buck cover, it's you." Known as "Mr. October" for his playoff heroics, Jackson gave a roar of laughter and turned over a five.

Hockey player Tom Reid was a rough and tumble defenseman for the Minnesota North Stars. He recalls a certain camaraderie that existed between opposing teams when they gathered at Eddie Webster's Peanut Bar. "The North Stars were there all the time, and sometimes we would have a bunch of the guys from the other team in the place at the same time. Back then, you could be

Bud Grant, Minnesota Vikings head coach

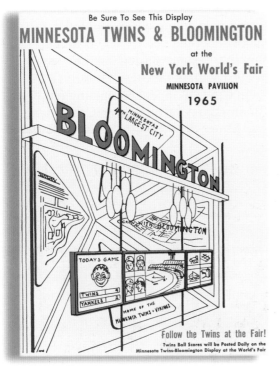

Follow the Twins at the Fair!

Twins Ball Scores will be Posted Daily on the Minnesota Twins-Bloomington Display at the World's Fair

Bloomington and the Minnesota Twins advertised themselves during the 1965 New York World's Fair.

The National Hockey League expanded into Minnesota in 1967. Ray Cullen, pictured, was a leader of the Minnesota North Stars whose home ice was in the Met Sports Center.

pounding each other out on the ice during the game, but still get together over a beer afterwards. I don't think any rough stuff ever broke out at Webster's." Reid smiled at the recollection. "Well, maybe once or twice, but nothing too bad!"

As Bloomington continued to flower, competition in the hospitality industry developed. Howard Wong's, Steak and Ale and Max McGee's Left Guard were among the newcomers. Added to that mix was the emergence of a thriving hotel sector with its lounges and restaurants. There seemed to be plenty of business to go around.

Construction of the Met Center, next to Met Stadium, not only brought professional hockey to Bloomington in the form of the NHL's Minnesota North Stars, it also became a venue for major entertainers. The Carleton Celebrity Room, just south of the Strip, also featured national headliners that drew great crowds.

In August 1965 some 30,000 screaming teenaged fans, along with others more than a few years older, gathered at Metropolitan Stadium for a musical performance by four young men from Great Britain. The Beatles, the hottest act in the entertainment world, had come to Bloomington and the Met.[18]

Ten local teenaged girls with staff connections were allowed to gather in an inside Met hallway through which the Beatles would pass. Assistant Concessions Manager, Jess Masener, reminded them, "You can see 'em if you don't squeal." Then the young Englishmen appeared and the girls began screaming, one with her hand clapped over her

mouth. Sixteen-year-old Sandy Olson of Bloomington was in tears. She snapped a picture of the scene but was now sobbing, "My flash didn't go off!"[19]

Magnetic Bloomington

Producers of national television broadcasts of the Twins and Vikings games during the early 1960s enjoyed pointing their cameras away from the games to the farm fields that lay just beyond Metropolitan Stadium. "Bucolic Bloomington" drew chuckles from the national media. Such scenes had disappeared from the nation's television screens as the decade ended. Housing developers, business owners (there were 85 businesses in the city in 1955, 800 by 1965) and industrial firms including Toro, John Deere, Thermo King, Zeigler, Donaldson, Control Data, Xerox and ADA had discovered Bloomington's appeal.[20]

The hospitality industry and pro sports clubs continued to seek a place in the growing city. Bloomington passed the 50,000 mark in population in 1960 and had 82,000 residents 10 years later. The Registry Hotel and the Marriott Inn opened, along with Southtown, a major shopping center. The National Bowling League started operations in 1961 with the Eastern Division's Twin Cities Skippers competing on Bloomington's Convention Center lanes. The Minnesota Muskies became charter

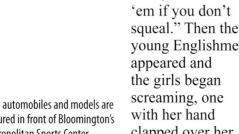

New automobiles and models are pictured in front of Bloomington's Metropolitan Sports Center.

members of the new American Basketball League Association in 1967 and played their games at Met Center, while the Minnesota Buckskins, of the World Team Tennis League, also called Met Center home when they debuted in spring 1974. These clubs and the leagues in which they played soon faded from the scene.

Professional soccer came to Bloomington in 1976 and, to the surprise of many, became an instant hit. A devoted fan base and legendary pre-game tailgating parties in the Met Stadium parking lot produced an average of 20,000 fans per game in the team's first North American Soccer League season. More than 49,000 packed the Met for a playoff game that year, and the Minnesota Kicks appeared destined for a long run. The franchise was unable to sustain that early pace and operated for just six years.[21]

Adding to the excitement of these years of phenomenal growth in Bloomington was an expanded international airport just north of Interstate-494. Minnesota readied for the coming Jet Age, opening the new Lindbergh Terminal in 1962. Designers planned to have it ready to serve four million passengers annually by 1975, but more than that number were using the airport in 1967. Other modernistic air terminals arose across America, from New York's stunning Pan American and TWA Flight Center terminals at John F. Kennedy Airport to Los Angeles International and its signature Theme Building.[22]

Bloomington was in excellent position for the onset of the new wave in national and international travel. The glamour, sophistication and ease of jet flights and their comparatively moderate cost created an expanding market for the airline industry. The stars of this remarkable air show, as depicted

by the public relations campaigns of their employers, were the capable and trustworthy pilots. Flight attendants were portrayed as attractive, fashionable and competent—a stereotype not unlike the young woman described at the beginning of this piece. Some pilots and

Lindbergh Terminal around 1965

stewardesses made Bloomington their home, and others stayed there during stopovers. They added a touch of glamour to Bloomington night life, especially when they appeared in uniform.

Betty Webster commented about air crews who visited Eddie Webster's. "We used to have a number of airline employees who would stop," she said, referring to the crews of the jetliners now frequenting the airport across the highway. "There were a lot of people who enjoyed the restaurant (with two large dining rooms) and the dancing. Remember, we had a piano bar and the peanut bar, but the evening could really get going downstairs. We did have a very attractive clientele at times."[23]

With a youthful population exceeding 80,000, a healthy industrial and commercial base, major league sports, an international airport next door and a prominent and popular, entertainment district, Bloomington in the 1970s was indeed a "swinging" place to be.

Section 1: Dominion of the Dakota

Cloud Man's Daughters and Their Anglo-American Husbands

1 Ohiyesa (Charles Eastman) cites his grandmother, Wakaninajinwin, as the source of this quotation; transcription of a Charles Eastman letter to H.H. Hitchcock of Minneapolis, September 8, 1927, in *Minnesota Archaeologist*, 12 (January 1949): 1.

Cloud Man's mother was a descendant of two Mdewakanton chiefs, and his father was a French nobleman. His great-grandson described a still active but aging Cloud Man as "…a fine looking old man, his hair pure white, silky and wavy." See Charles Eastman to H.H. Hitchcock.

2 Bruce M. White, "The Power of Whiteness or, the Life and Times of Joseph Rolette Jr.," *Minnesota History,* 56 (winter 1998–99): 180.

3 Rhoda R. Gilman, *Henry Hastings Sibley: Divided Heart* (St. Paul: MHS, 2004), 48. Gary Clayton Anderson, *Little Crow: Spokesman for the Sioux* (St. Paul: MHS, 1986) 26. Anderson reports Cloud Man was related to Taoyateduta, the future Little Crow. Frederick L. Johnson, *Richfield: Minnesota's Oldest Suburb* (Richfield: Richfield Historical Society), 3–4. Taliaferro named the Mdewakanton village Eatonville in honor of John Eaton, the then U.S. Secretary of War.

4 Mark Dietrich, "A 'Good Man' in a Changing World, Cloud Man, the Dakota leader and his Life and Times," *Ramsey County History*, 36 (spring, 2001): 4, 12. Coen, *Minnesota History*, 52: 150. Dillon, at about age thirty-seven, was two years older than her bridegroom.

Anderson, *Little Crow*, 26. Anderson reviews Taliaferro's links to the Mdewakanton Dakota and how his marriage to The Day Sets affected the agent's status with the Indians.

5 Coen, *Minnesota History*, 52: 147–148, 150. If young Mary stayed with the Taliaferros, she would have certainly encountered their house servant, black slave Harriet Robinson, who married another slave at the fort in 1836. His name was Dred Scott, and his celebrated 1856 Supreme Court case dealing with ownership of slaves in free territory captured America's attention.

6 Jane Lamm Carroll, "Who Was Jane Lamont? Anglo-Dakota Daughters in Early Minnesota," *Minnesota History*, 59 (spring 2005): 189–190. Coen, *Minnesota History*, 52: 148, 150. It is possible that at some time Mary Taliaferro lived with her father and Eliza at Fort Snelling. Rev. Jedediah Stevens ran the Lake Harriet mission located near Cloud Man's 1835 village.

7 Taliaferro to Samuel W. Pond, August 26, 1839, Pond papers.

8 Carroll, *Minnesota History*, 59: 190.

9 Lawrence Taliaferro to Samuel Pond, January 1, 1846. Taliaferro hoped Mary could stay with the Ponds, "be steady" and "not cause me grief of shame on her account." He had appointed himself trustee for Mary, Nancy Eastman and Elizabeth Williams, and assigned Benjamin Baker, a trader at Camp Coldwater near Fort Snelling, to be a trustee for Jane Lamont, Winona Culbertson and several others; see Carroll, *Minnesota History*, 59: 190 *n*25.

10 Here and below, Carroll, *Minnesota History*, 59: 190–191. The reference to the Gideon Pond letter is found on 196, *n*31. The last recorded mention of Mary's mother, The Day Sets, is found in a letter from Gideon Pond to his brother dated January 15, 1844. In it Gideon sends love to "Jane [Lamont], Mary and their mothers."

11 Carroll, *Minnesota History*, 59: 191–192. Coen, *Minnesota History*, 52: 151.

12 Clement A. Lounsberry, *Early History of North Dakota* (Washington, D.C., Liberty Press, 1919), 170–173. The Upper Missouri Outfit based itself at Fort Tecumseh at the mouth of the Bad River (present day South Dakota) in 1822. They moved to Fort Pierre and higher ground in 1832. Carroll, *Minnesota History*, 59: 186.

13 Carroll, *Minnesota History*, 59: 186–187. Author Carroll believes that Lamont had more children with Hushes the Night, 195, *n*11. Lounsberry, *North Dakota*, 173.

14 Here and below, Carroll, *Minnesota History*, 59: 187. Lucy Prescott Pettijohn, the mixed-blood daughter of Philander Prescott, said she attended the mission school with Mary Taliaferro and Jane Lamont, see "Lucy Prescott Pettijohn," "Fragment—no title," and "Early Minnesota History," box 1 folder 2, John H. Case Papers, MHS.

15 Patricia C. Harpole and Mary D. Nagle, *Minnesota Territorial Census, 1850* (St. Paul: MHS, 1972), 9. That census shows newlyweds Moses S[tarr] Titus, age thirty, living at Oak Grove with Jane, twenty-three. Gideon was aware that Moses and Jane did things together before announcing their impending marriage. On June 29, 1849, he wrote in his diary that they "went strawberring" (sic) together and on March 1, 1849, noted Starr and Jane went to Prairieville [Shakopee] probably to see Samuel and Cordelia Pond. Starr returned alone. Carroll, *Minnesota History*, 59: 187–188

16 Samuel Pond to Ruth Riggs, January 17, 1853, Pond papers.

17 Carroll, *Minnesota History*, 59: 188–189.

18 William L. Bean, "Eastman, Cloud Man, Many Lightnings, an Anglo-Dakota Family," (compiled for the Eastman family reunion), July 4, 1989, at Flandreau, South Dakota, 21, 23. Eastman's military specialty was topographical analysis.

19 Holcombe, *Minnesota in Three Centuries*, I: 41. Charles Eastman to H.H. Hitchcock, September 8, 1927.

20 Charles Eastman to H.H. Hitchcock, September 8, 1927. The friendship between Henry Sibley and Seth Eastman became stronger when Eastman was reassigned to Fort Snelling (1841–1848). See Gilman, *Henry Sibley*, 90. Holcombe, *Minnesota in Three Centuries*, I: 41 relates Samuel Pond's version of Stands Sacred's request. Charles Eastman gives the name of his mother's mother-in-law, Uncheedah, in Charles Alexander Eastman, *From the Deep Woods to Civilization*, ed. A. LaVonne Brown Ruoff (Chicago: R.R. Donnelley & Sons, 2001), 12–13.

21 Holcombe, *Minnesota in Three Centuries*, I: 41.

22 Eastman, *From the Deep Woods to Civilization*, 8–9. Eastman wrote of his mother, "…she had every feature of a Caucasian descent with the exception of her luxuriant black hair and deep black eyes…." Chris C. Cavender, "The Dakota People of Minnesota," *Hennepin County History*, 47 (summer 1988): 13.

23 Mary Henderson Eastman, *Dacohtah or Life and Legends of the Sioux around Fort Snelling*, (Afton, MN: Afton Historical Society Press, 1995), first published by John Wiley, New York, 1849, see Coen's preface, xv.

24 Ibid.

25 Ibid. Coen quotes from George Turner to William C. Baker, January 1, 1846, George Franklin Turner correspondence, 1840–1847, MHS.

26 Eastman, *From the Deep Woods to Civilization*, 12–13. Many Lightnings, Charles Eastman's father, had likely been the source of this story. In son Charles's version of the incident, Nancy discovered the ruse but decided to stay with Many Lightnings, believing The Great Spirit was punishing her for being disobedient to her parents.

27 Carroll, *Minnesota History*, 59: 193–194. Red Blanket Woman was a member of the Black Dog band of Mdewakanton.

Anglo-Dakota Marriage

1 Jane Lamm Carroll, "Who Was Jane Lamont? Anglo-Dakota Daughters in Early Minnesota," *Minnesota History*, 59 (spring 2005): 184–185. Sylvia Van Kirk, *Many Tender Ties, Women in the Fur-Trade Society in Western Canada, 1680–1870* (Winnipeg: Watson and Dwyer, 1980), 4–8, 28–36. By mid-nineteenth century, French traders continued a long and successful tradition of intermarriage with Indian people of the region that endured British, and then American, control of the area, see Jennifer S. H. Brown, *Strangers in Blood: Fur Trade Company Families in Indian Country* (Vancouver: University of British Columbia Press, 1980), 51–90.

2 Helen M. White and Bruce White, *Fort Snelling in 1838: an ethnographic and historical study* (St. Paul: Turnstone Research, 1998), 164. Col. John Stevens, "Early Hennepin County History" [last of three parts] *Hennepin County History* 18 (summer 1958): 17–18; the article is based on an 1856 address by Stevens at the Minneapolis Lyceum. Stevens employs the term "half breed," common usage at that time.

3 Jane Lamm Carroll, "The McLeods, an Anglo-Dakota Family in Early Minnesota," *Minnesota History*, 60 (summer 2007): 219.

4 Lawrence Taliaferro, Auto-Biography of Maj. Lawrence Taliaferro, *Minnesota Collections*, 6 (St. Paul, 1894): 217–218. J. Fletcher Williams, "Henry Hastings Sibley, a Memoir," *Minnesota Collections*, 6 (St. Paul, 1894): 258. Rhoda R. Gilman, *Henry Hastings Sibley, Divided Heart* (St. Paul: MHS, 2004), 3–6.

5 Carroll, *Minnesota History*, 59: see 195, *n*6 for quotation.

6 Barbara Stuhler, *Gentle Warriors: Clara Ueland and the Minnesota Struggle for Woman Suffrage* (St. Paul, MHS Press, 1995), 15. Stone and husband, Henry Blackwell, read the prenuptial agreement. Stone also retained her maiden name.

7 Angela Cavender Wilson, "The Role of Women in Eastern Dakota Society in the Early 1800s," (revision of a 1994 paper by Anne Float), in City of Bloomington, David O. Born, director, *A Dakota Perspective: Pond-Dakota Mission Park*, June 1996. The Wilson quote is from Mari Sandoz, *They Were Sioux* (New York: Hastings House, 1961), 80.

8 Samuel W. Pond, *The Dakota or Sioux in Minnesota as They were in 1834* (St. Paul: MHS reprint 1986),141.

9 Mary Henderson Eastman, *Dahcotah or, Life and Legends of the Sioux around Fort Snelling* (Afton, MN: Historical Society Press, 1995), first published by John Wiley, New York, 1849). Rena Neumann Coen wrote the preface for this reprint and notes Eastman's feelings about the status of Dakota women on x–xi. See also Eastman's introduction to the book, 3, 5.

10 Ruth Landes, *The Mystic Lake Sioux: Sociology of the Mdewakantonwan Santee* (Madison: University of Wisconsin, 1968), 96–104. Pond, *The Dakota as They Were in 1834*, 26–29, 39–49, 140–142. Carroll, *Minnesota History*, 59: 185.

11 Philander Prescott, "Autobiography and Reminiscences of Philander Prescott," *Minnesota Collections*, 6 (St. Paul: 1894): 476–477.

12 Pond, *The Dakota as They Were*, 31–34. David Humphrey to Dear Friends, July 9, 1855, David W. Humphrey Papers, MHS. Jon Willand, *Lac Qui Parle and the Dakota Mission* (Madison, MN: Lac Qui Parle Historical Society, 1964), 29–30. Eastman, *Dahcotah*, 3.

13 Stevens, *Personal Recollection of Minnesota*, 43. Prescott, *Minnesota Collections*, 6: 481.

14 Gilman, *Henry Hastings Sibley,* 61.

15 Ibid.

16 Carroll, *Minnesota History*, 59: 192. While Helen was still a child, Sibley had her adopted by William Reynolds Brown and his wife, Martha. The Browns raised her with financial assistance from Sibley, who kept in contact with Helen for the remainder of her life. Helen also received income from treaty money that her father had invested for her. Well-educated, attractive, and a pious Christian, she married Sylvester Sawyer, an Anglo-American physician, in 1859, with Henry Sibley, now governor, giving her away. Helen died less than a year later from scarlet fever contracted just after giving birth. Her daughter died shortly after her mother. Helen's husband said Sibley "mourned her loss sincerely and truly." See Carroll, *Minnesota History*, 59: 192–193, 196, *n*35–44.

17 Bruce M. White, "The Power of Whiteness or the Life and Times of Joseph Rolette, Jr.," *Minnesota History* 56 (winter 1998–99): 180. The quotation is from the beginning of John Wesley Bond's 1853 guidebook, *Minnesota and Its Resources*.

18 N[athaniel] M'Lean, "My Dakota Children," *The Dakota Friend*, January 1851, 4. Samuel Pond asked the Dakota to "…turn their attention to planting and make an earnest effort to adopt the habits of civilized people [so] they can dwell in the neighborhood of the Americans, see S[amuel] W. Pond, *The Dakota Friend*, February 1851, 1.

19 Anderson and Woolworth, *Through Dakota Eyes*, 24.

A Missionary's Mission and "The Dakota Friend"

1 "Memorial Notices of Rev. Gideon H. Pond," by messrs. Riggs (Stephen), Williamson (Thomas) and Sibley (Henry), *Minnesota Collections* (St. Paul: 1880), 3: 360. S[amuel P. Pond, Jr., *Two Volunteer Missionaries Among the Dakota* (Chicago: Congregational Sunday School and Publishing Society, 1893), vi.

2 Here and below, *The Dakota Friend*, Vol. 1, no. 1, p. 4, November, 1850. Pond described the first issue of the newspaper as making "a more acceptable appearance that I anticipated and yet I saw sufficient in it to mortify me. The blunders of my composition added to my own awkwardness [is] anything but gratifying to me," see Gideon Pond Diaries, November 27, 1850, Hennepin County History Museum collections, (hereafter HCHM). Transcriptions of Pond's diaries and some original fragments are available at HCHM. Pond charged twenty-five cents for a year's subscription.

3 *The Dakota Friend*, November 1850, 4. Pond listed himself as editor and the Dakota Mission as publishers. This issue also carried news from Lac qui Parle mission written by "S.R.R" (Stephen Return Riggs).

4 Jon Willand, *Lac qui Parle and the Dakota Mission* (Madison, MN: Lac qui Parle Historical Society, 1964), 11–13. Pond, Jr., *Two Volunteer Missionaries*, 19–20. Samuel's words are found in a letter to his brother dated December 3, 1833. He had gone west before Gideon in search of a proper mission for them. Samuel got the idea to go to the Dakota during a stay in Galena, Illinois.

5 Charles M. Gates, "The Lac Qui Parle Indian Mission," *Minnesota History* 16 (June 1935): 133–138, 148. Pond worked as a farmer and carpenter at Lac qui Parle. Although concerned with spreading the Gospel to the Dakota, he was not an ordained minister until 1848.

6 Willand, *Lac qui Parle and the Dakota Mission*, 13. Jedediah D. Stevens believed the Pond brothers to be eccentric, and quoted Thomas Williamson as saying, "They have a way of doing things on their own, and do not like to be directed by others." Williamson also thought them to be pious and industrious. Both Stevens and Williamson were colleagues of the brothers.

7 Gates, "The Lac Qui Parle Indian Mission," 148. Gideon Pond Diaries, November 28, and December 5, 7, 1848.

8 Gates, "The Lac Qui Parle Indian Mission," 148. Holcombe, *Minnesota in Three Centuries*, II: 307–308. Folwell, *A History of Minnesota*, I: 284–287.

9 Willand, *Lac qui Parle and the Dakota Mission*, 26.

10 On November 3, 1850, a confident Henry Sibley incorrectly claimed to have the land sale to the Dakota wrapped up, writing, "The Indians are all prepared to make a treaty when we tell them to do so, and such a one as I may dictate." Congress had little interest in remote frontier Minnesota but did set aside, in September 1850, fifteen thousand dollars for expenses related to the arranging of a treaty with Dakota. See Folwell, *A History of Minnesota*, I: 274–276, and 20*n* on 275.

11 Here and below, *The Dakota Friend*, February 1851, page 1, see article by S.W.P. [Samuel W. Pond]. Good Road took Pond's first option and, according to *The Dakota Friend*, "…abandoned his summer mansion and farm at Oak Grove, and has located himself on the Credit river…." Good Road took seven or eight families with him, according to Pond, who wrote the chief would be "out of the reach of the Chippewas [Ojibwe], but he has heard their bullets whiz by too often to fear them," *The Dakota Friend*, January 1851, 3.

12 Here and two paragraphs below, *The Dakota Friend*, January 1851, 3.

13 N. M'Lean, "The Agent to his Dakota Children," *The Dakota Friend*, February 1851, 3.

14 N. M'Lean, Ind. Sub. Agent, "A Letter from the Sub-Agent to the Dakotas," *The Dakota Friend*, March 1851, 3. Gideon Pond printed parts of a gratifying letter to the editor in the March issue. Stephen Riggs had written from Lac qui Parle mission that the Dakota liked the newspaper and that Riggs was using it in his school there. The missionary had also sold thirty-five subscriptions and believed he would "reach fifty easily," news that, no doubt, warmed the editor's heart. Editor Pond modestly admitted in words printed below those of Riggs that there "are probably more Dakota readers at Lac qui Parle" than among all other bands combined. He did seem pleased that "either full Indian or mixed" read the *Friend* aloud to those Dakota in the area unable to read, "The Dakota Friend at Lac qui Parle," *The Dakota Friend,* March 1851, 3.

15 "A Letter from the Sub-Agent to the Dakotas," *The Dakota Friend*, March 1851, 3.

16 Folwell, *A History of Minnesota*, I: 278–287, see 287 *n*43 for detail on the amount of land sold.

17 Michael C. Coleman, "Presbyterian Missionaries and Their Attitudes Toward the American Indians, 1837–1893," 88, University of Pennsylvania dissertation, 1977. From this study, Coleman developed a book by the same title (Jackson: University of Mississippi Press, 1985). Regarding the quotation, Ramsey wrote on July 16, 1846, about his speech before students in Spencer Academy, a school founded in 1844 "to transform the minds and manners of Choctaw citizens into well-educated European Americans," see Joel H. Spring, *The Cultural Transformation of a Native American Family and Its Tribe, 1763–1995* (Mahwak, NJ: Lawrence Erlbaum Assoc., 1996), 3.

18 Reid's words are quoted in Coleman, "Presbyterian Missionaries," 95.

19 M.J. Hichock, *Spiritual Prosperity Conditioned upon the Missionary Work* (New York: Mission House, 1865), 23.

20 In February 1994 Cavender was interviewed by Jonathan Ritter and Claire Schommer on the subject of Dakota missionary relations at the Pond Mission, see City of Bloomington (MN), David O. Born, study director, *A Dakota Perspective: Pond-Dakota Mission Park*, 1996, 24. See also, Linda M. Clemmons, *Satisfied to Walk in the Ways of Their Fathers, Dakota and Protestant Missionaries, 1835–1862* (Urbana: University of Illinois, 1998), 43. Author Clemmons noted that the Dakota often saw missionaries and the government as one entity.

21 Anderson and Woolworth, *Through Dakota Eyes*, 23. Big Eagle added, "The Indians wanted to live as they did before the treaty of Traverse des Sioux [1851]—go where they pleased when they pleased; hunt

game where they could find it, sell their furs to the traders and live as they could."
22 Ibid. 24.
23 Willand, *Lac qui Parle and the Dakota Mission*, 209.
24 Ibid. The quotation is found in Pond, Jr., *Two Volunteer Missionaries*, 212.
25 Stephen R. Riggs, *Mary and I, Forty Years with the Sioux* (Boston: Congregational House, 1880), 368–370, the quotation Riggs used is from Gideon Pond's diary. See also "Memorial Notices of Rev. Gideon H. Pond," 368–369; in his memorial to Gideon Pond, Thomas Williamson reported Dakota prisoners accepted the gospel, saying the Pond brothers "had told us these things long ago." This, wrote Williamson, occurred on February 3, 1863, five weeks after the executions in Mankato.
26 Riggs, *Mary and I*, Riggs quotes Gideon Pond's diary.
27 Here and below, Folwell, *A History of Minnesota*, II: 208–210. The late reprieve of Round Wind reduced the number executed to thirty-eight.
Lincoln met with Minnesota Episcopal Bishop Henry Whipple, a strident opponent of sentencing the three hundred Dakota to death. The President said he felt Whipple's eloquent words in defense of the Dakota "down to my boots," Carley, *The Sioux Uprising of 1862*, 73–74.

Bet On Six: Ball-Play Tournament Brings Hundreds to Oak Grove

1 Here and below, Gideon Pond printed an account of the game in *Dakota Tawaxitka Kin*, or *The Dakota Friend*, a bi-lingual monthly newspaper he published; see "Dakota Ball-Play," *The Dakota Friend*, July 1852, p. 3. The bands of Wabasha and Shakopee were the largest of the Mdewakanton, see Anderson, Gary Clayton Anderson, *Little Crow: Spokesman for the Sioux* (St. Paul: MHS Press, 1986), 11–13.
2 Ibid.
3 Alexander M. Weyand and Milton R. Roberts, *The Lacrosse Story* (Baltimore: H & A. Herman, 1965), 5–6.
4 *The Dakota Friend*, July 1852, p. 3. Weyand and Roberts, *The Lacrosse Story*, 6–7. The Carver quote is from "La Crosse or the Game of Ball," *Hennepin County History* (January 1955): 7
5 "La Crosse or the Game of Ball," 6–7. Seth Eastman, the soldier-artist who sketched Dakota life in the Minnesota area, made a December 1849 etching of a ball-game on the Minnesota River.
6 Here and three paragraphs below, *The Dakota Friend*, July 1852, p. 3. Pond reported Little Six's athletes added another thousand dollars worth of goods to their haul.

George Quinn's Decision: "I Went With My People Against the Whites."

1 Gary Clayton Anderson and Alan R. Woolworth, eds., *Through Dakota Eyes: Narrative Accounts of the Minnesota Indian War of 1862* (St. Paul: MHS Press, 1988), 6.
2 Kenneth Carley, ed., "Account of George Quinn," *Minnesota History* 38 (September 1962): 147–49.
3 Anderson and Woolworth, *Through Dakota Eyes*, 93–94. Anderson and Woolworth brought together eyewitness accounts of the 1862 Minnesota Dakota War. Quinn's interview was among those receiving attention and serves as a foundation for this piece. It is possible that William L. Quinn, Holcombe's interpreter, was George Quinn's half-brother.
4 As a young man, Quinn lived at Ft. Garry (today's Winnipeg) in the early 1820s. Quinn married the mixed-blood, Mary Louise Finley. They later settled near Fort Snelling in the late 1820s and eventually moved to the future Bloomington in 1842; Isaac Atwater and John H. Stevens, *History of Minneapolis and Hennepin County, Minnesota* (New York: Munsell Publishing, 1895), 1207–1209.
5 Anderson and Woolworth, *Through Dakota Eyes*, 94–95, 157–158.
6 Kenneth Carley, *The Sioux Uprising of 1862* (St. Paul: MHS, 1976), 64–67.
7 Board of Commissioners, *Minnesota in the Civil and Indian Wars, 1861–1865* (St. Paul, 1890, 1899), II: 165, carries correspondence of Ramsey and Sibley as they attempted to organize to fight the Dakota.
8 Here and two paragraphs below, Anderson and Woolworth, *Through Dakota Eyes*, 258–259; Folwell, *A History of Minnesota*, II: 177–182.
9 Carley, *The Sioux Uprising of 1862*, 64–67; Anderson and Woolworth, *Through Dakota Eyes*, 258–259.
10 Anderson and Woolworth, *Through Dakota Eyes*, 94, 259.
11 Ibid. 93–94

Parallel Lives, Parallel Deaths: Philander Prescott and Peter Quinn

1 Here and below, "Philander Prescott: One of the First Hennepin County Settlers Whose End Was Tragic," *Hennepin County History*, 21 (spring 1962): 3–4. Prescott, "Autobiography and Reminiscences," *Minnesota Collections* (St. Paul, 1894), 6: 475–479. Folwell, *A History of Minnesota*, I: 137–140. Zacariah Prescott, already trading with the soldiers, was on hand to greet his younger brother. Regarding deaths from scurvy, some estimates of fatalities were somewhat smaller, see Folwell, *A History of Minnesota*, I: 138, *n*20.
2 Prescott, *Minnesota Collections*, 6: 480–481. John H. Stevens, *Personal Recollection of Minnesota and its People: and early history of Minneapolis* (Minneapolis: Tribune Job Printing, 1890), 43. The marriage temporarily broke down when Prescott abandoned his young family and headed south where he roamed for about two years. A contrite Philander returned to Mary and found she was willing to take him back; they recommitted to each other in a marriage sanctioned by law. Missionary Samuel Pond officiated. See also Merle Potter, *101 Best Stories of Minnesota* (Minneapolis: Schmitt Pub. 1956 reprint), 242–245.
3 Stevens, *Personal Recollection*, 5. Roy W. Meyer, *History of the Santee Sioux: United States Indian Policy on Trial* (Lincoln: Univ. of Nebraska, 1967), 49–50.
4 "Philander Prescott," *Hennepin County History*, 21: 4–5. Eli Pettijohn married Prescott's daughter Lucy in 1850. She reported that Eli built the Pond and Quinn log homes during the winter of 1842–1843, see "Lucy Prescott Pettijohn," "Fragment—no title," and Early Minnesota History," box 1 folder 2, John H. Case Papers, MHS.
Before moving his family to Oak Grove, Peter Quinn took possession on May 6, 1840, of the Mississippi River east bank claim of Pvt. Thomas Brown, a Fifth Infantry soldier. This well-sited parcel was just above St. Anthony Falls, and Quinn held onto it until established in his new home. Quinn sold the site on May 1, 1845. See Marion Daniel Shutter, ed., *History of Minneapolis, Gateway to the Northwest*, Vol. I. (Minneapolis: S.J. Clarke Pub., 1923), 80.
5 Here and below, Edward D. Neill and J. Fletcher Williams, *History of Hennepin County and the City of Minneapolis* (Minneapolis: North Star, 1881), 225.
6 "Philander Prescott," *Hennepin County History*, 21: 4–5. Folwell, *A History of Minnesota*, I: 159–160. The parcel included territory ranging north to include south sections of the future Crow Wing and Aitkin counties along with north Pine County. See map on page 324 for this and other acquired tracts of Indian land.
7 Frederick L. Johnson, *Richfield: Minnesota's Oldest Suburb* (Richfield: Richfield Historical Society, 2008), 9, 14. Philander and Mary Prescott built a home overlooking the creek at today's E. 45th Street and Snelling Avenue. Foster Dunwiddie, "The Six Flouring Mills on Minnehaha Creek," *Minnesota History* 44 (spring 1975): 166.
8 Col. John Stevens, "From Col. John Stevens 1856 Address before the Minneapolis Lyceum," *Hennepin County History*, 18 (spring 1958): 10, 18.
9 P. Prescott to Governor Ramsey, September 28, 1860, copy in Richfield Historical Society Prescott file.
10 The quotation is found in United States Army Military Commissions, "Proceedings of the Military Commission for the 1863–64 Trial of Dakota Prisoners; Records relating to the trial of Medicine Bottle and Little Six," MHS Collections. See testimony of Mar-pe-he-de-awin [court recorder's spelling], a sister-in-law of Prescott.
11 Anderson and Woolworth, ed., *Through Dakota Eyes*, 30–31. Perhaps the nervous Prescott remembered the words he heard from the Dakota concerning the fighting style of Anglo-American soldiers. In his own words, Prescott reported, "I have heard them [the Dakota] acknowledge before a white and Indian assembly that they thought the whites excelled them in a few things, but the moment they assembled by themselves they would say the whites were the greatest fools they ever saw, and particularly when standing straight up in battle to be shot at." See Prescott, "Autobiography and Reminiscences," 491.
12 Carley, *The Sioux Uprising*, 15. Capt. Marsh had already fought in the Battle of Bull Run but had no experience with Indian fighting. He sent a message to a nearby unit asking for assistance, writing, "It is absolutely necessary that you should return with your command immediately…The Indians are raising hell at the Lower Agency."
13 Holcombe, Minnesota in Three Centuries, III: 316. Neill and Williams, History of Hennepin County, 227.
14 Here and below, Minnesota in the Civil and Indian Wars, see Lt. Thomas P. Gere, "Battle of Redwood," I: 248–250. Gere, then a young lieutenant, became temporary commander at Fort Ridgely following the death of Capt. Marsh. Carley, The Sioux Uprising, 16.
15 Just two weeks before Quinn's death, Indian agent Thomas J. Galbraith wrote to a Lt. T.J. Sheehan, an officer with the 5th Regiment, warning, "Your interpreter, Quinn, is a man whom I cannot trust to communicate…with my Indians." Galbraith asked that Quinn be "ordered off the reservation."
Charles E. Flandrau, a major figure in the 1862 war, defended Quinn from this "grievous wrong," asserting he had seen "a good deal of the old man" and his work as an interpreter. Wrote Flandrau, "…I never knew a man in…military life who enjoyed to such an extent not only the absolute confidence but the friendship of all officers, enlisted men and citizens with whom he came in contact." Flandrau reported he still held (in 1890) a saber that Quinn wore for many years "…as a memento of a good and brave man, whose name and fame I will defend against all assaults while I live." See Minnesota in the Civil and Indian Wars, "Notes to Judge Flandrau's Narrative" (Addendum) 818i, j.
16 "Proceedings of the Military Commission," Medicine Bottle's Trial. There were reports that the Dakota severed Prescott's head after shooting him. Gabriel Renville, a Dakota mixed-blood and later a chief, who helped whites escape from the fighting in 1862, reported in *Minnesota Collections*, (St. Paul, 1905), 10: 605*n* that Prescott was "intercepted and killed and his gray head cut off and stuck on a pole."
17 "Lucy Prescott Pettijohn," "Fragment—no title," John H. Case Papers, MHS.
18 Roger Kennedy, *Men on the Moving Frontier* (Palo Alto: American West, 1969), 51–52.

Medicine Bottle On Trial

1 Alvin C. Gluek, Jr., "The Sioux Uprising, A Problem in International Relations," *Minnesota History* 34 (winter, 1955) 318. Alexander Dallas reminded officials in London of the 1857 Sepoy Rebellion in India during which native troops rose up against whites.
2 Here and below, for an account of Hatch's march to Pembina and ensuing operations see Board of Commissioners, *Minnesota in the Civil and Indian Wars, 1861–1865* (St. Paul, 1891). Maj. C. W. Nash, "Narrative of Hatch's Battalion of Cavalry," I: 594–601. Gluek, Jr., *Minnesota History* 34: 320.
3 A.G. Dallas to Thomas Fraser, January 15, 1864, in "Copies or extracts of all the correspondence between the commanding officers of the United States troops in Minnesota and resident governor of the Hudson's Bay Company at Red River, respecting a tribe of Sioux Indians who were refugees within the British territory…and of the correspondence between the Hudson's Bay Company…and Her Majesty's government…." MHS collections. See also A.G.B. Bannatyne to Maj. Hatch, December 19, 1863 in *Minnesota in the Civil and Indians Wars*, II: 546.
4 Folwell, *A History of Minnesota*, Appendix 16, "Little Six and Medicine Bottle," II: 444. John MacKenzie, a leader in the capture of the two chiefs, described his role in a 1912 letter to E. Southworth, MHS Microfilm Collection, M582. Major C.W. Nash, "Narrative of Hatch's Independent Battalion of Cavalry," *Minnesota in the Civil and Indians Wars*, I: 599–600.
5 For the Toronto *Globe* citation see "Copies or extracts of all the correspondence…" 'Extracts from the Canadian *News*, 3 March 1864.' Folwell, *A History of Minnesota*, II: 448. Maj. Hatch still wished to pursue Dakota remaining in Canada. Although under direct orders not to cross the border, Hatch was itching to move against Dakota so near his grasp. He wrote to the governor asking permission to "pursue and capture these savages," and quickly received approval for a raid. The major then decided not to cross the border, see Gluek, Jr., *Minnesota History* 34: 323–324.
6 Here and two paragraphs below, United States Army Military Commissions, "Proceedings of the Military Commission for the 1863–64 Trial of Dakota Prisoners; Records relating to the trial of Medicine Bottle and Little Six," MHS Collections. Medicine Bottle's trial began at Fort Snelling on November 26, 1864, 10 a.m.
7 Court records identified the forty-five-year-old woman as "Mar-pe-he-de-sawin."
8 Here and below, the names of the first two men testifying on November 29 were written as Mack-a-pee-ah-wak-kan-za and Wak-ke-an-wash-ta.
9 "Statement of the accused in his defense," p. 1–2 (marked "A") attached to the document "Records relating to the trial of Medicine Bottle and Little Six."
10 "Statement of the accused," 3; Shelby Foote, *The Civil War, a Narrative, Fort Sumter to Perryville*, (New York: 1958) 158–163, Lincoln famously said in regard to the Trent Affair, "One war at a time."
11 Folwell, *A History of Minnesota*, II: 449.
12 *Saint Paul Pioneer*, September 26, 4, November 12, 1865, 4.
13 *Saint Paul Pioneer*, November 12, 1865

The Extraordinary Life of Charles Eastman

1 See transcription of a Charles Eastman letter to H.H. Hitchcock of Minneapolis, September 8, 1927, in *Minnesota Archaeologist*, 12 (January 1949): 1. Capt. Seth Eastman, born January 14, 1808, in Brunswick, Maine, was a sixth generation descendant of English immigrant Roger Eastman. His military career, enhanced by a West Point education, brought him to Fort Snelling in 1830. He would return in 1841 as fort commander. His talents as an artist brought him greater prominence than his years as a soldier.
2 Charles A. Eastman, *Indian Boyhood* (Garden City: Double Day, Page, 1910), 3, 13–16. Regarding his name, Eastman wrote, "I had to bear the humiliating name 'Hakadah,' meaning "the pitiful last," until I should earn a more dignified and appropriate name."
3 Here and three paragraphs below, Charles Alexander Eastman, *From the Deep Woods to Civilization, Chapters in the Autobiography of an Indian*, ed. A. LaVonne Brown Ruoff (Chicago, R.R. Donnelley & Sons, 2001), 2–7, 50, 54, 113–117.
4 "I was trained…" page 5 and "Your father has come…" page 6, Eastman, *From the Deep Woods to Civilization*."
5 "Our own life…" Eastman, *From the Deep Woods to Civilization*, 8.
6 "…a stranger…" Eastman *From the Deep Woods to Civilization*," 54. For more on Eastman's genealogical background see William L. Bean, "Eastman, Cloud Man, Many Lightnings, an Anglo-Dakota Family," compiled for the Eastman family reunion, July 4, 1989, Flandreau, South Dakota.
7 Here and below, Eastman, *From the Deep Woods to Civilization*, 65–66, 105–106, 125–126.
8 Eastman, *From the Deep Woods to Civilization*, 65–66.
9 Eastman, *Indian Boyhood*, pages 3, xxii and 49. Eastman, *Indian Boyhood*, pages 3, xxii and 49. Charles A. Eastman, *The Soul of an Indian* (New York: Dover Publications, 2007 reprint). Eastman's book was first published in 1911.

Section Two: Patrons of Agriculture

Squatters in South Hennepin County

1 Carl Waldman, *Atlas of the North American Indian* (New York, Facts on File, 1985), 114–120. Scott L. Malcomson, *One Drop of Blood: The American Adventure of Race* (New York: Farrar Straus Giroux, 2000), 55–56. Malcomson asserts the alliance of Indian tribes fighting at Fallen Timbers was "the largest organized racial uprising in American history."
2 Francis Paul Prucha, *The Sword of the Republic: The United States Army on the Frontier, 1783–1846* (Lincoln: University of Nebraska Press, 1986). Prucha discusses the use of the army to promote American sovereignty over Indian lands by speeding settlement. Paul S. Boyer, ed., *Oxford Companion to United States History* (New York: Oxford University, 2001), 379. Waldman, *North American Indian*, 115–120.
3 Roy W. Meyer, *History of the Santee Sioux* (Lincoln: University of Nebraska Press, 1975), 87.
4 For views regarding the treaty process and other issues of the Dakota, see Gary Clayton Anderson and Alan R. Woolworth, ed., *Through Dakota Eyes: Narrative Accounts of the Minnesota Indian War of 1862* (St. Paul: MHS, 1988), 19–33. Franklyn Curtiss-Wedge, ed., *History of Goodhue County* (Chicago, H.C. Cooper, Jr. & Co.), Chapter VII: 7, 74–87, provides a summary of Minnesota treaties with the Dakota from 1825 to the 1851 agreements at Traverse des Sioux and Mendota.

5 Folwell, *History of Minnesota*, 1: 353–355.

6 Daniel J. Boorstin, *The Americans: The National Experience* (New York: Random House, 1965), 74. Writes Boorstin, "The Western 'squatter' was usually the actual first settler, the preemptor, the man who had got their first." For the Ramsey quotation, see Folwell, *History of Minnesota*, 1: 354–356.

7 Gov. Ramsey also believed many settlers would be temporary Minnesotans staying on "until another wave of hardy adventurers, a little less restless in spirit, arrive to purchase their places…while they resume their never-ceasing journey towards the setting sun," see Folwell, *History of Minnesota*, 1:354–355.

8 Article 7, *Equal Right and Impartial Protection Claim Association of Hennepin County, Constitution and By-Laws*, c. 1852. The original document is in the collections of the Hennepin County Historical Society, along with a list of members. George E. Warner and Charles M. Foote, *The History of Minnesota: From the Earliest French Explorations to the Present Time* (Minneapolis: Minnesota Historical Soc., 1882), 174.

The fifth name on the claim association membership roster is "McLeod," with no first name given. Might this be Bloomington's Martin McLeod, a city founder and territorial representative who moved to Oak Grove in 1849? See "Membership List," c. 1852, *Equal Right Protection Association*.

9 Article 7, *Equal Right Protection Association*.

10 "Membership List," c. 1852, the membership list is found on two separate handwritten documents that accompany the association's constitution. They are written in the same hand but vary in clarity and penmanship. The first page is more readable and most always provides first and last names or first and middle initials. The second appears to have been written at a later time, although no dates appear on either sheet.

11 Articles 7 and 8, *Equal Right Protection Association*.

12 Folwell, *History of Minnesota*, 1: 359. Thomas Hughes, "History of Steamboating on the Minnesota River," *Minnesota Collections* (1905) 10: 141–145, shows that navigation on the Minnesota River in 1855 included 119 steamboat arrivals at St. Paul. Hughes includes a list of steamboats using Minnesota waters from 1850 to 1897, 158–163.

13 Warner and Foote, *The History of Minnesota*, 174. Folwell, *History of Minnesota*, 1: 362–363. Wrote Folwell regarding townsite organizers, "No form of speculation was more alluring, and for a time more profitable than operations in townsites…in the years from 1855 to 1857, inclusive, at least seven hundred towns were platted into more than three hundred thousand lots—enough for one and a half million people."

14 Here and below, Warner and Foote, *The History of Minnesota*, 172–173. Pierce served in the Territorial House in 1856.

New England of the West

1 John G. Rice, "The Old Stock Americans," in June Drenning Holmquist, ed., *They Chose Minnesota, a Survey of the State's Ethnic Groups* (St. Paul: MHS, 1981), 58–59. Maine lumbermen, millwrights and bridge builders reached the east side of the Mississippi at St. Anthony in the late 1840s.

2 *Eighth Census of the United States, 1860*, Hennepin County, Richfield, 130–152.

3 Rice, "The Old Stock Americans," 58–59, see also Table 3.4. "Minnesotans Born in New England, 1850–80," 61. Rhoda R. Gilman, "How Minnesota Became the 32nd State, *Minnesota History* 56, (winter 1998–99): 165.

4 Here and below, *Eighth Census of the United States, 1860*, Minnesota, Hennepin County, Richfield, pages 130–152. Rice, "The Old Stock Americans," Table 3.4, "Minnesotans Born in New England, 1850–1880," 61, lists Richfield among the communities with "concentrations" of New Englanders.

According to 1860 population statistics, others among the most affluent in Richfield were Vermonters Asa and Laura Keith, Able and Mahala Wilson; Bowen and Phoebe Briggs, and Ezra and Sarah Hubbard from Connecticut; Jesse and Lucy Richardson of Maine, and New Yorkers George and Merribeth Irwin,

5 Johnson, *Richfield*, 9–13.

6 *Eighth Census of the United States, 1860*, Hennepin County, Richfield, 130–152. Other early Irish in the area were Daniel and Catherine Clifford, John and Margaret Dugan, William and Mary Fogerty, Hugh and Ella Dasey. The land in the section known as the Cahill community was of somewhat poorer quality yet still productive. The acreage owned by the families mentioned averaged twenty-three hundred dollars in value.

7 Ann Regan, "The Irish," June Drenning Holmquist, ed., *They Chose Minnesota, a Survey of the State's Ethnic Groups* (St. Paul: MHS, 1981), 130, 140 and Table 7.1 "Irish in Minnesota by County," 1860–1970, 131.

The Irish community built St. Patrick's Catholic Church, Cahill School and the Cahill post office, and the farming community grew. The Cahill Irish settled along and around the south branch of Nine Mile Creek and lived on modest farms ranging from forty to 150 acres. A distinctly Irish tint to the neighborhood lasted through the 1920s, with the store and school surviving into the 1960s. Paul D. Hesterman, *Suburban Growth in Edina, 1900–1930*, 9, manuscript in MHS Collections.

8 "Memorial Notices of Rev. Gideon H. Pond," by messrs. Riggs (Stephen), Williamson (Thomas) and Sibley (Henry), *Minnesota Collections*, 1880, 360. S[amuel P. Pond, Jr., *Two Volunteer Missionaries Among the Dakota* (Chicago: Congregational Sunday School and Publishing Society, 1893), 166–169. For McLeod's reading habit see, "The Diary of Martin McLeod," Grace Lee Nute, ed., *Minnesota History Bulletin* 4, (May–November, 1922). Entries of November 1840 provide insight into McLeod's reading habits and his preference for Byron, "…my favourite of all English poets." Judith A. Hendricks, ed., *Bloomington on the Minnesota* (Bloomington: Bicentennial Committee, 1976), 30–35.

9 Holmquist, ed., *They Chose Minnesota*, 1.

10 Isaac Atwater, ed., *History of Minneapolis*, 498. *Eighth Census of the United States, 1860*, Hennepin County, Bloomington, 158. Hendricks, ed., *Bloomington on the Minnesota*, 36, 38, 48. Dean became a member of Hennepin County's first board in October 1852.

11 Here and two paragraphs below, *Eighth Census of the United States, 1860*, Hennepin County, Bloomington, 153–163. Hendricks, ed., *Bloomington on the Minnesota*, 36–49. Martin and Mary McLeod, owning real estate and personal property valued at $29,400, ranked as Bloomington's wealthiest couple in 1860, while R.B. and Margaret Gibson followed with $12,500.

12 Rice, "The Old Stock Americans," in June Drenning Holmquist, ed., *They Chose Minnesota*, 57.

Jonathan and Eliza Grimes: An Edina First Family

1 Henry David Thoreau, *Thoreau's Minnesota Journey: two documents*, edited by Walter Harding (Geneseo, NY: Thoreau Society, 1962), 17. Henry David Thoreau, *Wild Fruits: Thoreau's Rediscovered Last Manuscript*, Bradley P. Dean, ed. (New York: W.W. Norton, 1999), 315–316.

Thoreau's journals speak of his love for the "great west and north west stretching on infinitely far and grand and wild, qualifying all our thoughts." Yet in Minnesota he became preoccupied with the study of plants and animals. Edwin S. Fussell writes, "Minnesota and Henry Thoreau, standing face to face, found nothing to say to one another." See Daniel J. Philippon, "Thoreau's Notes on the Journey West: nature writing or environmental history," 18 (*Transcendental Quarterly*, June 2004).

2 Deborah Morse-Kahn, *Edina: Chapters in the City History* (Edina: City of Edina, 1998), 47–49. Ella A. Eustis, "Out of My Mind," 1959 manuscript at Edina Historical Society, 7. Eustis, Grimes's daughter, said Jonathan decided he would not live in a slave state. See also Eustis, "There Were Wolves in Those Days," *Hennepin County History* 50 (winter 1990–91), for an excerpt of her manuscript.

3 Here and below, Alden R. Grimes, "Descendents of Jonathan Taylor Grimes," pre-publication manuscript, Evanston, Illinois, 1988. 6.

4 Here and below, Grimes, "Descendents of Jonathan Taylor Grimes," 6. James D. Parsons, "The Morningside District of Edina," 14–15, manuscript in Edina Historical Society collections. Richard Strout became better known for his role in the 1862 Dakota War in western Minnesota. See Section One of this book, "Courage or Cowardice," for more.

Ella Grimes Eustis tells the story of the Ames saloon in "Out of My Mind," 13. Ames later became a Minneapolis mayor disgraced by scandal, 1901–1903.

5 Folwell, *History of Minnesota*, I: 363. "Fortunes seem to be dropping…" Folwell, 363, "so engrossed in speculating..." Kenneth Stampp, *America in 1857: A Nation on the Brink*, (New York: Oxford University Press, 1990) 218.

6 For a helpful view of the immediate effects of the Panic of 1857, see Stampp, *America in 1857*, Chapter 8, "Flush Times and Autumn Panic," 214–238. Frederick L. Johnson, *Goodhue County, Minnesota, A Narrative History* (Red Wing: Goodhue County Historical Society), 363–364.

7 Parsons, "The Morningside District of Edina," 23–24, manuscript in the Edina Historical Society collections. Richard Strout, et. al., to Jonathan Grimes and William C. Rheem, January 31, 1859, Book L of Deed Records, 577, Hennepin County Registrar of Deeds and Strout to Grimes and Rheem, January 31, 1859, Book L of Deed Records, 578.

8 "Today and Yesterday, The Mills of Edina," undated copy of a *Northwestern Miller* magazine article in Edina Historical Society collections. Foster Dunwiddie, "The Six Flouring Mills on Minnehaha Creek," *Minnesota History* 44 (spring 1975): 164–168. Grimes, "Descendents of Jonathan Taylor Grimes," 6.

9 Grimes quote from Parsons, "The Morningside District of Edina," 26, 28. For this and more on the Marsh Harvester, see Elvira H. Vinson, "Pioneer Women of Edina, Grimes family," 2, Edina Historical Society. One of the Marsh brothers demonstrated the machine to an audience of farmers at the Grimes farm.

The late summer 1862 Dakota uprising in western Minnesota touched Edina. According to Ella Grimes Eustice, "many" of the Grimes neighbors fled in fear to Fort Snelling while her family stayed behind. She adds, we were "packed and ready to go," Eustice, "Out of My Mind," 15–16.

10 Parsons, "The Morningside District of Edina," 28–29. Eustis, "Out of My Mind," 14. During the blizzard, the team circled in the ravine while Grimes, covered in buffalo robes, tried to stay warm.

11 Parsons, "The Morningside District of Edina," 29–31. The sheriff's sales are documented in Richard Strout to Peter Wolford in Book U of Deed Records, 417–418, Hennepin County Registrar of Deeds and Richard Strout to Edwin S. Jones, Book R, 429. Jonathan's land purchase is found in Book 9 of Deed Records, August 5, 1865, 16, Walter Harriman to Jonathan Grimes.

Grimes would later write that he sold the Bairds the mill around 1866, but Hennepin County mortgage records show he lost control of it after the 1862 sheriff's sale. The Bairds did continue to run the mill with Grimes still possibly involved.

12 See the biography of "Jonathan T. Grimes," *Minnesota Horticulturist* 23 (May 1895): 130. Grimes became a Society representative at America's successful 1876 Centennial Exposition in Philadelphia, traveled in 1882 to St. Louis on behalf of the Mississippi Valley Horticultural Association, and was a delegate to the 1888 American Horticultural Society gathering in San Jose, California.

13 Return I. Holcombe, *A Compendium of History and Biography of Minneapolis and Hennepin County* (Chicago: H. Taylor & Co., 1914), 328–329.

14 The Grimes house at 4200 West 44th Street still exists and is privately owned. It is listed on the National Register of Historic Places. Morningside's Grimes Avenue and Alden Drive are named for Jonathan Grimes and his son, Alden.

15 "Nickel Limit is Pushed Westward Replatting of Grimes Farm," Minneapolis *Journal*, April 11, 1905, 4.

The Split: Edina Divorces Richfield

1 Frederick L. Johnson, *Richfield: Minnesota's Oldest Suburb*, 13–14. The name "Harmony" was first applied to the mill. This came from James Dunsmoor, an early notable Richfield settler and its postmaster. He used the name of his hometown Harmony, Maine, as a post office address. The mill was sited at present-day Lyndale and 53rd.

Those in attendance couldn't know it, but Congress had formally accepted Minnesota into the union on that same day. The residents left the meeting in the knowledge they now lived in the town of Richfield. It is a coincidence of history that Richfield and Minnesota share March 11, 1858, as a "birth date." See Folwell, *History of Minnesota*, II: 14–23 for the final congressional actions regarding Minnesota statehood.

2 Richland Mill was sited near the geographic center of the proposed incorporation. Philander Prescott, his son-in-law Eli Pettijohn, and William Moffat built the mill in the summer and fall of 1855 at the Bloomington Road ford on Little Falls Creek, Johnson, *Richfield*, 13–14. Parsons, "The Morningside District of Edina," 21–25, manuscript in the Edina Historical Society collections.

3 Johnson, *Richfield*, 14. Folwell, *A History of Minnesota*, 3: 66. In those days, as soon as Minnesota farmers broke ground, they planted spring wheat and also typically grew some corn and oats. By 1860, the state's wheat crop reached five million bushels; five years later it was nearly ten million.

4 Prominent east Richfield farmers, including Charles and Ann Hoag, Cornelius and Nancy Coulliard, and Riley and Fanny Bartholomew, typically patronized Richfield Mill, while leading westerners such as James and Mary Bull, George and Merribeth Irwin, and Michael and Mary Delaney preferred Waterville. For more information on the families named here, see Johnson, *Richfield*, index 159–161.

5 Hopkins's claim is found in a December 1860 letter to *Minnesota Farmer and Gardener*. He is credited with founding the city now named for him, but in 1860 his land was within Richfield's boundaries. *Minnesota Farmer and Gardener*, L[yman] M. Ford and John H. Stevens, eds., 1 (December 1860): 13. Hopkins also reported his oat yield varied from forty to seventy-five cents per acre. Parsons, "The Morningside District of Edina," 27–28.

6 Parsons, "The Morningside District of Edina," 25. James Pratt to Ches. (Chesley) Pratt, November 16, 1864, Chesley Pratt and Family papers, MHS collections.

7 Johnson, *Richfield*, 27–28. The Richfield Historical Society has a photocopy of *Records of the Town of Richfield* [hereafter *Richfield Records*] that contains minutes from annual town meetings and specially called gatherings from 1858 up to 1899. Town meetings were briefly held at Richardson's Hall, owned by Jesse R. Richardson, from May 1874 until construction of the new town hall, *Richfield Records*, 142, May 10, 1874.

8 See "A Shrinking Richfield," a map with explanatory narrative detailing the many losses Richfield sustained between 1867 and 2000, Johnson, *Richfield*, 54–55. David J. Butler, a Richfield attorney, conducted detailed research regarding Richfield's long history of land loss and documented it for use in Johnson's *Richfield*.

9 *Richfield Records*, for those periods in which land was lost, contain no mention of these changes. Town and Board of Supervisors meeting records show concern about taxes, road building, legalizing liquor, building a town hall, etc., but not about encroaching Minneapolis.

10 "A Shrinking Richfield," Johnson, *Richfield*, 54. In the wake of those losses, voters at a Richfield town meeting designated several localities as "public places" for meetings, elections or other business, apparently to make local government more accessible. That March 8, 1887, resolution named as those locations the town hall, Edina Mills, and Hohag's Corners. On March 22 the Board of Supervisors met to reorganize Richfield's road districts, a meeting "made necessary on account of the loss of territory taken by the city of Minneapolis," *Richfield Records* March 8 and March 22, 1887: 265–267.

11 Here and below, Minnesota State Grange, Minnehaha Grange, No. 398 (Edina) Record, Box 1 MHS. A *Secretary's Book* from the Minnehaha Grange Assn., Richfield Township (1879–1907), contains information on the Edina Hall Association and the Minnehaha Grange. See *Secretary's Book*, March 7, 1879, entry for details on the local Grange's organizational meeting held at the Yancey residence.

There was considerable debate over the naming of the new community. When Andrew Craik bought the local mill in 1869 he renamed it "Edina Mills" the poetic name of Edinburgh, Scotland, his birthplace. Strong resistance to the name created hard feelings and heated debate but in the end all involved accepted Edina. Paul D. Hesterman, *From Settlement to Suburb, the History of Edina* (Edina: Edina Historical Society, 1988), 22–27.

12 Hesterman, *From Settlement to Suburb*, 22–27. *Richfield Records*, town meeting March 13, 1888: 270, 280.

Sarah Gates Baird and the Grangers

1 *Eighth Census of the United States, 1860*, Minnesota, Hennepin County, Richfield, pages 130–152. Minneapolis *Morning Tribune*, July 23, 1926, 10. Foster W. Dunwiddie, "The Six Flouring Mills on Minnehaha Creek," *Minnesota History* 44 (spring 1975): 163–166.

2 Rhoda R. Gilman and Patricia Smith, "Oliver Hudson Kelley, Minnesota Pioneer, 1849–1868," 40, *Minnesota History* (fall 1967): 330–338. Oliver H. Kelley, *Origins and Progress of the Order of the Patrons of Husbandry in the United States; a history from 1866 to 1873* (Philadelphia: J.A. Wagenseller, 1875), 11–90. Kelly credits his niece, Miss C.A. Hall, with suggesting that women receive full memberships. Paul S. Boyer, ed., *Oxford Companion to United States History* (New York: Oxford University, 2001), 318–318.

3 Here and below, James D. Parsons, "The Sarah Baird Diary," 1995 manuscript in the Edina Historical Society Collections, 4–5. Johnson, *Richfield*, 55.

4 Kelley, *Patrons of Husbandry*, 11–90. Solon J. Buck, *The Granger Movement, a study of agricultural organization and its political, economic and social manifestations, 1870–1880* (Cambridge: Harvard University Press, 1913), vol. 19: 50–58. Folwell, *History of Minnesota*, 3: 47.

5 Paul S. Boyer, ed., *The Oxford Companion to United States History* (New York: Oxford University Press, 2001), 183.

6 Elvira H. Vinson, "Pioneer Women of Edina, Sarah Baird," 4–5. Vinson wrote a series brief biographies during the 1920s. They along with some of Vinson's notes on her subjects are found in Edina Historical Society folder 70.3.5.

7 Minnesota State Grange, Minnehaha Grange, No. 398 (Edina) Record 1873–1985, Box 1, vol. 1, MHS collections. For more on James Bull see Coates P. Bull, "Time, Luck, Stamina," *Ramsey County History* 4 (spring 1967), 21. The author was Bull's son and a faculty member of the University of Minnesota's College of Agriculture.

8 Folwell, *History of Minnesota*, III: 38–51. Carl H. Chrislock, *The Progressive Era in Minnesota, 1899–1918* (St. Paul: MHS Press, 1917), 9–10. John D. Hicks, "People's Party Platform, 1892," in Daniel J. Boorstin ed., *An American Primer* (Chicago: University of Chicago, 1996), 533. Lawrence Goodwyn, *The Populist Movement, A Short History of the Agrarian Revolt in America* (New York: Oxford University Press, 1978), 3–9.

9 Minnesota State Grange, Minnehaha Grange, No. 398 (Edina) Record, Box 1 MHS. A minute book, *Secretary's Book*, Minnehaha Grange Assn., Richfield Township (1879–1907), contains information on the Edina Hall Association and the Minnehaha Grange.

10 Johnson, *Richfield*, 32. A map showing Richfield's original boundaries is found on page 55.

11 *Secretary's Book*, Minnehaha Grange Assn., see March 7, 1879, entry for details on the meeting at the Yancey residence. Paul D. Hesterman, *Suburban Growth in Edina, 1900–1930*, manuscript in MHS collections, 10. B[everly] C[assius] Yancey and Ellen Yancey played important roles in Edina history, see Deborah Morse-Kahn, *Edina: Chapters in the City History* (Edina: City of Edina, 1998), 60–62.

12 Sarah G. and George W. Baird diaries and account books, 1862, 1870–1918, MHS. Sarah's notebooks vary in size, and the text in some can be difficult to read. Volume two carries the story of the 1888 winter.

13 *A History of Minnehaha Grange No. 398, 90 years young* (Edina: Minnehaha Grange, 1963), 7. S[arah] G[ates] Baird, "Address to the Grange of Minnesota," 1912, p. 16, Minnesota State Grange Record, Box 1 MHS.

14 Baird, "Address to the Grange of Minnesota," 1.

15 Ibid. 6–11.

16 The Minnesota Grange reached its zenith in September 1874 but two years later saw the number of Granges nearly halved. Fowell, *History of Minnesota*, 3: 55. Theodore C. Blegen, *Minnesota: A History of the State* (Minneapolis: University of Minnesota Press, 1963), 386–387.

17 Baird, "Address to the Grange of Minnesota," 16.

Boom, Bankruptcy, Bust—Steele, King and Menage

1 Return I. Holcombe, *Minnesota in Three Centuries* (New York: Publishing Society of Minnesota, 1908), II: 96. Rodney C. Loehr, "Franklin Steele, Frontier Businessman," *Minnesota History* 27 (December 1946): 309–311. Franklin Steele Papers, MHS collections, contain a manuscript dealing with Steele's life in Minnesota.

2 William C. Folsom, "Lumbering in the St. Croix Valley," in *Collections of the Minnesota Historical Society* (St. Paul: MHS) 9: 323. Folsom, speaking at the annual MHS meeting on January 16, 1899, cited a letter from Steele as his source for the information.

3 Folsom, *Minnesota Historical Society Collections* 9: 324. Loehr, "Franklin Steele," 310–311.

4 Willam Watts Folwell, *History of Minnesota*, 1: 452–453. In this appendix to volume one of his study ("Steele's Preemption at the Falls of St. Anthony"), Folwell examines the conflicting stories that swirled around the incident.

5 Folwell, *History of Minnesota*, 1: 453–454. Return I. Holcombe, *Compendium of History and Biography of Minneapolis and Hennepin County, Minnesota* (Chicago: H. Taylor, 1914), 60. Holcombe reports Capt. Martin Scott accused Steele of jumping a claim he established with Plympton, Capt. Martin Scott and another officer sometime around July 16, 1838. Steele's brother-in-law, Gen. Richard W. Johnson, says that Steele and prominent fur trader, Norman Kittson, crossed the frozen Mississippi and built a rough shack on Steele's St. Anthony claim. They slept on hay and used buffalo robes for warmth and were awakened by the knocks of Plympton and Scott. See Richard W. Johnson, "Fort Snelling from its Founding to the Present Time," *Minnesota Historical Collections* (St. Paul, MHS, 1898), 8: 437.

6 Loehr, *Franklin Steele*, 314–315. Folwell, *History of Minnesota*, 1: 503–504. Folwell notes an act of Congress in March 1819 authorizing the secretary of war to sell military bases that "may have been found, or become useless for military purposes." Part of the problem for Steele was that most believed the 1819 law no longer was in effect. Minnesota Senator Henry M. Rice disposed of that issue by attaching an obscure paragraph of the army appropriation bill legislation. This March 3, 1857, action restored the government's power to sell off unneeded military bases.

7 *House of Representatives, 40th Congress, Sale of the Fort Snelling Reservation, Letter from Secretary of War transmitting papers relative to the sale of Fort Snelling*, Washington D.C., 1868, 2–8. Folwell, *History of Minnesota*, 1: 504–509.

8 Paul Wallace Gates, "Southern Investment in Northern Lands before the Civil War," *Journal of Southern History* (May 1939): 174–175. Gates notes Archibald Graham recognized the Fort Snelling sale as "an opportunity of a lifetime and Graham did not neglect it." Gates asserts the ninety-thousand-dollar price tag for the land was "well below the estimated value of the land." There was dispute about the value. See Folwell, *History of Minnesota* 1: 510. Steele produced ten thousand dollars for the down payment, while Mather added eight or nine thousand, and Schell ponied up the remainder.

9 Here and below, Folwell, *History of Minnesota* 1: 513–515. Steele had platted the town site of Fort Snelling in 1857 before the nationwide financial collapse forced him to await further developments.
Secretary of War John B. Floyd wrote to officers at Fort Snelling on November 11, 1858, noting that since Franklin Steele was "…in default of the second installment, which should have been paid on the 10th of July last, I desire that you will, at once, institute suit, and prosecute it with all vigor and dispatch, so as to subject the land to sale for the payment of the purchase money." "Consolidated correspondence file relating to Fort Snelling, 1819–1868," [microform], MHS collections.

10 Here and below, Folwell, *History of Minnesota*, 3: 90–91.

11 "Lyndale Farm," Minneapolis Daily *Tribune*, December 4, 1870, 3. This long and detailed news story carries specific information about Lyndale Farm and King's plans for it. The writer rated King's massive barn the "best" in the west.

12 William S. King papers, MHS, see Jay Cooke's letter to King, September 21, 1870. Cooke wrote that capital needed "for the building of the road, necessitates the disbursement of large sums hence we are desirous of calling in all amts due." *Down at the Lake, A Historical Portrait of Linden Hills and the Lake Harriet District* (Minneapolis: Linden Hills History Study Group, 2001), 19.

13 See William King's testimony in *State of Minnesota Supreme Court, William S. King Plantiff and Respondent against Philo Remington, Caroline A. Remington, Robert S. Innes, Louis F. Menage and Amanda A. Menage*, 191.

14 Here and two paragraphs below, Loring Staples, "The Decline and Fall of Louis Menage," *Hennepin County History* 42 (spring 1983): 6

15 David A. Lanegran and Ernest R. Sandeen, *The Lake District of Minneapolis, A History of the Calhoun-Isle Community* (St. Paul: Living Historical Museum, 1979), 36–37. Staples, "The Decline and Fall of Louis Menage," 8. Menage agreed to pay Innes in installments on or before June 1, 1882, and on or before November 1, 1887, with a mortgage of $411,000 for the remainder.

16 Staples, "The Decline and Fall of Louis Menage," 8–9. Thomas W. Pierce and John T. Blaisdell, among Richfield's founders, testified for King regarding the 1878 value of his land. Pierce lived on the west shore of Lake Calhoun across from Lyndale Farm, and said the land should have brought $700 per acre. Blaisdell testified land prices were depressed at the time, but the King property still was worth about a half-million. See *William S. King against Philo Remington,et.al.*, 417–418, 434–435.

17 Charles M. Loring, "The Parks and Public Grounds of Minneapolis, *Minnesota Collections*, 602–603. Walter B. Dahlberg, Minneapolis Parks—Their Early History," *The Civic Digest, A Cyclopedia of the Governments of Minneapolis, Hennepin County and State of Minnesota* (Minneapolis: 1949), 16. King also deeded a forty-foot-wide and a mile-long strip of land to a road today known as "King's Highway.

18 Staples, "The Decline and Fall of Louis Menage," 11.

19 Larry Millet, *Lost Twin Cities* (St. Paul: MHS, 1992), 222–224. The Northwestern Guaranty and Loan Building on 3rd Street and 2nd Avenue South became known to future generations as the Metropolitan Building. It was destroyed in a 1961–62 urban renewal effort. Author Millet ranked its demolition as "perhaps the most inexcusable act of civic vandalism" in Minneapolis history. Lanegran and Ernest R. Sandeen, *The Lake District of Minneapolis*, 37–38.

20 Staples, "The Decline and Fall of Louis Menage," 12.

21 Here and three paragraphs below, Staples, "The Decline and Fall of Louis Menage," 14. The losses in the Puget Sound portion of the scheme amounted to $1,667,000. Minneapolis *Journal*, March 17, 1924, 1 and Minneapolis *Morning Tribune*, March 18, 1924, 10 provided historical background on Menage in his obituaries.

The Poet and the Park

1 Steven J. Keillor, *Grand Excursion: Antebellum American Discovers the Upper Mississippi* (Afton, MN: Afton Historical Society Press, 2004), 17–18. Artist George Catlin touted the idea of a "fashionable tour" on the upper Mississippi in 1835, and small numbers of sightseers took excursions during the 1830s and 1840s. Theodore C. Blegen, "The Fashionable Tour on the Upper Mississippi," *Minnesota History* 20 (December 1939): 377–396, considers earlier versions of this kind of excursion.

2 Mark W. Seely, "Mother Nature Smiled: The Grand Excursion of 1854," *Minnesota History* 49 (spring 2004) provides a detailed review of weather conditions at the time of the excursion. Keillor, *Grand Excursion*, 178–179 describes the interest and delight of the travelers and quotes their reports about "Little Falls."

3 Samuel Pond to Herman Hine, January 19, 1835, in Helen White and Bruce White, *Fort Snelling in 1838: An Ethnographic and Historical Study* (St. Paul: Turnstone Historical Research, 1998), 5. Mary Jones to Dearest Rebeca [sic], November 7, 1855, MHS Manuscript Notebooks. For the Mann quotation, see Henry David Thoreau, *Thoreau's Minnesota Journey: two documents*, edited by Walter Harding (Geneseo, NY: Thoreau Society, 1962). 50.

4 Longfellow used an updated version of Schoolcraft's *Algic Researches, comprising inquiries respecting the mental characteristics of the North American Indians, first series, Indian tales and legends* (Philadelphia: Harper, 1839). For an overview of Schoolcraft's work, see Theodore C. Blegen, *Minnesota: A History of the State* (Minneapolis: University of Minnesota Press, 1975 edition), 117–118. MHS has sixty-nine reels of Schoolcraft's papers on microfilm (M296).

5 Through the nineteenth century's later decades, the success of Longfellow and his contemporaries, such as John Greenleaf Whittier and William Cullen Bryant, led some to call them the "school room" poets—their work could be found in nearly every American school. Longfellow was a lion in American literature with *The Courtship of Miles Standish*, *Paul Revere's Ride*, and *The Wreck of the Hesperus* joining a growing list of his most popular works.
Teachers used daily recitation—oral responses to teacher questions about lessons—as an instructional and evaluative tool in American classrooms well into the twentieth century. Recitation and memorization were combined when a student learned a passage and then repeated it verbatim for the teacher, the class or adult audiences. A.N. Raub, *School Management: Including a Study of School Economy, School Ethics and School Government, and Professional Relations of the Teacher* (New York: Raub & Co., 1882), see chapter III, Objects and Methods of Recitation, 111–121. George Gould and Gerald Yoakam, *The Teacher and His Work: A First Course in Education* (Chicago: Ronald Press, 1954), discuss nineteenth-century education practice and memorization.

6 Here and below, Dana Gioia, "Longfellow in the Aftermath of Modernism," *Columbia History of American Poetry*, Jay Parini, ed., 64–67, 80–83. Maine Historical Society, Henry Wadsworth Longfellow website, www.hwlongfellow.org accessed March 21, 2009. His words inspired composers and artists; communities named schools, geographic locations, even cigars for him and characters from his writings.

7 Federal Writers' Project, *The WPA Guide to Minnesota* (St. Paul: MHS Borealis Press, 1985 edition), 193. This update of the 1938 book reports that a Longfellow friend, George Sumner, gave the poet an 1852 daguerreotype of the falls. Longfellow, according to Sumner "took it out in the woods with him and from it conceived the thought and the poem of Hiawatha." Charles E. Doell, "History of Minnehaha State Park," *Hennepin County History* 3 (October 1943): 2.

8 Charles M. Loring, "History of Parks and Public Grounds of Minneapolis," *Minnesota Collections* 15 (1915): 602. Walter B. Dahlberg, "Minneapolis Parks–Their Early History," *The Civic Digest, A Cyclopedia of the Governments of Minneapolis, Hennepin County and the state of Minnesota* (Minneapolis, 1949), 15–16. Johnson, *Richfield*, 54–55.

9 Johnson, *Richfield*, details the annexation of the Richfield land, 54. Doell, "History of Minnehaha State Park," 16. Loring, "History of Parks and Public Grounds of Minneapolis," 601–602, tells of the opposition to the Park Act and its eventual passage.

10 C.M. Loring, Geo. A. Brackett, William H. Yale, Chas. H. Strobeck, Wm. A. Van Slyke, "Report of the Commissioners for the State Park at Minnehaha," November 1886, 1–2. The legislation establishing Minnehaha, backed by Hennepin County politicians, had attached to it a search for a "Horticultural and Mechanical State Exhibit Grounds" (state fairgrounds) favored by St. Paul lawmakers.

11 "Minnehaha Park Syndicate," 5–6, an 1891 advertising booklet, MHS collections.

12 Here and below, "The Minnehaha Case," and "Supt. of HaHa Park Accused," April 12, 1905, Minneapolis *Journal*, 4. Charges against O'Brien included mistreating animals, stealing feed for his cows, selling park stone, threatening employees, and sleeping on duty. See also, Janet Whitmore, "The John Stevens House, Birthplace of Minneapolis," *Hennepin County History* 56 (summer 1997): 17.

13 R[obert] F. Jones, *The Story of Longfellow Gardens*, (Minnehaha Falls: self-published, 1912). This photo-filled promotional booklet shows Jones with his animals and describes the Gardens' features. Joseph W. Zalusky, "Fish Jones and His Irresistible Longfellow Gardens," *Hennepin County History* 27 (fall 1967): 7–8. Minneapolis *Journal*, October 16, 1930, 15, contains Jones' obituary. It notes his fish market was at 308 Hennepin Avenue.

14 Jones, *The Story of Longfellow Gardens*, 1912 and 1922 editions. Jones' 1922 publication contains twelve pages of photos showing him and zoo animals. Loring, "History of Parks and Public Grounds of Minneapolis," 603.

15 Here and below, Zalusky, "Fish Jones," 8–10. The Longfellow House was moved and renovated in 1994 and may still be visited, as can the statues, at Minnehaha Park. The weather-beaten, toga-clad tribute to Longfellow is located in the lagoon area of the park.

Section Three: Looking South

Streetcar Suburb: Edina's Rail Links to the Twin Cities

1 David L. Ames and Linda Flint McClelland, "Historic Residential Suburbs," National Register Bulletin, U.S. Department of Interior, September 2000, 16–26.

2 Folwell, History of Minnesota, III: 1–3. Bertha L. Heilbron, The Thirty-Second State: A Pictorial History of Minnesota (St. Paul: MHS Press, 1966), 99–101. Johnson, Richfield, 29–30.

3 Here and below, Eric Foner and David Garraty, eds., The Reader's Companion to American History (Boston: Houghton Mifflin, 1991), 881–883. Nationwide there were 415 horse car companies in operation by the mid-1880s. Calvin G. Goodrich, A History of the Minneapolis Street Railway Company (Minneapolis: 1909), 3–6. David Lanegran and Biloine W. Young, "How the trolleys came and went," Mpls.St. Paul, 24 (June 1996): 60. Minnesota historians Lanegran and Young based this magazine article on their 1996 book Grand Avenue: the Renaissance of an Urban Street.

4 Denis Murphy, "Colorfully Critical: Newspapers and the Horsecars of the 1870s," Ramsey County History 18 (winter 1983): 11–13.

5 Isaac Atwater, History of the City of Minneapolis Minnesota (New York: Munsell & Co., 1893), 341–342. Atwater interviewed Lowry for this biographical sketch and was effusive with praise for the businessman. See also Rev. Marion Daniel Shutter, ed., History of Minneapolis, Gateway to the Northwest (Chicago-Minneapolis: S.J. Clarke Publishing, 1923), II: 20–24 for another glowing tribute, this one posthumous, of Thomas Lowry.

6 Goodrich Lowry, "Tom Lowry and the Launching of the Street Railway System," Ramsey County History 18 (winter: 1983): 6–7. Author Goodrich Lowry, who became a prominent Twin Cities banker, was Tom Lowry's grandson.

7 Goodrich Lowry, Street Car Man: Tom Lowry and the Twin City Rapid Transit Company (Minneapolis: Lerner Publishing, 1979), 49, 61.

8 Lanegran and Young, Minneapolis St. Paul 24: 60; by 1890, horse cars rolled across 120 miles of Twin City tracks. Lowry, Ramsey County History 18: 7–8.

9 Goodrich, A History of the Minneapolis Street Railway Company, 7. Atwater, History of the City of Minneapolis, 339.

10 Here and below, See Goodrich, "The Old 'Motor Line,'" in A History of the Minneapolis Street Railway Company, 8–10. David A. Lanegran and Ernest R. Sandeen, The Lake District of Minneapolis (St. Paul: Living Historical Museum, 1979), 21–22.

11 Atwater, History of the City of Minneapolis, 339.

12 Here and below, Goodrich, A History of the Minneapolis Street Railway Company, 8–9. The power problem on Nicollet hill grew worse at about six p.m. when heaviest passenger loads occurred. Lanegran and Sandeen, Lake District of Minneapolis, 24–26.

13 Elvira H. Vinson, "Pioneer Women of Edina Morningside," Brown file, 35, Edina Historical Society Collections.

14 Paul D. Hesterman, The History of Edina, from Settlement to Suburb (Edina: Edina Historical Society, 1988), 22. Goodrich, A History of the Minneapolis Street Railway Company, 10. See Motor Line Time Card, September 10, 1885, at the bottom of the page for the Edina stops.

15 Lowry, Ramsey County History 18: 7–8. Experiments with steam-powered "cable cars," an 1885 San Francisco invention, had added more red ink to Tom Lowry's ledgers. In that system a streetcar grips a moving cable in the street and is pulled along to its destination. Minnesota weather overwhelmed cable technology. Extreme cold caused the slot in the track to shrink and a cable car's "gripper" could not access the cable. Conversely, the slot expanded in the summer and became a trap for passing carriages. Weathering also damaged the cable itself.

Lowry's St. Paul cable line opened on January 16, 1888, and ran west from downtown along 3rd up today's Cathedral Hill area to Selby Avenue and beyond. Damaged cables frayed and could cause dreaded cable car "runaways." Shortly after the line's debut, a runaway car killed one passenger while injuring others; see Lanegran and Young, Mpls.St. Paul 24: 61.

16 Lowry, Ramsey County History, 18: 8–9. Lanegran and Young, Mpls. St. Paul 24: 61. Archbishop of St. Paul, John Ireland, and Macalester trustee,Thomas Cochrane, asked Thomas Lowry to extend and electrify St. Paul Street Railway lines leading west from downtown. The prominent St. Paul men desired better access to the schools they helped establish—Ireland was a founder of St. Paul Seminary—and the land they owned in the largely undeveloped areas west of Lexington Avenue. Cochran and Ireland raised money to advance this admittedly new and yet to be fully tested electric rail concept and agreed to insure Lowry against potential losses. See Lanegran and Young, Mpls.St. Paul 24: 61.

17 Lowry, Ramsey County History 18: 9. "Trudging up and down Wall Street…" Lowry, Street Car Man, 132.

18 Atwater, History of the City of Minneapolis, 340. A triple financial whammy clobbered Tom Lowry during the 1890s. The scandalous collapse of Minneapolis mogul Louis Menage's financial empire (Lowry was a large stockholder), the national financial Panic of 1893, and the bicycle fad that blossomed from 1893 to 1896 and crowded Minneapolis streets and emptied streetcars, damaged Lowry severely. The New York Times reported he "rented his palatial home to those who could afford to live in luxury and moved his family into more modest quarters. Lowry, Street Car Man, 81, 125, 132. "Thomas Lowry Dies after Long Illness," New York Times, February 5, 1909, 7.

19 Here and below, John W. Diers and Aaron Isaacs, Twin Cities by Trolley: the Streetcar Era in Minneapolis and St. Paul (Minneapolis: University of Minnesota Press, 2007), 113.

The Greatest Race Course in the World

1 Wheeler was part owner of the Wheeler-Schebler Carburetor Co. in Indianapolis. *Twin City Motor Speedway Official Programme*, September 4, 1915, 17, copy in MHS pamphlet collection. "Centennial Era Moments, Gala, Reflections," www.Indianapolismotorspeedway.com/centennial (accessed April 7, 2009).

2 Alvin W. Waters, "The Twin City Motor Speedway," *Minnesota History* 60 (winter 2007–08): 306. Quotations are from F.W. Wheeler to C.E. Dutton, September 17, 1914, letter in author Waters' collection.

3 Noel Allard, "Ill-fated Twin City Auto Speedway," *Hennepin County History* 35 (spring, 1976): 29. Johnson, *Richfield*, 45. Allard's more comprehensive study of the race (Noel Allard, *Minneapolis 500*, 2007) is online at www.gotomn.com/racing/minn500.htm.

4 "Million Dollar Speedway will Attract Thousands Saturday," Minneapolis *Journal*, September 2, 1915, 16. An Ingvolstad Lumber Company ad, also on page 16, provides details on building supplies. Allard, *Minneapolis 500*, chapter 5.

5 Allard, *Minneapolis 500*, chapter 5. "Salutatory," *Twin City Motor Speedway Official Programme*, 4.

6 Allard, *Hennepin County History* 35: 29.

7 Here and below, Minneapolis *Journal*, September 2, 1915, 16. The advertisement referring to ticket costs is also found on this page.

8 Ibid.

9 St. Paul *Pioneer Press*, September 5, 1915, 1–2. Minneapolis *Journal*, September 5, 1915, 1. Not everyone in the crowd was apathetic. National Guard troops on hand for security turned back a group of about one hundred men who broke through a fence in a bid for free admission. Allard, *Minneapolis 500*, chapter 5.

10 St. Paul *Pioneer Press*, September 5, 1915, 1.Minneapolis *Journal*, September 15, 1915, Sports Section, 1.

11 Minneapolis *Journal*, September 15, 1915, 2. Frank G. Force, director of publicity, announced the number of paid admissions. Wheeler pointed out to reporters that the Indianapolis racetrack had opened in 1909 with just twenty thousand fans, a number that grew to more than eighty thousand in the years ahead.

12 "Speedway Workers Angry when Told to Wait," Minneapolis *Journal*, September 7, 1915, 1. Capron played halfback for the Gophers and briefly joined the Chicago Bears in 1920. He also had appeared in several baseball games during a two-year career with the Pittsburgh Pirates and Philadelphia Phillies in 1912–1913, www.baseball-almanac.com/players.php?p=caprora, accessed April 13, 2009.

13 "Special Race for Speedway Sunday," Minneapolis *Journal*, September 6, 1915, 12 and September 9, 1915, 8. St. Paul *Dispatch*, September 8, 1915, 1, makes note of Wheeler's activities.

14 Waters, *Minnesota History* 60: 310. Waters quotes the correspondence between Frank Wheeler and Charles Dutton.

15 Minneapolis *Journal*, July 15, 1917, Sports Section, 1. A subhead to the newspaper story read, "Speedway Revival a Great Success From Racing Standpoint—Crowd Small." Allen E. Brown, ed., *The History of the American Speedway: Past and Present* (Marne, Michigan: Slideways Pub. 1989), 25, 203.

16 Johnson, *Richfield*, 28, 47. Gus's parents were Charles and Emily Hohag. Charles served on the Richfield town board for thirty consecutive years, twenty as chairman. He became the community's first president in 1908 when Richfield formally organized as a village.

17 "Nostalgic Memories Haunt Metro Runway," Richfield *News* (Special Section) January 11, 1962, 2. Karen Fadden, a Hohag descendant and a family historian, supplied information on the land sale to Gus Hohag. See also Jerry Sandvick, "Early Airport Development and the Emergence of the Metropolitan Airports Commission," *Hennepin County History* 43 (fall 1984): 2–3.

18 Sandvick, "Early Airport Development," 3–4. *Minnesota Statutes 1927*, Chapter 62. Johnson, *Richfield*, 55.

19 "Resident Recalls Richfield History," Richfield *News*, January 19, 1973, 1. This interview with Jack Hohag provides an overview of his family's relationship with the airport and aviation.

20 Johnson, *Richfield*, 128.

A Disastrous Inaugural: The Arrival of Airmail Service

1 Speedway Field, later Wold-Chamberlain, was built on the site of the 1915 Twin Cities Auto Speedway. When that auto racetrack failed, pilots began using the interior of the two-and-one-quarter-mile track as a landing strip. The Minneapolis Aero Club bought the field in December 1919. In 1923, the airfield was renamed to honor Ernest Wold and Cyrus Chamberlain, local pilots killed in France during World War I; see Short History of the Minneapolis Municipal Airport (Wold-Chamberlain Field) a mimeographed 1937 report describing operations at the field, MHS Manuscript Notebooks, Minneapolis Board of Park Commissioners. See also, Frederick L. Johnson, Richfield: Minnesota's Oldest Suburb (Richfield: Richfield Historical Society, 2008), 47–48.

2 Minneapolis Journal, "U.S. Launches Minneapolis-Chicago Air Mail Monday," June 6, 1926, 1. Dave G. Stiff, "Final Flight: Reconstructing an Early Airmail Accident," Minnesota History 50 (fall 1986): 99. The June 7, 1926, St. Paul Pioneer Press carried extensive coverage about the airmail service and the city's new airport.

3 "Death and Gale Fail to Halt Air Mail," Minneapolis Journal, June 8, 1926, 1. "Air Mail Pilot Killed in Crash," St. Paul Pioneer Press, June 8, 1926, 1.

4 Minneapolis Journal and St. Paul Pioneer Press, June 7, 1926, page one accounts. For the Stiff quote, see Stiff, Minnesota History 50 (fall 1986): 100; Dave Stiff, who wrote this article is the grandson of Albert Stiff, Sr., into whose field Elmer Partridge crashed.

5 For the information on Charles Dickinson, see Century of Flight, "Aviation between the wars: the start of airmail," http://www.century-of-flight.net/index.html (accessed January 31, 2009). Camille Allaz, The History of Air Cargo and Airmail, from the 18th Century (London: Christopher Foyle, 2005), 60–68. Dickinson's flyers included Billy Brock, Matty Laird, Dan Kaiser, H.J. Keller, and Nimmo Black. Elmer Partridge served as a substitute pilot; see "More on the First Airmail Flights," History Matters, newsletter of NWA History Centre 1 (fall/winter 2003): 3–4.

6 Stiff, Minnesota History 60:100.

7 Joe Cristy and LeRoy Cook, American Aviation, an Illustrated History (Blue Ridge Summit, PA: McGraw-Hill, 1994), 9–13. Partridge had designed aircraft with Henry Warner, a colleague and friend, as early as 1913. He built a plane for Katherine Stinson of the flying Stinson family in 1915, and she used that aircraft to become the fourth American to complete an aerial loop maneuver.

8 St. Paul Pioneer Press, June 8, 1926, 2.

9 "Merrill K. Riddick, 93, Politician and Aviator," New York Times, March 12, 1988. Besides his flying exploits, Riddick ran for U.S. president three times as the candidate of the Puritan Ethic and Epic, Magnetohydrodynamics and Prohibition Party.

10 Here and below, Stiff, Minnesota History, 60: 100–101. Minneapolis Journal, June 8, 1926, 8. Billy Brock reported Partridge's initial confusion over Wold-Chamberlain.

11 Minneapolis Journal, June 8, 1926, 19.

12 "Airmail Pilot Killed in Crash," St. Paul Pioneer Press, June 8, 1926, 1. "Death and Gale Fail to Halt Air Mail, Minneapolis Journal, 1.

13 St. Paul Pioneer Press, June 8, 1926, 2. Stiff, "Final Flight," 101; author Stiff interviewed one of the eyewitnesses, Sig J. Letendre, in September 1977.

14 Stevens's interview appears in the St. Paul Pioneer Press, June 8, 1926, 2.

15 St. Paul Pioneer Press, June 8, 1926, 2.

16 Ibid. Dr. R.A. Schnacker arrived with the ambulance and declared Partridge dead. Along with the head injuries, he found that both of the flyer's legs were broken in several places.

17 Minneapolis Journal, June 8, 1926, 1. William Kidder operated the Curtiss-Northwest Airport and Flying School on the southeast corner of Snelling and Larpenteur Avenues in St. Paul. Pop Dickinson secured two of Kidder's aircraft for his airmail operation.

18 Allaz, The History of Air Cargo and Airmail, 60–68. Dickinson operated his airmail service from Chicago's Blackstone Hotel. He died in 1935 following a heart attack; "More on the First Airmail flights," History Matters, 3–4.

19 "In the Beginning," History Matters, newsletter of NWA History Centre, 3 (September, 2007): 2. Of Northwest's five original officers, all but Britten, vice-president and general manager, were from Michigan.

20 Here and below, "More on the First Airmail Flights," History Matters, newsletter of NWA History Centre, 2 (June 2004): 1–2.

Fly Northwest Airlines, Circa 1932

1 Air trips from Minneapolis to Chicago were known to be bumpy. When the federal government authorized bids to deliver airmail as part of its newly privatized Contract Air Mail (CAM) system, the Minneapolis to Chicago route, aka CAM 9, was considered more challenging. The first successful bidder for CAM 9, sixty-eight-year-old "Pop" Dickinson, soon failed because of air crashes. Northwest Airways was organized in 1926 to claim the open CAM; see Camille Allaz, *The History of Air Cargo and Airmail, from the 18th Century* (London: Christopher Foyle, 2005), 60–68 and "More on the First Airmail Flights," *History Matters, newsletter of NWA History Centre* 1 (fall/winter 2003): 3–4.

2 Susan Duxbury, "Captain Joe Kimm, Quiet Birdman," *Journal of the Airline Pilots Association* 71 (May/June 2002) 24–26. The Green Bay, Wisconsin, route had stops at Fond du Lac, Oshkosh, Neenah and Appleton. Northwest added service to Rochester, Minnesota, in 1929 and to Elgin and Rockford, Illinois, Sioux City and Iowa City, Iowa, and Omaha, Nebraska, in 1930.

In 1934 Northwest Airlines was based at St. Paul's downtown airport, Holman Field. It continued mail and passenger service from Wold-Chamberlain, however.

3 Joe Kimm was one of Northwest's first stewards and told about that job in several interviews. The information here is from "A Conversation with Joe Kimm," *History Matters, newsletter of NWA History Centre* 3 (March 2005): 3–4.

Northwest began hiring female stewardesses in the late 1930s. They were required to be registered nurses between twenty-one and twenty-five years old, five-feet-two to five-feet-five, with weight not more than one hundred-twenty pounds; "Helen Jacobson, Northwest's Third Stewardess Recalls the Exciting Early Days," *History Matters, newsletter of NWA History Centre* 6 (September 2008): 2.

4 Ibid.

5 "Triple Inquiry Opens on Plane Crash Here," St. Paul *Dispatch*, June 25, 1924, 1–2. Ernest Von Lorenz owned the house struck by the plane. He and other neighbors rushed to assist the stunned passengers. See also, St. Paul *Pioneer Press*, June 25, 1929, 1–2.

6 Frederick L. Johnson, *Richfield: Minnesota's Oldest Suburb* (Richfield: Richfield Historical Society, 2008), 50–51. Gus and Lottie Hohag would hold onto their land at the edge of airport until they died. The Metropolitan Airports Commission finally got control of it upon Lottie's death in February 1970.

7 Here and below, George E. Hopkins, "Transcontinental Air Transport, Inc." *American Heritage* 27 (December 1975).

8 "A Conversation with Joe Kimm," 4. Hopkins, "Transcontinental Air Transport, Inc."

9 Duxbury, "Captain Joe Kimm," 27. Kimm claimed landing planes in farm fields did not cause problems with farmers. "Farmers were more than happy to see us and were glad to give us a ride to town." See also, "A Conversation with Joe Kimm," 4–5.

10 Hopkins, *American Heritage* 27.

11 "Captain Leon S. "Duke" Delong," *History Matters, newsletter of NWA History Centre* 1 (summer 2005): 3–4. Regarding Holman "looping" a Tri-Motor, see "Holman and Bullock; Born to be Airborne and Flying Legends in Their Own Time," *History Matters, newsletter of NWA History Centre* 3 (June 2005): 4–6.

12 Here and five paragraphs below, "A Conversation with Joe Kimm," 5. The author relies heavily upon Joe Kimm's account here and the five paragraphs below. His words, in quotations, best tell the airsickness story.

Indestructible Mal Freeburg

1 Susan Duxbury, "Captain Joe Kimm, Quiet Birdman," *Air Line Pilot* 71 (May/June 2002): 24–25.

2 Noel Allard, "Charles W. 'Speed' Holman," *Hennepin County History* 34 (summer 1975): 3–5. Walter Bullock, Fred Whittemore, Homer Cole, Deke Delong, J.F. Malone, Joe Ohrbeck, Russ McNown, C. Les Smith, Jerry Sparboe, Cass Chamberlain, and Carl Luethi were among Northwest's other early pilots. Eddie Middagh died in a June 24, 1929, crash in St. Paul; see "In the Tough 1930s, Pay Day was a Great Day for Northwest Families," *History Matters, newsletter of NWA History Centre* 1 (fall/winter 2003): 5.

Northwest hired Freeburg on December 5, 1928, see "[Northwest] Seniority List," October 8, 1943, Northwest Airlines History Centre (Bloomington) collections.

3 Interview with James Freeburg, March 19, 2009, notes in author's possession. Jim Freeburg became a pilot for Northwest in 1948 and flew for forty-two years.

4 Frederick L. Johnson, *Richfield, Minnesota's Oldest Suburb* (Richfield: Richfield Historical Society), 48.

5 "Hero," *TIME Magazine* 24 (October 1, 1934). Kenneth D. Ruble, *Flight to the Top, How a hometown airline made history…and keeps making it* (no city given: Viking Press, 1986), 27–28.

6 St. Paul *Dispatch*, April 13, 1932, 1; a *Dispatch* reporter was a passenger and told the story in print the following day. Joe Kimm also discussed the incident in an interview, see Susan Duxbury, *Air Line Pilot* (May/June 2002): 28–29.

7 Here and one paragraph below, St. Paul *Dispatch*, April 13, 1932, 1. Ruble, *Flight to the Top*, 28. Duxbury, *Air Line Pilot*, 28–29.

8 St. Paul *Dispatch*, April 13, 1932, 1. Freeburg and his wife, Ruth, divorced in 1934, James Freeburg interview.

9 Ruble, *Flight to the Top*, 28–29, 38. During the 1930s Freeburg flew Santa Claus to St. Paul's Holman Field on behalf of Schuneman's department store.

10 Duxbury, "Captain Joe Kimm, Quiet Birdman," 27–28. Also on the flight with the pilots and Earhart were Hunter and his wife, Anne, Col. Lewis Britten, head of the airline, and mechanic Heinie Wahlstrom, who sat in the cabin.
11 Robert L. Johnson, "Joe Kimm Remembers Amelia Earhart and the Northwest Transcontinental Survey Flight," *History Matters, newsletter of NWA History Centre* 4 (March 2006): 5.
12 Ruble, *Flight to the Top*, 45.
13 Minneapolis *Journal*, September 19, 1934, 2.
14 Here and below, "7 in Plane Periled When Gear Halts Landing 90 Minutes," St. Paul *Pioneer Press*, September 19, 1934, 1.
15 "Hero," October 1, 1934. *TIME* reported the plane's propellers suffered the worst damage and would take fifty dollars to repair. It also noted that Northwest kept its record of eight years without a single passenger fatality. They were not counting the death of pilot Eddie Middagh in the June 24,1929, crash in St. Paul.
16 Here and below, Ruble, *Flight to the Top*, 69–70. The aircraft oxygen mask developed was named "BLB" for the physicians who invented it, Arthur H. Bulbulian, William H. Lovelace and Walter Boothby.
17 Richfield *News*, December 17, 1942, 1; July 8, 1943, 1. The quotation is in an unnamed magazine photo caption c. 1941, see "Flight Attendants Archives, 1935–1943," Northwest Airlines History Centre (Bloomington) collections.
In 1941 Minneapolis had Freeburg cap its 1941 Aquatennial celebration by "spiraling up to 5,000 feet in a plane and dropping two magnesium flares on 18-foot parachutes into the lake [Calhoun]," newspaper clipping c. July 1941 in "Flight Attendants Archives, 1935–1943," Northwest Airlines History Centre (Bloomington) collections.
18 James Freeburg interview.
19 Ibid. For more on Transocean Air Lines, see Richard Thruelsen, "The Daring Young Men of Transocean," *Saturday Evening Post*, August 2, 1952.
20 James Freeburg interview.

Louise Whitbeck Fraser Starts Over

1 "Dry Agent Shot Dead on So. St. Paul Job," St. Paul *Pioneer Press*, January 3, 1928, 2.
2 "Our Founder, Louise Whitbeck Fraser," www.fraser.org/about_fraser/LWF (accessed February 27, 2009). "Soldier Rites Ordered for Slain Agent," St. Paul *Dispatch*, January 3, 1928, 2. Fraser's assailant, a South St. Paul butcher, surrendered to police and admitted to the crime. See also, The Officer Down Memorial Page, www.odmp.org/officer/5085 (accessed, December 22, 2008).
3 St. Paul *Dispatch*, January 3, 1928, 1–2. Fraser attended Valley City (North Dakota) Normal School, as did his future wife, Louise Whitbeck. He taught and coached football at Redwood Falls, Minnesota, before serving in France as a sergeant in the U.S. army during World War I. S.B. Kvale, Northwest Division administrator for prohibition enforcement, said of Fraser, "He was one of the finest men in the department."
4 Here and two paragraphs below, "Our Founder, Louise Whitbeck Fraser."
5 "Soldier Rites Ordered for Slain Agent," St. Paul *Dispatch*, January 3, 1928, 1. Louise Fraser endured Wesley Fraser's exhausting military funeral. Soldiers from Company I, Minnesota National Guard, a unit in which he was a captain, escorted the widow and the body to Redwood Falls for burial.
6 Thomas W. Balcom, "Fraser School celebrates Louise Whitbeck Fraser and 50 years of caring for special children," *Hennepin County History* 44 (winter 1985–86): 5.
7 Ibid.
8 "Our Founder, Louise Whitbeck Fraser." Balcom, *Hennepin County History* 44: 5–6.
9 Dan Olson, Minnesota Public Radio, News and Features, "Turning Setbacks into Stepping Stones," March 26, 2001. A copy of the text is available at www.news.minnesota.publicradio.org/features/200103/27_olsonnd_fraser/ (site accessed December 23, 2008).
10 Here and two paragraphs below, Balcom, *Hennepin County History* 44: 6–7. "Our Founder, Louise Whitbeck Fraser."
11 Here and below, Balcom, *Hennepin County History* 44: 11–13.
12 Carol Ratelle Leach, "Seven Wonders of Minnesota," *Minnesota Monthly* (September 2006).
13 "People," 103 (*TIME* magazine, June 24, 1974). The "People" section carries the story about Muriel Humphrey who was quoted saying, "At no time did any officer of the State Department or any other agency of Government inform me that gifts received by me…should be placed in the custody of the department."

Safety in the Suburbs, Augsburg and its move toward Richfield

1 Here and below, Merrill E. Jarchow, *Private Liberal Arts Colleges in Minnesota, Their History and Contributions* (St. Paul: MHS, 1973), 17–18, 25. By 1860 there were 3,178 Swedes, 7,738 Norwegians and 164 Danes living in Minnesota. Those numbers mushroomed in the decades to follow.
2 Frederick L. Johnson, *Goodhue County, Minnesota: a Narrative History* (Red Wing: Goodhue County Historical Society Press, 2000), 118–121. Minnesota's Scandinavians could choose from three Minneapolis newspapers to fit their language or ideological needs: *Minneapolis Tidende*, a Norwegian daily and weekly; *Vikingen-Minneapolis*, a Danish-Norwegian paper; and the Swedish weekly *Svenska-Amerikanska Posten*.
3 Jarchow, *Private Liberal Arts Colleges in Minnesota*, 25, credits Rev. Ole Paulson with being the prime mover in establishing Augsburg in Minneapolis. Sven Oftedal claimed to have secured Murphy's land contribution for a seminary, "without the payment of any consideration therefore by anyone," see Charles Lillehei, *Augsburg Seminary and the Lutheran Free Church* (Minneapolis: no publisher, 1928), 29. Blegen's quote is found in Theresa Gervais Haynes, "Augsburg Park, a forgotten dream," *Minnesota History* 40 (winter 1967): 375. Isaac Atwater, ed., *History of the City of Minneapolis* (New York: Munsell Pub., 1895), 34, 396–397 provides more detail on the Murphy Addition. Author Atwater lived near the Augsburg campus.
4 Carl G. O. Hansen, *My Minneapolis* (Minneapolis, privately published, 1956), 315–316.
5 Lincoln Steffens, *The Shame of the Cities* (New York: McClure, Phillips & Co. 1904), 64–65. Alfred E. Ames was a member of the Equal Right and Impartial Protection Claims Association, a group of early settlers mostly from south Minneapolis and Richfield. See "Squatters in South Hennepin County," Section Two.
6 Steffens, *Shame of the Cities*, 72.
7 Haynes, *Minnesota History* 40: 376–377.
8 Steffens, *Shame of the Cities*, 64. Sondra Herman, *Eleven against War: Studies in American International Thought, 1898–1921* (Stanford: Hoover Institute, 1969), 152, 162–164. Herman writes of Veblen's complaints about Yankee business owners who made the village life of youth "the perfect flower of self-help (selfishness) and cupidity." Yet when his parents sent Veblen to college in nearby Northfield, Minnesota, they chose the city's Yankee stronghold, Carleton College, instead of the predominantly Norwegian-American St. Olaf College.
9 Jarchow, *Private Liberal Arts Colleges in Minnesota*, 79. In 1921 five women enrolled, and the student newspaper, *Echo*, reported no problems were caused by their presence.
10 Here and below, Haynes, "Augsburg Park," 378. Jarchow, *Private Liberal Arts Colleges in Minnesota*, 79. Johnson, *Richfield*, 44, 52–53. For the opening of Augsburg Park tracts see Minneapolis *Journal*, July 13, 1924, Real Estate and Building section, 1. College treasurer Fred Paulson issued the announcement that twenty-five acres of land overlooking Wood Lake was available.
11 Johnson, *Richfield*, 52–53. Haynes, *Minnesota History* 40: 379, the quotation is found in the *Lutheran Free Church Messenger*, April 15, 1922, 3.
12 "Mystery Tips Fail to Locate Missing Pastor," Minneapolis *Morning Tribune*, December 1, 1925, 9. This article appeared the day before Birkeland's body was found and reported that leads provided to police about his disappearance had been "fruitless."
"Birkeland Believed Slain," Minneapolis *Morning Tribune*, December 2, 1925, 1 reported the discovery of the body, that Birkeland had been missing since November 24, and claimed evidence indicated he had been murdered. "Physician Believes Pastor Slain," Minneapolis *Journal*, December 2, 1925, 1, noted an examination of the body pointed to murder.
Minneapolis *Journal*, December 3, 1925, 1, 33, looks at the continuing search for the woman who rented the apartment and considers reports that witnesses saw Birkeland four days *after* he disappeared, near the apartment.
13 "Secrecy Shrouds Birkeland Inquest," Minneapolis *Journal*, December 9, 1925, 1.
14 George H. Mayer, *The Political Career of Floyd B. Olson* (Minneapolis: University of Minnesota Press, 1951), 182. Howard Birkeland continued efforts to prove his father was a murder victim. He published a series of pamphlets detailing his version of events, with the eighth used here as a source, Harold Birkeland, *Floyd B. Olson in the First Kidnapping Murder in "Gangster Ridden Minnesota,"* (Minneapolis: self published, 1934), copy in MHS collections. By then, Olson was in his third year of service as governor of Minnesota.
15 Mayer, *Floyd B. Olson*, 182. Haynes, *Minnesota History* 40: 379.
16 Ibid. Haynes quotes *Folkebladet* 46: 824–826 (December 29, 1926) and 47:10 (January 5, 1927]).
17 See interview with Paulson from the Minneapolis *Star*, December 15, 1964. Paulson later became Richfield city clerk and at the time of this interview was ninety-five and the community's oldest citizen. Johnson, *Richfield*, 53, 154 *n*45.
18 Here and below, Haynes, "Augsburg Park," 381–382.

The Country Club District

1 Details about Nichols and the development of the Kansas City Country Club district are found in the *Speeches of J[esse] [Clyde] Nichols* (1880–1950), Western Historical Manuscript Collection, University of Missouri–Kansas City. Accessed online at www.wmkc.edu/WHMCKC/publications/JCN/JCNintro.htm, May 7, 2009. Samuel Thorpe notes in the foreword of his 1924 *Thorpe Brothers County Club District* that he had "many conferences with his intimate friend, J.C. Nichols of Kansas City."
2 Marion Daniel Shutter, *History of Minneapolis: Gateway to the Northwest* (Chicago-Minneapolis, S. J. Clarke Publishing Co, 1923), 2: 15–16.
3 Kenneth T. Jackson, *The Crabgrass Frontier: the suburbanization of the United States* (New York: Oxford University Press, 1985), 177–178. Jackson provides an overview on the history and significance of the J.C. Nichols's Kansas City Country Club district. See also the *Speeches of J.C. Nichols* for his observations on the creation his exclusive housing development. See *Thorpe Brothers County Club District*, c. 1924 for references to the nation's other leading housing subdivisions, copies at Edina Historical Society and MHS.
4 Shutter, *History of Minneapolis*, 15–16.
5 "District Founder Buried October 5, *The Crier* 7 (November 1936): 5, 6, 12. George P. Morrill, *The Millionaire Straphanger, A Life of John Emory Andrus* (Middletown, CT: Wesleyan University Press, 1971). *TIME* magazine's January 7, 1935, obituary of Andrus. John Andrus was notoriously careful with his money. He built the Andrus Building in Minneapolis "over and around" an 1880s building known as the Sidle Block. See Larry Millett, *Twin Cities Then and Now* (St. Paul: MHS Press), 30–31.
6 Here and below, *New York Times*, October 4, 1889, 4, carried the wedding notice. Morrill, *The Millionaire Straphanger*, 62, 164–165.
7 *The Crier* 7 (November 1936): 12.
8 Shutter, *History of Minneapolis*, 15–16.
9 Paul D. *Hesterman, Suburban Growth in Edina, 1900–1930*, manuscript in MHS collections, 28–29.
10 Robert D. Sykes, "The Country Club District: a model for suburban life in Edina," *Minnesota Common Ground* 3 (fall 1995): 3.
11 Sykes, *Minnesota Common Ground* 3 (fall 1995): 3. Anthony Morell and Arthur Nichols (not to be confused with Kansas City developer, J.C. Nichols) planned Duluth's Morgan Park neighborhood and worked for Thorpe on the Country Club's Sunnyside and Wooddale Additions as well as on Washburn Park in Minneapolis. Morell and Nichols designed a number of Edina neighborhoods including the 120-acre "residential colony" Rolling Green (1936), Indian Hills (1947), Edina Highlands (1948), Parkwood Knolls (1948) and Brookview Heights (1951); see Greg Kopischke, "Elite, elegant and expensive: Morell & Nichols' Edina Projects, 1936–1951," *Minnesota Common Ground*," 1996, copy n.d., in Hennepin County History Museum.
12 "Country Club, 11 Years Old, One of the Nation's 4 Finest Subdivisions," *The Crier* 6 (July 1935): 1, 3, 8.
13 Here and three paragraphs below, William W. Scott and Jeffrey Haas, *History and Architecture of Edina* (Edina: City of Edina, 1981), 66. In *The Crier* 6 (July 1935): 8, Sam Thorpe asserts that restrictions helped sales.
14 Kevin Boyle, *Arc of Justice: A Saga of Race, Civil Rights, and Murder in the Jazz Age* (New York: Henry Holt and Company, 2004), Klan statistics found on page eight. Boyle's Prologue provides a feel for the racial tensions in the Midwest and nation in the wake of World War I. In the mid-20s, Chicago's Klan numbered fifty thousand, Detroit's thirty-five thousand. A parade of fifty thousand Klan members paraded past the White House in 1925.
15 *Thorpe Brothers County Club District*.
16 Scott and Haas, *History and Architecture of Edina*, 66–67. Among the works of brothers-in law Liebenberg and Kaplan are the Granada (Suburban World, 1927–28), the Wayzata (1932), the Edina (1934), the Hollywood (1935), the Uptown (1937), the Varsity (1938), as well as Adath Jeshurun Synagogue (1927) and Beth El Synagogue (1926, razed in 1995), Minneapolis Heritage Commission website, www.ci.minneapolis.mn.us/hpc/landmarks/Liebenbergandkaplan.asp accessed May 22, 2009.
17 Here and below, David McDonald, *"Successful" suburbanization in Edina*, 1974, 11–17, manuscript at MHS. *Hesterman, Suburban Growth in Edina*, 66–67. The community sent council members and farmers, James Delaney and J.J. Duggan, to a League of Minnesota Municipalities meeting in June 1926. That organization was dedicated to modernizing the governance of the state's municipalities.
18 Scott and Haas, *History and Architecture of Edina*, 67.
19 *The Crier* 6 (July 1935): 1. The Country Club's May 1935 issue of *The Crier* noted "every phase of activity in the Country Club has been more brisk this spring than at any time in the last six years."

Section Four: Boomlet to Boom

"Automobility" and Hennepin South

1 Isaac Atwater, *History of the City of Minneapolis, Minnesota* (New York: Munsell & Co., 1893), 340. Goodrich Lowry, *Street Car Man: Tom Lowry and the Twin City Rapid Transit Company* (Minneapolis: Lerner Publishing, 1979), 81, 125, 132. St. Paul held a Good Roads convention in 1893, and the Minnesota State Fair staged its first Good Roads Day in 1893 and followed it with another in 1894. See Frederick L. Johnson, *Goodhue County, Minnesota: A Narrative History* (Red Wing, MN: Goodhue County Historical Society Press, 2000), 188.
The author uses the word "automobility" in the title of this piece, an apt term applied by Kenneth T. Jackson in chapter nine of his book *Crabgrass Frontier: The Suburbanization of the United States* (New York: Oxford University Press, 1985).
2 Mark Sullivan, *Our Times: America at the Birth of the Twentieth Century*, edited by Dan Rather (New York: Scribner, 1996), 56. Eric Foner and John A. Garraty, editors., *The Readers's Companion to American History* (Boston: Houghton Mifflin, 1991), 694.
3 David L. Nass, *Minnesota in a Century of Change: The State and its People since 1900*, Clifford E. Clark, Jr., ed. (MHS: St. Paul, 1989), 136. Sullivan, *Our Times*, 56.
4 *Automobile Club of Minneapolis* (Minneapolis: The Club, c.1915): 5–8 in MHS collections. A June 27, 1916, letter to Solon J. Buck, newly appointed superintendent of the Minnesota Historical Society and member of the auto club, is found with this pamphlet.
An Auto Club membership card worked as a "bail bond" recognized by the Minneapolis and St. Paul police departments "in the event of a member's arrest for alleged [law] violation…."
5 *Automobile Club of Minneapolis*, 5–6. Sullivan, *Our Times*, 339. Jackson, *Crabgrass Frontier*, 164.
6 Frederick L. Johnson, *Richfield: Minnesota's Oldest Suburb* (Richfield: Richfield Historical Society, 2008), 44. Jackson, *Crabgrass Frontier*, 164. C.M. Babcock, state highway commissioner declared the renaming of the southern leg of Lyndale Avenue in June 1922. This occurred in spite of resistance from some south Minneapolis residents who preferred that south Cedar Avenue would become the new Highway 50. Babcock said Lyndale was "the logical choice. See Minneapolis *Morning Tribune*, June 24, 1922, 26.
7 Yale Realty was marketing Waleswood and encouraged potential buyers to take a Bryant Ave. S. streetcar to the end of the line at 50th where the realty firm's autos awaited. Customers received a "free ride over a paved highway" (Lyndale). See Minneapolis *Morning Tribune*, June 12, 1921, A 6. Other Waleswood ads are found in May 22 (A 8), June 4 (D 5) and July 10 (A 8) editions.
The Wales residence included twenty-eight rooms connected to a large guest hall by a 125-foot-long pergola under which two passageways, one for guests the other for servants, were located. It included bowling alleys, a swimming pool, barns and an observatory. The Great Depression cut into the Wales fortune and the home was torn down in 1933 due to high maintenance costs. See "Notes in

Reference to the Waleswood Properties on the Minnesota River," (a rough plat map is also included) in a folder with cover note, "From C.E. Wales, 205 Transportation Building, Mpls. Minn," in the collections of the Hennepin History Museum. See also, Scott Donaldson, *The Making of a Suburb: An Intellectual History of Bloomington, Minnesota* (Bloomington: Bloomington Historical Society, 1964), 39–40.

8 Minneapolis *Journal*, April 8, 1923, Real Estate and Building Section, 2. Minneapolis *Journal*, April 27, 1924, Real Estate and Building Section, 1.

9 Minneapolis *Journal*, April 27, 1924, Real Estate and Building Section, 1. The following lists the new 1924 Richfield plats, their location and firms involved in development, as cited in *Journal* article:

(1) Sheldon Blair, Wood Dale First Addition, 20 acres at Lyndale Avenue between 68th and 69th (2) Gerard & Kimball, Ford Town Addition, 100 acres at Cedar Avenue between 62nd and 66th (3) J.S. Hooper Co., Morris Park, Fourth Addition, 40 acres at 28th Avenue between 58th and 60th (4) Kvall Realty Co, Ingelside Addition, 20 acres at Humboldt Avenue between 56th and 58th (5) Kelly & McKusick, Wood Lake Highlands Addition, 80 acres on Penn Avenue between 68th and 70th (6) Francis A. McGillis, five acres at Colfax Avenue between 56thth and 57th (7) National Suburban Home Development Co., 40 acres on Lyndale Avenue between 70th and 72nd (8) Peri-Reed Co., 10 acres on Lyndale Avenue between 57th and 58th (9) C.F.E. Peterson Co., 50 acres on 34th Avenue between 58th and 66th (10) Tracker and Co., Fairview Park Addition, 70 acres at Humboldt Avenue between 64th and 66th (11) Tingdale Brothers, Goodspeed Addition, 200 acres at Lyndale Avenue between 66th and 68th.

Morningside Secedes From Edina

1 James D. Parsons, "The Morningside District of Edina," 51, manuscript in Edina Historical Society collections. Melvin Grimes still lived on the family farm when he became council president in 1895.

2 Here and below, "Nickel Limit is Pushed Forward," Minneapolis Journal, April 11, 1905.

3 Parsons, "The Morningside District," 52–53, 53 n133. Charles Fuller owned the Massassoit Land Company that later purchased just thirteen lots in Morningside. Hennepin County Deed Records, Book 615, 11 and 628; Book 616, 49 and 354; Book 633, 628, Hennepin County Registrar of Deeds, Hennepin County Government Center, Minneapolis

4 Edward Grimes, et al., to Charles Reynolds, Lots 8 and 9, Hennepin County Deed Records, Book 596, 184.

5 "Morningside Grew Out of 'Hole in Mud,'" Minneapolis Star, December 30, 1954. Dan A. Nelson, a veteran Morningside city clerk, is the source of the quote.

6 Paul D. Hesterman, Suburban Growth in Edina, 1900–1930, manuscript in MHS collections. Historian Paul Hesterman traced Morningside's long history of problems with the Edina village council. Village Clerk, Edina, Ordinances and Resolutions, 1889–1930, May 9, 1904.

7 Village Clerk, Village of Edina, Minutes of the Village Council of Edina, Minnesota, 1888–, August 9, 1908.

8 Hesterman, Suburban Growth in Edina, 24–25. Harriet News, October 1, 1920, 3. Deborah Morse-Kahn, Edina, Chapters in the City History (Edina, City of Edina, 1998) 89.

9 Ibid.

10 Village Clerk, Council Minutes, July 16, August 7, 1920. Leerskov, a house builder, owned six properties with frontage on 44th and owed $291.

Dan A. Nelson claimed the village's often muddy streets irritated residents, particularly those living on Scott Terrace, Branson Street, and Morningside Road, see Minneapolis Star, December 30, 1954.

For the quotation, see undated newspaper article, "Morningside's First Mayor Recalls Secession," R.L. Jensen Papers, Edina Historical Society.

11 Here and below, "In the Morning Mail," The Harriet News, September 17, 1920, 1, the author of the letter is an anonymous "Morningside Resident." E. Dudley Parsons, a regular contributor to the News and a capable, sometimes colorful writer, might have created it.

12 "Morningside's Civic League Meeting on Incorporation," Harriet News, October 1, 1920, 4. The meeting was held September 18, 1920. J.F. Main, a future Morningside official, and attorney Walter Whitan were among the speakers.

Long supplied the words to the community anthem. The first of four verses opens "I say to thee with loyalty, Morningside! My Morningside! In all my thought thou hast a part, Morningside! My Morningside!" see Edina Historical Society's Morningside File, 70.3.11.

13 Harriet News, October 1, 1920, 3.

14 Ibid.

15 Harriet News, October 8, 1 and October 15, 1, 1920.

16 Hesterman, Suburban Growth in Edina, 25. Harriet News, October 29, 1920, 1. The Morningside ticket for the October 30 election included R.L. Jensen and Emil Nelson for president, George Woodling and Ben Hoerger, recorder, Joseph Cowing, Wyman Elliott, J.H. Main, Alfred Bjorklund, Alex Nelson and Mr. Capler, directors, Nils Leerskov and J.H. Vander Bie, treasurer. Jensen, a Denmark native, moved into Morningside in 1914 and built on an Elmer Avenue lot he bought for $500, "Diary of Mr. R.L. Jensen," 23–25, Edina Historical Society, 2002.6.1.

17 Village Clerk, Council Minutes, November 5, 1920. Village Clerk, Morningside, Minnesota, Minutes of the Council of the Village of Morningside, November 10, 1920.

18 The safecracking incident occurred following a May 1922 election regarding the contentious school construction incident. The safe had been broken open, but a check by school board members found the ballots still inside. See "School Ballots Believed Stolen by Safe-Crackers are Discovered Intact," an unidentified May 25, 1922, newspaper clipping in Parsons, "Morningside Notes" (Part II).

19 Here and below, "Feelings ran high when Morningside married Edina," Minneapolis Tribune, April 14, 1979, B 2–3.

20 Ibid.

Rubbing Out Richfield

1 Frank Blackwell Mayer, *With Pen and Ink on the Frontier in 1851,* edited by Bertha L. Heilbron (St. Paul: MHS, 1986), 143.

2 David A. Lanegran and Ernest R. Sandeen, *The Lake District of Minneapolis: A History of the Calhoun-Isles Community* (St. Paul: Living History Museum, 1978), 36–40. The authors provide background of the development of south Minneapolis during its late nineteenth-century growth boom.

3 *Richfield Minute Book, 1908–1926*, Richfield (Minn.) Records, MHS state archives, May 29, June 26, August 28, and October 11, 1911. The motion to buy a Minneapolis map is found in the October 11 minutes. Frederick L. Johnson, *Richfield, Minnesota's Oldest Suburb* (Richfield: Richfield Historical Society, 2008), 42–43.

4 Johnson, *Richfield*, 43.

5 *Richfield Minute Book, 1908–1926*, February 26, March 25, July 28, August 26, 1912.

6 *Richfield Minute Book, 1908–1926*, names of new plats are in the minutes of May 29, 1922 and January 19, February 27, March 26, April 9, June 25, July 18, and September 20, 1923. Richfield Civic Association, *Richfield Minnesota*, not paginated, c. 1920, copy at RHS.

7 Minneapolis *Journal*, April 8, 1923, Real Estate and Building Section, 2. The newspaper reported 157 building permits had been issued for the 13th ward in the first quarter of 1923.

8 Minneapolis *Journal*, April 22, 1923, Real Estate and Building Section, 1.

9 "Richfield to Hold Vote on Annexation of Part of Village to Minneapolis," Minneapolis *Tribune*, March 9, 1924, Sect. II, 6.

10 Ibid.

11 Minneapolis *Tribune*, March 9, 1924, Sect. II, 7. "Petitions to Annex Richfield are Filed, Minneapolis *Journal*, April 13, 1924, Real Estate and Building Section, 1.

12 "Richfield to Vote on Taxes Tuesday," Minneapolis *Journal*, May 25, 1924, Editorial Section, 9. "Voters of Richfield Reject Plan to Join Minneapolis," Minneapolis *Tribune*, May 28, 1929, 2. The *Tribune* reported the vote as 1150–297, and the *Journal* called it 1150–396.

In "The Cue From Richfield," an editorialist in the *Tribune* wrote, "There is no doubt that the main reason for the large adverse vote in Richfield [was that] taxes in the city are much heavier than taxes in Richfield." The writer claimed city taxes raised land costs and "In that case [small home-owners] look to the suburbs for a home site." Minneapolis *Tribune*, May 29, 1924, editorial section, 14.

13 "Bachman Farm Lots on Sale Today," Minneapolis *Journal*, May 25, 1924, Real Estate Section, 1. The advertisement for Bachman Estates is found on page 4 of this section. Two years earlier, the Richfield council approved a Bachman plat for Lynnhurst Terrace development, *Richfield Minute Book, 1908–1926*, May 29, 1922.

14 Ibid.

15 Petition to the Richfield Village Council, February 19, 1926, 1, copy at Richfield Historical Society. For Minneapolis ward boundaries in 1910 and 1920, see maps by George F. Cram in Connie Murray, "Richfield: A Classic 50's Suburb," manuscript at RHS. Laura Nelson Baker, *Not So Long Ago* (Richfield: American Legion Post #435, 1951), 23.

16 Baker, *Not So Long Ago*, 31.

17 *Richfield Minute Book, 1908–1926*, December 13, 1926. *Minneapolis City Directory*, Vol. LIV, 1926, 689, 981.

18 Ibid. Joe H. Clark, village clerk, wrote in the minute book, "...Richfield consents to detachment."

19 For detail on the land annexed, see F.E. Johnson and E.H. Farmer, *Atlas of the Territory Annexed to the City of Minneapolis from the Village of Richfield in the Year of 1927*, MHS collections.

The Boom Begins

1 Here and below, Kenneth T. Jackson, *The Crabgrass Frontier: the suburbanization of the United States* (New York: Oxford University Press, 1985), 232–233. William Manchester, *The Glory and the Dream: A Narrative History of American*, 1932–1972 (Boston: Little, Brown and Co., 1974), 428. Harold Evans, *The American Century* (New York: Alfred A. Knopf, 1998), 384–385.

2 Manchester, *The Glory and the Dream*, 428–429. Jackson, *The Crabgrass Frontier*, 232. Jackson reports that an Omaha newspaper ad offered a 7 x 17-foot ice box as a living space; Atlanta bought one hundred trailers for vets, and North Dakota turned surplus grain bins into apartments. In New York City, newlyweds lived in a department store window, hoping the notoriety would bring them a place to live. Harold Evans, *The American Century* (New York: Alfred A. Knopf, 1998), 437.

3 Jackson, *The Crabgrass Frontier*, 233. Lisa Plank and Thomas Saylor, "Constructing Suburbia: Richfield in the Postwar Era," *Minnesota History*, 61 (Summer 2008): 48.

4 David Halberstam, *The Fifties* (New York: Fawcett Columbine, 1993), 131. Manchester, *The Glory and the Dream*, 397.

5 Manchester, *The Glory and the Dream*, 424, 583–589.

6 Halberstam, *The Fifties*, 116. Oscar T. Barck, Jr., and Nelson M. Blake, *Since 1900: A History of the United States in Our Times, 4th ed.* (New York: MacMillan, 1959), 752–753.

7 Frederick L. Johnson, *Richfield: Minnesota's Oldest Suburb* (Richfield: Richfield Historical Society, 2008) 147. Judith A. Henricks, ed., *Bloomington on the Minnesota* (Bloomington: Bloomington Bicentennial Committee, 1976), 103. Paul D. Hesterman, *The History of Edina, Minnesota: From Settlement to Suburb* (Edina: Edina Historical Society, 1988), 73.

8 Hesterman, *History of Edina*, 79–80.

9 Johnson, *Richfield*, 76–79, 80–81. Richfield's League of Women Voters led the charge to bring water and sewer issues to a vote and an eventual resolution. Henricks, *Bloomington*, 104, 119. The 1959–1960 installation of city water and sewage facilities finally resolved the Bloomington question. One thousand block leaders worked to develop support for public water and sewer programs.

10 Here and below, Henricks, *Bloomington*, 91–92, Hesterman, *History of Edina*, 84, Johnson, *Richfield*, 99–101, 147.

11 Ibid.

12 Henricks, *Bloomington*, 105. Manchester, *The Glory and the Dream*, 784.

13 Vonda Kelly, "Bloomington Growth," 2007, historical texts on the community's growth, copy at Bloomington Historical Society. Between 1950 and 1970, Bloomington opened twenty-five schools. In 1970, the community held twenty-one elementary schools, five junior highs, and three senior high schools, *Bloomington, Edina, Richfield*, (Bloomington Chamber of Commerce: Windsor Publications, 1970), 4. Henricks, *Bloomington*, 93.

Let Marv Anderson Build it for You

1 Minneapolis *Star Tribune*, February 19, 1998, see Anderson's obituary on page B9 and a news story on his death on B7. An excellent account of the American army's initiation into World War II combat, including the service of the 34th Division, is found in the first two books of Rick Atkinson's Pulitzer Prize-winning Liberation Trilogy, *An Army at Dawn* (2002) and *The Day of Battle* (2007) published by Henry Holt and Company. See also, *Legislative Manual of the State of Minnesota, 1949*, 484 for biographical information on Anderson. For a summary of the 34th Division and its combat operations, see http://www.globalsecurity.org/military/agency/army/34id.htm, accessed May 2, 2009.

2 Val Bjornson, *The History of Minnesota* (West Palm Beach: Lewis Historical Pub., 1969), IV: 673. *Legislative Manual, 1949*, 484. Minneapolis *Star Tribune*, February 19, 1998, B7.

3 Connie Murray, *Richfield: A Classic 50's Suburb*, 1992,18, 20, map 9.

4 Paul Hesterman, *The History of Edina: From Settlement to Suburb* (Edina: Edina Historical Society, 1988).

5 *Bloomington Ten Year Report, 1953–1963* (Bloomington: City of Bloomington, 1963), 4.

6 Interview with Mark Anderson, Marv Anderson's nephew, June 24, 2009, notes in author's possession.

7 Here and below, "Rambler Homes Stand the Test of Time in Bloomington, *Bloomington Briefing,* December 2007.

The Murder of Fred Babcock

1 Here and three paragraphs below, "Killing Denied by Suspect," Minneapolis *Sunday Tribune*, June 5, 1949, 13. The eyewitness accounts of Officer Poulter and Mr. and Mrs. Jay Peterson, who lived across Garfield from the murder scene, were used to recreate the attack on Babcock. Said Mrs. Peterson, "I saw it all." See also, Babcock's death certificate, Hennepin County Miscellaneous Records, "Birth and Death Record. Jan. 1948–Dec. 1950," Richfield.

2 "Search for Killers Shifts to Nebraska," Minneapolis *Star*, June 6, 1949, 1, 8.

3 Ibid.

4 "Richfield Policeman Killed by Burglars," Minneapolis *Star*, June 4, 1949, 1, 3. Richfield *News*, June 9, 1949, 1, 6. Fred and Lorraine Babcock had two children, Cheri Louise, three, and Fred III, eighteen months old.

5 "Search for Killers Shifts to Nebraska," Minneapolis Star, 1, 8.

6 "Farm Wife Bares Day of Terror With Trio," Minneapolis *Star*, June 7, 1949, 1.

7 Ibid.

8 Here and four paragraphs below, "Last 2 Fugitives Caught as Car Hurtles Off Bridge," Minneapolis *Star*, June 7, 1949, 1, 10. Paul Presbrey, a reporter for the *Star*, followed in the wake of the fugitives and wrote first-hand reports from the scene.

9 Richfield *News*, June 9, 1949, 6. Fred Babcock is buried at Fort Snelling, Plot: C-6, 0, 8325.

Commies! The 1950s "Red Scare" in South Hennepin

1 The Union of Soviet Socialist Republics (USSR) or Soviet Union was made up of present day Armenia, Azerbaijan, Belarus, Estonia, Georgia, Kazakhstan, Kyrgyzstan, Latvia, Lithuania, Moldova, Russia, Tajikistan, Turkmenistan, Ukraine, and Uzbekistan, with Russia the controlling power. After World War II, the USSR helped create the Warsaw Pact, a military alliance of eastern European nations, functioning under Soviet domination. Those satellite states were Albania, Bulgaria, Czechoslovakia, East Germany (Germany had been partitioned into two states by the victorious allied nations after World War II), Poland and Rumania.

2 Army Capt. Bernie M. Pepper was killed in action September 22, 1950, and Marine Cpl. John L. Madvig died in combat on November 3, 1950. Both were from Richfield, Richfield *News*, October 5, 1950, 1 and November 9, 1950, 1. Korean War Casualty File, 1950–57, Records of the Office of the Secretary of Defense, Record group 330.

3 "The Bomb," Richfield *News*, September 14, 1950, 1.

4 "Civilian Defense Goes Forward in South Hennepin," Bloomington *News*, September 21, 1950, 1; "Bloomington Rapidly Shapes Plans for Civilian Defense," September 22, 1950, 1.

5 Oscar B. Strand, "The Election and the Atomic Bomb," Bloomington *News*, November 9, 1950, 2.

6 Ibid.

7 Here and below, "A Letter to Joe About Your Home!" Richfield *News*, November 16, 1950, 1. It appears likely that Oscar Strand, given his frustration with citizen apathy regarding local civil defense needs, wrote this letter from the future. If he did not compose the letter, he believed and approved its message, and put it into the newspaper.

8 Ibid.

9 "Bloomington Crowd Told Third War Real Threat," Bloomington *News*, November 16, 1950, 1.

10 "The Bomb, How will it Affect Us." Richfield *News*, November 16, 1950, 12. For more on the leadership role of Richfield women, see Johnson, *Richfield*, 95–98.

11 H.E. Kossow, "An Open Letter to Residents of the Town of Bloomington," Bloomington *News*, December 7, 1950, 1. Herman Kossow later became Bloomington's first mayor. He and his wife, Irene, moved to Bloomington in 1932 where Herbert operated Kossow Oil at 95th Street and Lyndale Avenue, see interview Bloomington *Sun*, January 27, 1972, 1, 12.

12 Richfield *News*, December 7, 1950, 4. John C. Chalberg, *Bloomington, a sesquicentennial celebration* (Encino: Cherbo Publishing, 2007), 47. Another incident at this time shook Richfield. An account of the arrest and detention of two Richfield men suspected of past membership in the Communist Party, appeared in the December 7 Richfield *News*. Immigration officers picked up Otto Skog, a Norwegian-born resident of the country for thirty-five years, and Norman Bernick, born in Russia but in America since turning eight. They faced deportation under new internal security laws.

13 Bloomington *Sun*, January 11, 1951, 1. The film was to be shown for three days—January 18–20. Richfield *News*, December 28, 1950, 1.

14 State of Minnesota, Office of Civil Defense, "Minnesota Civil Defense and Disaster Relief Plan, 1950," 3, 6, 22.

15 *The Atom Bomb and Your Survival, Twin Cities Civil Defense Manual*, printed and distributed by Bloomington-based WDGY radio station in 1951, carries rough plans for a bomb shelter. St. Paul *Pioneer Press*, June 14, 1999.

16 William Manchester, *The Glory and the Dream, A Narrative History of America, 1932–1976* (Boston: Little, Brown, 1973), 547–575. Advisory Bulletin No. 69, September 20, 1951, 1; from the compilation *Civil Defense Memorandum, No. 1–19*, Minnesota Office of Civil Defense, June 6, 1951, August 28, 1952, 1. The Army Quartermaster Corps recommended identification tags be made of "corrosion-resisting steel type 430 or other chrome-iron alloys.

17 "Edina Grows," Village of Edina report, 1955–56, 5, copy at Edina Historical Society. Edina did a remarkable job in constructing air raid shelters throughout the 1950s and 1960s. In 1964 the village could accommodate one-third of its population in federally approved shelters ("Village of Edina News Letter," May 1964, 8: 3).

Edina became "the first community in the United States" to have civil defense shelters stocked with emergency provisions for its entire population. Seventeen locations were available in case of an emergency, "Village of Edina News Letter," January 1, 1968, 2.

18 Civil Defense Museum website, www.civildefensemuseum.com, accessed March 12, 2009, provides background on fallout shelters including photographs of shelters and their contents. "Civil Defense Can Feed 11,000 for Two Weeks," unidentified newspaper clipping date July 2, 1964, found "Edina Police Department Scrapbook #1." Edina Historical Society.

Edina residents Steve Marston, Roger Olwin, Don Enger, Chip Schwartz, and Brandon Deshler provided details about their community's fallout shelters. Marston was involved in cleaning out shelters in 1972, three years after the program ended. He reports, "… I spent most of a day visiting the half-dozen or so sites, blowing the dust and cob webs from the boxes, and bringing them to 4801. One site was in the tunnel at 169 (then known as Co. Rd 18). That building is no longer there. The others included several churches and schools, but I don't specifically remember which ones. As I recall, the supplies were sold."

19 *The Atom Bomb and Your Survival*, 4, 6, 8. The letters quoted are found reproduced on these pages. WDGY, one of Minnesota's first radio stations, built a transmitter in Bloomington in 1948. Jerry Verne Haines, *The History of Radio Station WDGY*, 114, University of Minnesota graduate thesis, December 1970.

20 Ibid.

21 The first "Red Scare" (1917–1920) followed the successful Russian communist revolution of 1917 and the fear that "Reds" would try to stir a similar revolt in America. Allen Weinstein and Alexander Vassiliev, *The Haunted Wood: Soviet Espionage in American—the Stalin Era* (New York: Random House, 1999), 133, 332–333. Ronald Radosh, "Closed Case: The Rosenbergs were spies," Los Angeles *Times*, September 17, 2008.

22 The Twin Cities got some first-hand experience with the "Red Scare" when University of Minnesota physicist Frank F. Oppenheimer admitted in 1949 he had been a member of the Communist Party of the United States (CPUSA). The revelation that his more prominent older brother, Robert, known as the father of the atomic bomb, had also been a "Red" sympathizer brought more attention to the case. At about the same time, Joseph Weinberg, another U of M physicist and former graduate student of Robert Oppenheimer, was charged with being a communist and summoned to testify before the Red-hunting House Un-American Activities Committee (HUAC). Eventually, the university decided not to rehire Weinberg. Neither Oppenheimer nor Weinberg was convicted of taking actions against the interests of the United States. For information on the Minnesota cases of Frank Oppenheimer and Joseph Weinberg, see Iric Nathanson, "The Oppenheimer Affair, Red Scare in Minnesota," *Minnesota History* 60 (Spring 2007) and Gary Paul Henrickson, "Minnesota in the 'McCarthy Period,' 1946–1954," University of Minnesota PhD Thesis, December 1981.

Section Five: Suburban Satisfaction

Shopping Town, USA

1 Victor Gruen and Larry Smith, *Shopping Towns USA: The Planning of Shopping Centers* (New York: Reinhold Publishing, 1960), 11.

2 By 1960, the Twin Cities still ranked 19th in population density out of America's 20 metropolitan areas with a million or more residents. John S. Adams and Barbara J. Van Drasek, *Minneapolis-St. Paul: People, Places and Public Life* (Minneapolis: University of Minnesota Press, 1993), 90.

3 Ibid.

4 "Grand Opening of the HUB Shopping Center," advertising circular, copy in Richfield Historical Society collections. This ad ties Richfield and Bloomington together as a dual market. Richfield's growth outpaced Bloomington in the early postwar years, and HUB wanted a share of a dependent market. Growth to the south quickly exploded the notion that Bloomington shoppers needed HUB.

5 Adams and Van Drasek, *Minneapolis-St. Paul: People, Places and Public Life*, 109. Sylvia Porter, "Southdale: A Revolution in Retailing," Minneapolis *Tribune*, October 11, 1956, provides the "already are suffering" quotation.

6 Minneapolis *Star and Tribune*, promotional department, "Continuing Survey of Minnesota Living," April 24, 1961, 3. The newspaper conducted three home surveys of Hennepin County women in 1955, 1957 and 1959.

7 "Dayton Plans Stuns Edina," June 19, 1952, Edina Morningside *Courier*, 1.

8 "Southdale — a Complete Living Environment," Minneapolis *Tribune*, June 18, 1952, 14. Dayton's began selling lots for single-family housing in 1958, with costs ranging from $2,000 to $6,000. Peg Meier, "The Shopping Center that Spawned a Community," *Mpls.St. Paul* 1(August 1981): 68.

9 Meier, *Mpls.St. Paul* 1: 67.

10 Edgerton Martin, "From Southdale to the Mall of America: Urban Models of Cities of our Time," *Hennepin History* 51 (Summer 1992): 4.

11 "He Brought Charm to Southdale," Minneapolis *Sunday Tribune*, October 7, 1956, 25. Gruen was expressing his view on the automobile and its effect upon downtown shopping districts while asserting the movement to the suburbs had stifled "social and cultural" activity, see M. Jeffrey Hardwick, *Mall Maker: Victor Gruen, Architect of an American Dream* (Philadelphia: University of Pennsylvania Press, 2004), 119–220.

12 Minneapolis *Tribune*, June 18, 1952, 15.

13 Paul Lukas, "Our Malls, Ourselves: Malls Changed how Americans Shop—and how FORTUNE 500 Sells," *FORTUNE* Magazine (October 2004). Frederick L. Johnson, *Richfield: Minnesota's Oldest Suburb* (Richfield: Richfield Historical Society, 2008), 147. Paul D. Hesterman, *The History of Edina, Minnesota: From Settlement to Suburb* (Edina: Edina Historical Society, 1988), 89.

14 Meier, *Mpls.St. Paul* 1: 67.

15 Paul D. Hesterman, *The History of Edina: From Settlement to Suburb* (Edina: Edina Historical Society 1988), 66–67.

16 Edina *Morningside Courier*, April 21, 1955, 1. Bill McMahon, chairman of the Southwest Edina group, called for a mass meeting for April 21, 1955, at Wooddale Elementary regarding the highway construction cost issue.

17 Meier, *Mpls.St. Paul* 1: 67. Martin, *Hennepin History* 51: 4.

18 "Thorpe resigns from Planning Commission," Edina-Morningside *Courier*, June 19, 1952, 1. Minneapolis *Tribune*, June 18, 1952, 15. There was another history-related connection to Edina's early days. In 1856, settlers Jonathan and Eliza Grimes bought three-fourths of Minneapolis block 79 between Marquette and Second Avenue and 4th and 5th Streets. They later sold the land. Paul Boutell started a furniture store in the 1880s at 5th and Marquette, part of the former Grimes holding. Boutell's announced, in 1955, they would open a furniture outlet in Southdale, thus following the Grimeses to Edina, albeit nearly 100 years later. Alden R. Grimes, "Descendents of Jonathan Taylor Grimes," (pre-publication manuscript excerpt, *The Grimes Family*, Volume II, Evanston, Illinois, 1988) 6, copy at MHS. Edina-Morningside *Courier*, May 26, 1955, 1.

19 Marty Rud interview with Bob Reid, February 19, 2001, for the Edina Historical Society oral history collection.

20 Jame Holton, "Minneapolis Shopping Center Is the Last Word in Modernity," New York *World Telegram and Sun*, October 5, 1956. Lukas, *FORTUNE* magazine (October 2004). Minneapolis *Tribune*, October 11, 1956.

21 "Architect Says Southdale Planned as 'Cultural Center' for Its Patrons," Minneapolis *Tribune*, March 14, 1954,

22 "Pleasure-Domes with Parking, *TIME*, October 15, 1956.

23 "These are Southdale's Stores," Minneapolis *Sunday Tribune*, October 7, 1956, 30.

24 St. Louis Park *Dispatch*, October 11, 1956, 1.

25 Here and below, Marty Rud interview with Bob Reid.

26 Minneapolis *Star and Tribune*, "Continuing Survey of Minnesota Living," 3, 5.

27 Here and below, Lukas, *FORTUNE* magazine (October 2004).

28 Ibid.

29 "Architect Says Southdale Planned a 'Cultural Center' for Its Patrons," Minneapolis *Tribune*, March 14, 1954.

30 Hardwick, *Mall Maker*, 216–217.

31 "Opening," *Minnesota Real Estate Journal* 8 (August 3, 1992): 4.

32 *A Day in the Life: An Excursion through the Mall of America on One Day in the Near Future* (Indianapolis: Melvin Simon, n.d. c. 1991): 13. *Minnesota Real Estate Journal* 8: 33.

33 Martin, *Hennepin History* 51:6.

34 *Minnesota Real Estate Journal* 8: 4.

35 Ibid. 39–40.

36 Minneapolis *Star Tribune*, April 6, 1993.

The Met: Luring Big League Baseball to Bloomington

1 Harold Evans, *The American Century* (New York: Alfred A. Knopf, 1998), 435. William Manchester, *The Glory and the Dream, A Narrative History of America, 1932–1972*, 429–432, 721–725, 731–734. Oscar T. Barck, Jr., and Nelson M. Blake, *Since 1900: A History of the United States* (New York: Macmillan Co., 1959), 738–740.

2 Michael Shapiro, *Bottom of the Ninth: Branch Rickey, Casey Stengel, and the Daring Scheme to Save Baseball From Itself* (New York: Henry Holt and Co., 2009), 21.

3 Ibid.

4 Here and below, Jay Weiner, *Stadium Games: Fifty years of Big League Greed and Bush League Boondoggles* (Minneapolis: University of Minnesota Press, 2000), 2–3. Charles Johnson, *Midwest Federal Presents the History of the Metropolitan Center* (Minneapolis: Midwest Federal, 1970), 7. James Quirk and Rodney D. Fort, *Pay Dirt: The Business of Professional Sports Teams* (Princeton: Princeton University Press, 1997), 134–135.

5 Major league baseball statistics are from www.baseball-Almanac.com/teams/shtml, accessed March 23, 2009. Shapiro, *Bottom of the Ninth*, 22.

A study undertaken by Market Facts, Inc. of Chicago for the Minnesota baseball backers found the Wisconsin city realized as much as $5 million in new baseball-related trade. The typical Braves fan in 1953 spent $11 per game day, not counting ticket expense, and 54 percent of this audience came from outside the metro area, see *A Prospectus of a Metropolitan Sports Area for the Twin Cities* (Minneapolis: Chamber of Commerce, Major League Baseball Committee, 1954), n.p.

6 Johnson, *History of the Metropolitan Center*, 3. St. Paulites added to the committee were Harold Cummings, E.E. Engelbert, James Kelley and Robert Sanders. New Minneapolis members were Hugh Barber, Neil Messick, Sr., Wheelock Whitney, Joyce Swan, Don Knutson and Charlie Johnson.

7 Tommy Thompson interviews with Tom Tuttle, May–August 2009. Thompson discussed a number of significant Minneapolis and suburban issues during a series of interviews with Tuttle.

8 Weiner, *Stadium Games*, 8–9.

9 James B. Bell, *From Arcade Street to Main Street, A History of the Seeger Refrigerator Company, 1902–1984* (St. Paul: Ramsey County Historical Society, 2007).

10 Here and below, *A Prospectus of a Metropolitan Sports Area*, 1954), n.p. The Milwaukee *Journal* executive's letter serves as a cover page, and Jerry Moore's letter follows.

11 Michael D'Antonio, "The Wrong Man," *Sports Illustrated*, 110 (March 9, 2009): 56–59. Quirk and Fort, *Pay Dirt*, 134–135. Evans, "Emperor of a City," in *The American Century*, 438, provides a brief biography of Moses.

12 Peter Golenbock, *Amazin': The Miraculous History of the New York's Most Beloved Baseball Team* (New York: St. Martin's Press, 2003), 58. Steve Bitker, *The Original San Francisco Giants: The Giants of '58* (Champaign, Il: Sports Publishing Inc., 2001), 6.

13 Golenbock, *Amazin'*, 55.

14 Weiner, *Stadium Games*, 11. The author cited a November 12, 1998, interview with Brophy as the source of the Stoneham quote.

15 The editorial is found in Minneapolis *Star*, August 16, 1954, 10 and titled "We're on First."

16 Johnson, *History of the Metropolitan Center*, 3. "Dispute on Stadium Settled," Minneapolis *Morning Tribune*, June 20, 1955, 1.

17 Thompson interview with Tuttle.

18 Ibid.

19 Weiner, *Stadium Games*, 11–12. Frederick L. Johnson, *Richfield: Minnesota's Oldest Suburb* (Richfield: Richfield Historical Society, 2008), 78–81.

20 "Work Starts on New Baseball Stadium," Minneapolis *Morning Tribune*, June 21, 1955, 1.

21 Ibid.

23 Johnson, *History of the Metropolitan Center*, 3. Minneapolis *Star*, April 25, 1956, sports section, 1. Nicollet Park had lost ball issues, too. Said Minneapolis city engineer Tommy Thompson, "One of the problems it had were balls flying out of there into the street; not just home-run balls, but foul balls could shoot out of there in all directions," Thompson interview with Tuttle.

24 "Notables Hail 'Major League' Stature of Stadium," Minneapolis *Star*, June 28, 1956, 11C.

25 Minneapolis *Morning Tribune*, April 24, 1956, 14.

26 D'Antonio, *Sports Illustrated* 110: 59–60.

27 Thompson interview with Tuttle.

28 Bitker, *The Original San Francisco Giants*, 8.

On Being Goliath

1 *Richfield in the Postwar Era*, Bill Davis narrator and Thomas Saylor interviewer, part of Minnesota Historical Society's Richfield Oral History Project, 2007, 36.

2 Minneapolis *Tribune*, March 23, 1960, 22. "A *Tribune* survey of a quintet of leading high school basketball coaches found four choosing Richfield as the tournament favorite. Said Walt Williams of Minneapolis Southwest, "Richfield walked through the regional. I don't know who's going to stop them."

3 "Tournament Fans Like 'Little Ones,'" Minneapolis *Tribune*, March 26, 1960, 1.

4 Davis interview, *Richfield in the Postwar Era*, 33. Richfield *News*, March 31, 1960, sports section, 1.

5 Davis interview, *Richfield in the Postwar Era*, 34–35.

6 Minneapolis *Tribune*, March 26, 1960, 22.

7 Hartman's Roundup, "Davis: Edgerton Deserves State Title," Minneapolis *Tribune*, March 26, 1960. David and teammate Bob Sadek were named to the all-tournament team. The roster also included Denny Johnson, Bob Werness, Mac Lutz, Roger Alevizos, Bill Szepanksi, George Lary, Mark Gjerde, Doug Barton, Gary Bystedt and Harry McLenighan.

8 Ibid.

9 Here and below, Richfield *News*, March 10, 1960, 2, and March 31, sports section, 1. The *News* also provided brief biographies of each of the team's nine senior players. None had been born in the community.
10 Here and below, Bill Davis interviews with Thomas U. Tuttle, August–September, 2009.
11 Frederick L. Johnson, *Richfield: Minnesota's Oldest Suburb* (Richfield: Richfield Historical Society), 101.
12 Patrick Reusse, "Richfield loses one of those athletes that it holds so close," Minneapolis *Star Tribune*, June 17, 2007, C3. Bill Davis interview with Thomas U. Tuttle.
13 Marc Hugunin and Stew Thornley, *Minnesota Hoops: Basketball in the North Star State* (St. Paul: MHS, 2006), 116–117. The 1996 Edina championship basketball team had a 26–0 record; in 1967 it was 27–0, and in 1968, 26–1.
14 St. Paul *Pioneer Press*, March 22, 1968, C18.
15 "Non-Booing Fans Pay Tribute to Edina," Minneapolis *Star*, March 23, 1968, 12A.
16 Ibid.
17 Here and four paragraphs below, Bob Zender interview with Thomas U. Tuttle, August 12, 2009 and Jon Nicholson interviews with Thomas U.Tuttle, 2009.
18 Minneapolis *Tribune*, March 22, 1969, 15.
19 Minneapolis *Tribune*, February 24, 1969, 25.
20 Doug Long turned aside 52 Hornet shots on goal. Long helped keep his club in every game during the 1970 tournament, recording 124 stops, a record most saves in a state tourney action that still stands, Minnesota State High School League, *Boys Hockey Tournament Records*.
21 Minneapolis *Tribune*, March 10, 1974, 3C.

All-America Cities: Richfield and Bloomington Make the Grade

1 Richfield *News*, June 20, 1946, 4, June 27, 1946, 2, July 4, 1946, 1,11, July 11, 1946,1.
2 Minneapolis *Tribune*, July 7, 1949, 1. Richfield *News*, July 7, 1949, 1, 15, and July 21, 1949, 1.
3 LeRoy F. Harlow, *Without Fear or Favor: Odyssey of a City Manager* (Provo: BYU Press, 1977), 210–211. Richfield *News*, November 8, 1951, 1, November 15, 1951, 1, November 22, 1951, 1.
4 *Look Magazine*, February 8, 1955, 78. Connie Murray, *Richfield: A Classic 50s Suburb*, Master of Arts paper, copy in Richfield Historical Society collections.
5 Richfield *News*, September 7, 1944, 2, January 4, 1945, 1. Rumpel's advertisement calling for more support of public schools in Richfield is on page 5 of the July 4 issue.
6 *Look Magazine*, February 8, 1955, 78. See also *National Municipal Review*, 43 (October 1954): 613–616.
7 Mary McKenna, *Church of the Assumption, A History*, 1976, 2–11. Frederick L. Johnson, *Richfield: Minnesota's Oldest Suburb* (Richfield: Richfield Historical Society, 2008), 26–27.
8 "Grand Opening of the HUB Shopping Center," advertising circular, copy in Richfield Historical Society collections.
9 Here and below, Scott Donaldson, *The Making of a Suburb: An Intellectual History of Bloomington* (Bloomington: City of Bloomington, 1967 edition), 49.
10 Judith A. Hendricks, ed., *Bloomington on the Minnesota* (Bloomington: Bicentennial Committee, 1976), 119–20.
11 Here and below, Donaldson, *The Making of a Suburb*, 42. Hendricks, ed., *Bloomington on the Minnesota*, 119–120.

Edina and the "Cake Eater Syndrome"

1 Paul D. Hesterman, *The History of Edina, Minnesota: From Settlement to Suburb* (Edina: Edina Historical Society, 1988), 1. As early as 1937, a sociologist wrote that Edina was a "better-class residential district;" see Calvin F. Schmid, *Social Saga of Two Cities: An Ecological and Statistical Study of Social trends in Minneapolis and St. Paul* (Minneapolis: Minneapolis Council of Social Agencies, 1937), 101.
2 The Grimes family arrived in the Edina area bolstered by cash from the sale of their Indiana farm; Alden R. Grimes, "Descendents of Jonathan Taylor Grimes," pre-publication manuscript, Evanston, Illinois, 1988, 6. George Baird already owned 120 acres of well-sited land when he married school teacher Sarah Gates in 1865; *Eighth Census of the United States, 1860*, Minnesota, Hennepin County, Richfield, pages 130–152. A local historian rated James and Mary Bull's property as "among the best farms in this town;" Henry and Susan Brown owned a farm along Minnehaha Creek and specialized in raising shorthorn cattle; Hesterman, *The History of Edina*, 30. George E. Warner and Charles M. Foote, *The History of Minnesota: From the Earliest French Explorations to the Present Time* (Minneapolis: Minnesota Historical Co., 1882), 217. Foster W. Dunwiddie, "The Six Flouring Mills on Minnehaha Creek," *Minnesota History* 44 (spring 1975): 163–166.
3 *Thorpe Brothers County Club District*, c. 1924, promotional pamphlet, copy at Edina Historical Society.
4 Arthur M. Schlesinger, Jr., *The Crisis of the Old Order: The Age of Roosevelt, 1919–1933* (New York: History Book Club edition, 2002), 111–112. Workers had reason to be envious of the well off. Work weeks averaged around fifty hours in the 1920s, and by the end of the decade steel workers, by the tens of thousands, labored seven days a week. And the bosses wanted no reductions. The president of the National Association of Manufacturers said in 1929, "Nothing breeds radicalism more quickly than unhappiness unless it is leisure."
5 "Report of the Projects, Planning and Development Committee, Country Club Association, April 11, 1933, *The Crier* 3 (September 1930): 5–6. "Council Refuses to Entertain Motion for Fact Finding Survey," *The Crier* 3 (May 1930): 1. "Proposal Made for Making New Village Out of Country Club District," *The Crier* 4 (October 1931): 8–10.
6 "Thorpe Co-operates with Mpls Journal in Fine Home Exhibit," *The Crier* 3 (September 1930): 5. *The Crier* was published in Hopkins by the *Hennepin County Review*.
7 "Community Fund Begins on Nov. 2nd," *The Crier* 2 (November 1931): 1. By 1930 the Country Club District, with its 1,032 residents, made up about a third of Edina's population. It included 97 servants for the 935 adults and children and a ratio of one live-in servant for every 2.5 families. Servants, often teen-aged "hired girls" from working-class families, were typical in families of wealth. In 1880, 8.4 percent of the United States work force served as domestics, a figure reduced to 4.5 percent by 1920. See Hesterman, *The History of Edina*, 62. Paul Johnson, *A History of the American People* (New York: HarperCollins, 1997), 593–595.
8 William W. Scott and Jeffrey A. Haas, *History and Architecture of Edina, Minnesota* (Edina: City of Edina), 67–68.
9 Hesterman, *The History of Edina*, 73–75, 78. Schmid, *Social Saga of Two Cities*, 103.
10 Edina's modest population of 5,855 in 1940 was similar to that of its neighbors Richfield (6,750) and Bloomington (3,645).
11 Martha Mattson Johnson interview with author, March 26, 2009, notes in author's possession.
12 Hesterman, *The History of Edina*, 95–96.
13 Meier, *Mpls.St. Paul*, 1981, 9: 67–68.
14 The Associated Press (AP) awarded the 1960 University of Minnesota team its fourth national championship, the most received by any football program up to that point. The AP began selecting the top college football team in 1936. Minnesota won that year and again in 1940 and 1941. Prior to the AP poll, there was much speculation about which squad was the nation's best. Many experts chose the undefeated 1934 and 1935 teams as number one in the nation.
15 Marc Hugunin and Stew Thornley, *Minnesota Hoops: Basketball in the North Star State* (St. Paul: MHS, 2006), 116–117. The 1996 Edina championship basketball team had a 26–0 record, in 1967 it was 27–0, and in 1968, 26–1.
16 "Edina 'Mystery Man' Picks Edina," Minneapolis *Tribune*, March 20, 1968, 25. "Edina Hornets Sting Duluth Inside and Out," Minneapolis *Tribune*, March 23, 1968, 13.
17 Minneapolis *Tribune*, March 23, 1968, 13.
18 Minneapolis *Tribune*, March 24, 1968, fourth section, 1.
19 Ikola holds the Minnesota State High School League record for most victories by a hockey school coach.
20 John Tevlin, "An Attitude Called Edina," *Mpls.St. Paul* 11 (January 1992): 149.
21 Minneapolis *StarTribune*, Jim Klobuchar columns from March 17, 1988, October 19, 1988, April 30, 1989, October 26, 1986, January 26, 1995, carry the quoted material.
22 Richard Gordon Guindon, *Guindon* (Minneapolis: Minneapolis Tribune, 1977), 44.
23 Here and below, Dr. Anderson's "Edina Poll" was published in the *Edina Sun*, October 1971. Regarding satisfaction with Edina's public image, 22 percent were very satisfied, 25 percent somewhat satisfied, 16 percent indifferent, and 3 percent no answer.
24 "Building self image is commission's priority," Edina *Sun*, May 9, 1979, 1,7.
25 Canny Wright, a local committee member with knowledge of the survey, made the quoted statement. "Report claims Edina is pressured by own image," Edina *Sun*, March 19, 1980, 1.
26 Edina *Sun*, March 19, 1980, 1.
27 "New Median Income for Edina Families," Edina *Sun*, July 6, 1972.
28 Michael Farber, "Be True to Your School," *Sports Illustrated*, 110 (March 23, 2009): 26.

Swinging Bloomington

1 *Bloomington, Edina, Richfield, Minnesota*, (Chicago: Windsor Publications, Inc., 1970), 8. This 72-page book promoting south Hennepin County in general and Bloomington in particular was created for the Bloomington Chamber of Commerce.
2 Charles Johnson, *Midwest Federal Presents the History of the Metropolitan Stadium and Sports Center* (Minneapolis: Midwest Federal, 1970), 3–4.
3 Mortimer Adler, general editor, *The Negro in American History* (Chicago: Encylopaedia Brittanica Education Corp., 1969), see (Kerner Commission) "Report to the National Advisory Commission on Civil Disorders," 2: 5, 67. William Manchester, *The Glory and the Dream, A Narrative History of America, 1932–1972* (Boston: Little, Brown and Co., 1974), 1065.
4 Earl Spangler, *The Negro in Minnesota* (Minneapolis: T.S. Dennison & Co., 1961), 132.
5 Barbara Scott Giebnik, *A Sociological Study of Edina, Minnesota*, 1969, see "Suburbs in General," 1, copy at Edina Historical Society.
6 Scott L. Malcomson, *One Drop of Blood: The American Misadventure of Race* (New York: Farrar Straus Giroux, 2000), 379. *Minneapolis, State of the City, 2003*, (Minneapolis: The City), see "Population," 16. Frederick L. Johnson, *Richfield: Minnesota' Oldest Suburb* (Richfield: Richfield Historical Society, 2008), 118. When Robert and Mary Jane Samples moved their family to Richfield in 1951, there was only one other African American family in the city of 25,000.
7 Johnson, *History of the Metropolitan Stadium and Sports Center*, 4.
8 K.C. Joyner, "No Hype Review: Attendance in Times of Recession, *New York Times N.F.L. Blog*, December 16, 2008, http://fifthdown.blogs.nytimes.com/2008/12/16/html accessed April 4, 2009. Michael Shapiro, *Bottom of the Ninth: Branch Rickey, Casey Stengel, and the Daring Scheme to Save Baseball From Itself* (New York: Henry Holt and Co., 2009), 21.
9 James Quirk and Rodney D. Fort, *Pay Dirt: The Business of Professional Sports Teams* (Princeton: Princeton University Press, 1997), 41–42. Johnson, *History of the Metropolitan Stadium and Sports Center*, 9. For "merchandising his dreams," see Jim Klobuchar, *True Hearts and Purple Heads: An unauthorized biography of a football team* (Minneapolis: Ross & Haines, Inc. 1970), 13.
10 Johnson, *History of the Metropolitan Stadium and Sports Center*, 9. Johnson and Moore had arranged the secret meeting earlier in 1959 with Mrs. Walter Wolfner, owner of the NFL's Chicago Cardinals. They made a bona fide offer to buy the Cards but were turned down.
11 Ed Gruver, *The American Football League: A Year-by-Year History, 1960-1969* (Jefferson, NC, McFarland & Co., 1997), 16–23. Johnson, *History of the Metropolitan Stadium and Sports Center*, 9. Quirk and Fort, Pay Dirt, 41–42, Winter, Boyer and Skoglund owned 20 percent of the club, Ritter held 30 percent and Haugsrud 10. Their franchise fee was $600,000.
12 "Continental Shift," *Star Tribune* (Minneapolis) July 19, 2009, C1, 9. This article contains an interview with Wheelock Whitney, the key man in the attempt to bring a Continental League franchise to the Twin Cities. See also, City of Bloomington, *Bloomington Invites Industry*, 1959 booklet, 12.

The emergence of the Continental League presented Major League Baseball with the same choice the American Football League brought before the NFL: expand or let the newcomers take over some potentially lucrative markets. They chose expansion. On July 20, 1960, Wheelock Whitney stunned AFL officials with news that the Minnesotans were withdrawing. Two weeks later the major league owners formally announced they would expand from 16 to 24 teams, Shapiro, *Bottom of the Ninth*, 207–216. *StarTribune* (Minneapolis) July 19, 2009, C 9.

13 Johnson, *History of the Metropolitan Stadium*, 8.
14 Here and two paragraphs below, Betty Webster interview with Thomas U. Tuttle, June–July, 2009.
15 Bill Brown interview with Thomas U. Tuttle, August xx, 2009.
16 Here and below, Judith A. Hendricks, ed., *Bloomington on the Minnesota*, (Bloomington: Bicentennial Committee, 1976), 108–109. Johnson, *Richfield*, 99–100. Joe Sullivan, "Edina's Liquor Store Profits Have Supported Community Since 1951," *About Town*, 18 (Summer 2005): 6–9.
17 Here and below, Betty Webster interview with Tuttle, Tom Webster interview with Tuttle, September 6, 2009 and Tuttle interview with Tom Reid, September 8, 2009.

Betty Webster recalled a miscue regarding a visit by Hubert Humphrey, "Late one night, he (Humphrey) called the restaurant from the plane, introduced himself and asked if we could stay open a little longer until he arrived. Sometimes we would stay open late for a special guest. The problem was, he was talking to a new maître d' who had answered the telephone, didn't believe it was the Senator and hung up the phone on him! Hubert called back and I answered this time and told him there would be no problem if he wanted to stop by. He was a gentleman every time I saw him."

18 Bill Carlson, *The Beatles! A One-Night Stand in the Heartland* (Nashville: Cumberland House, 2007), 21–28, 81. The book provides a photo-filled review of the Beatles quick trip to Minnesota. See also, Steven R. Hoffbeck, "Instamatic Memories: The Beatles in Minnesota," *Minnesota History* 60 (Spring 2007): 190-204.
19 For the story of the ten teenage girls behind the scenes, see Allan Holbert's Minneapolis *Tribune* article from August 22, 1965, quoted in Carlson's *The Beatles!* 98–101.

Holbert's account also showed that teenagers weren't the only Minnesotans in the thrall of the Beatles. Upon the quartet's arrival at Minneapolis-St. Paul International Airport, a couple of heavy-set women, "who haven't been teen-agers for a number of years, crashed through the police lines…and touched Paul [McCartney] before being pushed back."

20 Hendricks, ed., *Bloomington on the Minnesota*, 103–105.
21 "Soccer is Kicking its way into Minnesota Sports," *Minnesota Sidekicker*, April 28, 1978, 5. The *Sidekicker* was the run by the team's Side Kicks Booster Club. It held more than puff pieces about the Kicks, reporting on the game of soccer and its reach in Minnesota.

A controversial 1977 newspaper article (Bob Ashenmacher "Kicks fans go for the gusto in Met lot," Minneapolis *Tribune*, July 27, 1977, Section B 1, 10) about rowdy parking lot behavior before games drew strong protests from the *Sidekicker* ("Side Kicks Unhappy about Kicks Coverage," May 6, 1977, 2).

22 Sudip Bose, "Flights of Fancy," *Preservation*, 61 (May/June 2009): 28-35. See also, http://mspairport.org/about–msp/history.aspx, accessed April 17, 2009.
23 Betty Webster interview with Thomas U. Tuttle.